The Renaissance of Roman Colonization

THE HISTORY AND THEORY OF INTERNATIONAL LAW

General Editors

NEHAL BHUTA
Chair in International Law, University of Edinburgh

ANTHONY PAGDEN
Distinguished Professor, University of California Los Angeles

BENJAMIN STRAUMANN
ERC Professor of History, University of Zurich

In the past few decades the understanding of the relationship between nations has undergone a radical transformation. The role of the traditional nation state is diminishing, along with many of the traditional vocabularies which were once used to describe what has been called, ever since Jeremy Bentham coined the phrase in 1780, 'international law'. The older boundaries between states are growing ever more fluid, new conceptions and new languages have emerged which are slowly coming to replace the image of a world of sovereign independent nation states which has dominated the study of international relations since the early nineteenth century. This redefinition of the international arena demands a new understanding of classical and contemporary questions in international and legal theory. It is the editors' conviction that the best way to achieve this is by bridging the traditional divide between international legal theory, intellectual history, and legal and political history. The aim of the series, therefore, is to provide a forum for historical studies, from classical antiquity to the twenty-first century, that are theoretically-informed and for philosophical work that is historically conscious, in the hope that a new vision of the rapidly evolving international world, its past and its possible future, may emerge.

PREVIOUSLY PUBLISHED IN THIS SERIES

The Laws of War in International Thought
Pablo Kalmanovitz

A History of International Law in Italy
Edited by Giulio Bartolini

The New Histories of International Criminal Law
Retrials
Edited by Immi Tallgren and Thomas Skouteris

Sovereignty
A Contribution to the Theory of Public and International Law
Hermann Heller, edited and introduced by David Dyzenhaus

The Battle for International Law
South-North Perspectives on the Decolonization Era
Edited by Jochen von Bernstorff and Philipp Dann

Rewriting the History of the Law of Nations
How James Brown Scott Made Francisco de Vitoria the Founder of International Law
Paolo Amorosa

The Renaissance of Roman Colonization

Carlo Sigonio and the Making of Legal Colonial Discourse

Edited by
JEREMIA PELGROM AND ARTHUR WESTSTEIJN

OXFORD
UNIVERSITY PRESS

OXFORD
UNIVERSITY PRESS

Great Clarendon Street, Oxford, OX2 6DP,
United Kingdom

Oxford University Press is a department of the University of Oxford.
It furthers the University's objective of excellence in research, scholarship,
and education by publishing worldwide. Oxford is a registered trade mark of
Oxford University Press in the UK and in certain other countries

First Edition published in 2020

Impression: 1

Published in the United States of America by Oxford University Press
198 Madison Avenue, New York, NY 10016, United States of America

British Library Cataloguing in Publication Data

Data available

Library of Congress Control Number: 2020940029

ISBN 978–0–19–885096–0

Printed and bound by
CPI Group (UK) Ltd, Croydon, CR0 4YY

Series Editors' Preface

The city of Rome became hegemonic in Italy over the fourth and third centuries BC. We tend to think of this as the beginning of the Roman empire. What we call the Roman empire, however, had originally developed without much in the way of direct Roman rule. Defeated former enemies retained their own government and domestic autonomy, but they were henceforth as allies permanently treaty-bound to Rome for defense, which meant that they owed Rome military support and had to provide contingents for the Roman army. The Romans through this mechanism had at their disposal very large militia armies. In addition to this kind of "empire light" and complementing it, the Romans developed a further device that allowed them to increasingly dominate the Italian peninsula: colonies. Roman colonies were settlements of Roman citizens or allies on land that had been conquered from enemies. These colonies were fortified and were populated by people who were very much committed to the success of Roman expansion—the settlers of these *coloniae* had, one might say, a lot of skin in the game since they tended to sit on land that had been expropriated and they were surrounded by local populations that had often been enemies of Rome. It was this aspect of the colonies that led Cicero to claim that they were really "bulwarks of empire." The colonies, strategically sprinkled all over Italy and soon connected with roads, projected military power and steadily enlarged a growing network of armed settlers who had a strong commitment to the Roman republic.

Early modern thinkers, most prominently Machiavelli, showed a vivid interest in this device of Roman imperialism. Machiavelli, too, thought of the colonies primarily as imperial fortresses that served to defend recently conquered lands and hold their native inhabitants in check. This much is well known. What the present volume reveals is that this strand of reception is far from the most interesting one, nor was it the most influential one. Another Renaissance scholar, Carlo Sigonio (1522/3-1584), put forward what the editors call a "specifically legal interpretation of the Roman model of the settler colony," an interpretation that proved to be groundbreaking both with regard to Sigonio's scholarly impact on the study of Roman history and the effect his interpretation had on political ideas more broadly speaking. Machiavelli had already noticed that the colonies' purpose was not exhausted by their strategic value, but that they might have contributed to Rome's domestic stability by providing land to those who lacked it. Sigonio, however, was able to base his investigation on a much broader source foundation than Machiavelli had done.

Using epigraphic as well as literary evidence, Sigonio put forward a novel, and far deeper, view of the Roman colonies. He emphasized especially the legal structure of the settlements, the fact that they were, within a Roman constitutional framework, largely self-governing entities of settlers working the land plots they had been allocated. Sigonio's emphasis on law and institutions and his systematic legal-historical research connected aspects of previous interpretations, such as the strategic dimension of the colonies and their value as social safety-valves, in ingenious ways. As the editors point out, there was also a subtle normative point resulting from Sigonio's comparative constitutional analysis. Sigonio seems to have thought the Roman model of settler colonialism vastly superior to contemporary early-modern models of imperial domination, such as the Venetian or Spanish ones, with which he was very familiar. Where the Republic of Venice gave imperial land to its nobility, which in turn built "bulwarks of empire" on imperial territory while having serfs work the fields and siphoning off the surplus, Sigonio's Roman colonies were models of republican self-government, with enfranchised and propertied citizen-farmers firmly in charge.

Carlo Sigonio's work retained its outsize influence on both antiquarian scholarship and more abstract political thought until the nineteenth century, when it was eclipsed by Theodor Mommsen's approach to studying Roman public law. Sigonio was formative for thinkers and scholars from Jean Bodin in the sixteenth century and some of the natural lawyers and the English republicans of the seventeenth to the Anglo-American writers on the British imperial constitution and some of the American founders in the eighteenth, and indeed for Mommsen himself. Some of the solutions Sigonio proposed turned out to be wrong or misguided, as the present volume demonstrates in light of the most up-to-date international research on Roman colonization, yet even beyond the nineteenth century, antiquarian scholarship in Sigonio's vein with its detailed yet systematic investigation of constitutional, legal and institutional aspects of the past lives on, not only in classics and ancient history, but also in political science, comparative legal history and political theory. Jeremia Pelgrom and Arthur Weststeijn and the learned contributors to this book show several of the important ways in which Sigonio and his analysis of Roman settler colonialism was groundbreaking and the ways in which Sigonio was crucial for the understanding and critical investigation not only of ancient Roman history, but also of early modern imperial expansion. The volume thus proves the extraordinary fruitfulness of combining the history of political and legal thought with the study of the classical tradition.

Benjamin Straumann
Sag Harbor, NY, July 17, 2020

Contents

List of Contributors

Mattia Balbo is a researcher in Roman history at the University of Turin. His studies concern the history of the Roman Republic, Roman economy, land division programmes, and the demography of ancient Italy.

Luigi Capogrossi Colognesi is Emeritus Professor of Roman Law at the University of Rome 'La Sapienza' and author of numerous works on Roman law and Roman agricultural history. He is a member of the Accademia dei Lincei, of the Academia Europaea, and of the Akademie der Wissenschaften of Göttingen.

Jeremia Pelgrom is an assistant professor at the University of Groningen. His research focuses on Roman Republican colonialism and Italian landscape archaeology. He is co-editor of *Roman Republican Colonization. New Perspectives from Archaeology and Ancient History* (2014).

John Rich is Emeritus Professor of Roman History at the University of Nottingham. He is the author of *Declaring War in the Roman Republic in the Period of Transmarine Expansion* (1976), *Cassius Dio, The Augustan Settlement* (1990), and numerous papers on Roman history and historiography.

Christopher Smith is Professor of Ancient History at the University of St Andrews, and was Director of the British School at Rome from 2009 to 2017. He works on the political and constitutional history of Republican Rome.

Mark Somos holds the Deutsche Forschungsgemeinschaft's Heisenberg position at the Max Planck Institute for Comparative Public Law and International Law. He is the author of *Secularisation and the Leiden Circle* (2011) and *American States of Nature: The Origins of Independence, 1761–1775* (2019).

William Stenhouse teaches history at Yeshiva University, New York. He works on the Renaissance study of Roman history, including the reception of material remains. His publications include *Reading Inscriptions and Writing Ancient History: Historical Scholarship in the Late Renaissance* (2005).

Arthur Weststeijn is a research fellow at the University of Padua. He is the author of *Commercial Republicanism in the Dutch Golden Age* (2012) and co-editor of *Ancient Models in the Early Modern Republican Imagination* (2017) and *The Dutch Empire between Ideas and Practice, 1600-2000* (2019).

1

Introduction

Settler Colonies between Roman Colonial Utopia and Modern Colonial Practice

*Jeremia Pelgrom and Arthur Weststeijn**

Colonization has been a crucial phenomenon in the making of the modern globalized world. From the fifteenth century onwards, European states expanded their power and population worldwide through the establishment of colonies from Asia to the Americas. The significance of this process for international law has been widely recognized in recent scholarship. European colonial expansion formed the context to the remaking of Roman *jus gentium* into modern international law, exemplified by Francisco de Vitoria, Alberico Gentili, and Hugo Grotius, while the legal norms and rules that gave shape to the Westphalian order served European claims to and practices of worldwide dominance in the eighteenth and nineteenth centuries which continue to inform contemporary normative accounts of global justice.[1] There is however a particular aspect of colonization that has been largely overlooked in this burgeoning historiography on the intertwinement of law and empire: the legal organization of the settler colony. This volume aims to include this dimension of colonial theory and practice in our understanding of the relationship between empire and legal history and theory. In particular, it highlights the importance of a specifically legal interpretation of the Roman model of the settler colony, focusing on the ground-breaking work of the Renaissance scholar Carlo

* This volume originates from a series of discussions at the Royal Netherlands Institute in Rome. We are grateful to Harald Hendrix, the director of the Institute from 2014 to 2019, for his support, and to Isabelle Buhre for providing an English translation of Sigonio's primary texts on Roman colonization.

[1] Authoritative contributions to recent scholarship include: Anthony Anghie, *Sovereignty, Imperialism and the Making of International Law* (Cambridge University Press 2004); Lauren Benton, *A Search for Sovereignty. Law and Geography in European Empires, 1400–1900* (Cambridge University Press 2010) (hereafter Benton, *A Search for Sovereignty*); Andrew Fitzmaurice, *Sovereignty, Property and Empire, 1500–2000* (Cambridge University Press 2014); Martti Koskenniemi, Walter Rech, and Manuel Jiménez Fonseca (eds), *International Law and Empire. Historical Explorations* (Oxford University Press 2017); Jennifer Pitts, *Boundaries of the International. Law and Empire* (Harvard University Press 2018); Duncan Bell (ed), *Empire, Race and Global Justice* (Cambridge University Press 2019).

Jeremia Pelgrom and Arthur Weststeijn, *Introduction* In: *The Renaissance of Roman Colonization*. Edited by: Jeremia Pelgrom and Arthur Weststeijn, Oxford University Press (2020).
DOI: 10.1093/oso/9780198850960.003.0001

Sigonio (1522/3–84). Tracing the context, making, and impact of Sigonio's vision on Roman colonization, the chapters of this volume explore the importance of the settler colony as a Roman colonial utopia that critically informed modern colonial discourse.

The Colonial Model of Carlo Sigonio

In the early modern world, European colonial expansion offered ideal contexts to test different forms of societal, political, and legal organization: the colony was not only an imperial tool, it increasingly became an experimental space for innovations that were difficult to realize in the metropolis. This development is illustrated by the rising popularity of the settler colony.[2] While more traditional and feudal forms of colonial rule, dominant for example in the Venetian territories in the Eastern Mediterranean, were based on the exploitation of a local workforce, settler colonies rose to prominence in the sixteenth century as an alternative or complement to existing colonial practices. Forming (semi) autonomous collectives intended to function largely independent from both the colonial centre and the indigenous communities they replaced, settler colonies required clear rules to function properly and to define their legal position towards the colonial mother-town. As a result, theories and practices of settler colonization were of crucial importance for the making of a colonial world order increasingly dominated by European metropoles and their overseas settlements. These colonial experiments were to a large extent (re)interpretations of classical socio-political theories and Roman colonial legal practices, as humanist scholarship in late sixteenth-century and early seventeenth-century Europe used classical sources and especially Roman law as its main source of inspiration and legitimation. Conversely, the fluid boundary between the academic and political spheres also facilitated new and creative readings of classical texts, instigated by contemporary colonial experiences and by developing political ideologies.[3]

[2] Settler colonialism developed progressively from the fourteenth century onwards, in tandem with the Spanish *Reconquista* and the occupation and exploitation of new territories in North Africa, South Asia, and the Americas: Patrick O'Flanagan, 'Mediterranean and Atlantic Settler Colonialism from the Late Fourteenth to the Early Seventeenth Centuries' in Edward Cavanagh and Lorenzo Veracini (eds), *The Routledge Handbook of the History of Settler Colonialism* (Routledge 2017) 37–48. For a definition of settler colonization see Lorenzo Veracini, *Settler Colonialism. A Theoretical Overview* (Palgrave Macmillan 2010) 1–15, with further references.

[3] For an exemplary discussion of the intertwinement of Roman law and empire around 1600, see Benedict Kingsbury and Benjamin Straumann (eds), *The Roman Foundations of the Law of Nations. Alberico Gentili and the Justice of Empire* (Oxford University Press 2010).

A key figure who illustrates the subtle interplay between ancient and early modern colonial practices and social theories was Carlo Sigonio (Latinized as Sigonius), born in the early 1520s in Modena (a city in the north of Italy founded as a Roman colony) and without doubt one of the most influential humanist scholars to attempt a reconstruction of Roman colonial legal history.[4] Sigonio's interpretation of Roman colonization, which he wrote in the mid-sixteenth century as part of his treatise *De antiquo iure Italiae* (first published in Venice in 1560), would be the standard reference work on this topic until the nineteenth century. The influence of his erudite and innovative description of Roman colonial practices and law was not limited to academic circles but extended to wider socio-political discussions about the legal status and organization of new colonies and the relationship between colonies and metropolis. At the same time, Sigonio's study illustrates how contemporary colonial experiences and social concerns found their way into authoritative interpretations of Roman colonial history, which would continue to dominate the scholarly and colonial discourse for centuries. As Giambattista Vico stated in 1725, 'the great Carlo Sigonio' should be considered for his study of Roman law 'the first torch of Roman erudition'.[5]

The task Sigonio set himself was not an easy one, as reconstructions of Roman colonization are necessarily of a rather hypothetical nature. Indeed, no coherent ancient text on Roman Republican colonial practices and law survives, if it ever existed. Therefore, Roman colonial history needs to be reconstructed from different scraps of information that can be found in a limited number of sources of different genres, scope, and date. Moreover, these sources sketch different and sometimes even contradictory images of Roman colonization.[6] In modern scholarship the fragmented Roman textual evidence has been used to support a wide range of different colonial scenarios. Following Cicero's statement that the Romans 'established colonies in suitable places in such a manner that guarded them against all suspicion of danger, so that they appeared to be not so much towns of Italy as bulwarks of an empire (*propugnacula imperii*)',[7] various (early) modern scholars, starting with Niccolò Machiavelli, have emphasized the strategic qualities of colonies, which are imagined to have been well-defended outposts that protected Roman interest abroad, keeping

[4] On Sigonio and his work see William McCuaig, *Carlo Sigonio. The Changing World of the Late Renaissance* (Princeton University Press 1989) 3–95 (hereafter McCuaig, *Carlo Sigonio*).

[5] Giambattista Vico, *The First New Science* (Leon Pompa ed, Cambridge University Press 2002) 137.

[6] For a useful overview, see John Patterson, 'Colonization and Historiography: The Roman Republic' in Guy J Bradley and John-Paul Wilson (eds), *Greek and Roman Colonization. Origins, Ideologies and Interactions* (Classical Press of Wales 2006) 189–219.

[7] Cicero, *De lege agraria* 2.73 (Loeb tr).

foreign subjects under control.[8] Others, however, have focused on an ambiguous passage of Aulus Gellius, which, combined with a passage of Tacitus on Roman rule in Britain, is taken to imply that Roman colonies were copies of Rome (*simulacra*) that brought civilized urban culture close to underdeveloped native peoples and as such were crucial tools in the cultural unification and stability of the Roman Empire.[9] This view was put forward strongly by the humanist scholar Justus Lipsius at the end of the sixteenth century, and it remains engrained in modern scholarship.[10] In sharp contrast, following late Republican moralist sources, colonies have also been imagined as sober rural spaces, the natural habitat of the much admired soldier–peasant, characterized by high morale, patriotism, and discipline.[11]

Within this many-sided scholarly tradition, Sigonio's study stands out for its erudition and completeness, discussing a wide range of available sources and underlining the multiple functions of Roman colonization.[12] Yet on closer inspection, his interpretation also includes a more political and polemical dimension that emphasizes especially the social benefits of Roman colonies. In the first paragraph of his chapter on Roman colonies, Sigonio immediately

[8] See for example Niccolò Machiavelli, *Discorsi sopra la prima Deca di Tito Livio* (Mario Martelli ed, Sansoni 1971) 1.1 (hereafter Machiavelli, *Discorsi*). In modern scholarship this interpretation of Roman colonial history is most clearly voiced by Edward Togo Salmon, *Roman Colonization under the Republic* (Thames and Hudson 1969). For further discussion, see Jeremia Pelgrom and Tesse D Stek, 'Roman Colonization under the Republic: Historiographical Contextualization of a Paradigm' in Tesse D Stek and Jeremia Pelgrom (eds), *Roman Republican Colonization. New Perspectives from Archaeology and Ancient History* (Palombi 2014) 10–44 (hereafter Pelgrom and Stek, 'Roman Colonization').

[9] Aulus Gellius, *Noctes Atticae* 16.13: 'because of the greatness and majesty of the Roman people, of which those colonies seem to be miniatures, as it were, and in a way copies' (Loeb tr). The Gellian passage is frequently connected with Tacitus *Agricola* 21, which discusses the cultural impact of Roman rule in Britain.

[10] See for example Justus Lipsius, *Admiranda, sive de magnitudine Romana* (Jan Moretus 1598) 1.6 (hereafter Lipsius, *Admiranda*), for the view that colonies distributed urban culture throughout the Roman Empire. In modern scholarship this view is expressed most clearly by Frank Brown, *Cosa. The Making of a Roman Town* (University of Michigan Press 1980). For further discussion, see Elizabeth Fentress, 'Frank Brown, Cosa and the Idea of a Roman City' in Elizabeth Fentress (ed), *Romanization and the City: Creation, Transformation and Failures* (2000) 38 Journal of Roman Archaeology Supplementary Series 11–24; Edward Bispham, 'Coloniam deducere: How Roman was Roman Colonization During the Middle Republic?' in Guy J Bradley and John-Paul Wilson (eds), *Greek and Roman Colonization. Origins, Ideologies and Interactions* (Classical Press of Wales 2006) 73–160; Tesse D Stek, 'The Impact of Roman Expansion and Colonization on Ancient Italy in the Republican Period. From Diffusionism to Networks of Opportunity' in Gary D Farney and Guy J Bradley (eds) *The Peoples of Ancient Italy* (De Gruyter 2017) 269–94.

[11] On the presumed moral and military superiority of the farmer class see for example Cicero, *Pro Sexto Roscio Amerino* 50; Cato, *De re rustica* 1.1. In modern scholarship, see especially Plinio Fraccaro, *Opuscula I. Scritti di carattere generale, studi catoniani, i processi degli Scipioni* (La Rivista 'Athenaeum' 1956) and the discussion in Jeremia Pelgrom, 'The Roman Rural Exceptionality Thesis Revisited' (2018) 130 Mélanges de l'École française de Rome—Antiquité 69–103 (hereafter Pelgrom, 'The Roman Rural Exceptionality Thesis').

[12] Carlo Sigonio, *De antiquo iure Italiae* (Giordano Ziletti 1560) 2.2, 63r (hereafter Sigonio, *De antiquo iure Italiae*). This passage is discussed in detail by John Rich in Chapter 3 of this volume.

declares the crucial importance of the Roman colonial resettlement programme, which in his view formed the key to Roman imperial success and even to lasting liberty:[13]

> Colonies, the topic I would like to start with, were places the Roman people led its own citizens to in order to inhabit them. Their origin is very old and goes back to King Romulus, as Dionysius testifies. Romulus, according to Dionysius, did not destroy places he conquered in wartime, nor punished their inhabitants with slavery. Instead, he generally brought over colonists from the city into the farmlands he took from them. Nothing could be more suitable to make liberty lasting and to enlarge his empire than this practice. It follows—Gellius also wrote this at a certain point—that colonies were communities of citizens, in some way sprung from the Roman state.[14]

The distinctive feature of the successful Roman colonial system, according to Sigonio, was that it was based on agricultural settler colonization: new rural polities created out of a fragment of the old one.[15] By consciously contrasting this allegedly successful colonial practice with another, and in his time, more widespread bulwark colonial model based on the exploitation of indigenous workforces, Sigonio discreetly advocated a colonial system based on semi-autonomous rather than subordinate colonial communities.[16]

Sigonio was not the first to emphasize the benefits of settler colonization over other imperial models. Machiavelli, for example, repeatedly stressed the benefits of detached colonial settlements over more costly imperial strategies that required permanent military control.[17] However, Machiavelli gave no clear guidelines as to how such settlements should be organized in legal and practical terms. This lacuna was filled by Sigonio, who offered by far the most detailed analysis of Roman colonial law of his time, discussing the benefits of

[13] Liberty in this context must be understood in the republican sense, thus as resulting from citizenship and political influence of the citizenry in opposition to autocratic systems of government that can develop within societies or that are the result of external domination. For a detailed analysis of Sigonio's republicanism, which was strongly influenced by Aristotelian social theory, see McCuaig, *Carlo Sigonio* (n 4) 96–250.

[14] Sigonio, *De antiquo iure Italiae* (n 12) 2.2.1, 63 (Isabelle Buhre tr).

[15] It is interesting to note that Sigonio used the passage of Gellius, *Noctes Atticae* (n 9) 16.13, not to emphasize the urban qualities of colonies but to underline the fact that they were communities of citizens.

[16] However, in *De antiquo iure Italiae* (n 12) 2.4.1–3 Sigonio adds that the autonomy of the colonists was not absolute. The cited Gellian passage makes it perfectly clear that colonies did not create their legal system and institutions on their own initiative, but received it from the Roman people.

[17] Machiavelli, *Discorsi* (n 8) 1.1.8; 2.6.8. For further discussion on Roman colonial studies before Sigonio, see Chapter 2 in this volume by William Stenhouse.

settler colonialism, land allocation procedures, the number and background of colonial settlers, the legal system of colonies, as well as providing an overview of all the colonies the Romans founded before the Social War. Moreover, Sigonio's analysis of Roman colonies not only stands out by its detail, it is also an innovative work that diverges from his predecessors especially in his emphasis on the connection between colonization and agrarian reform.[18] For Sigonio, the Roman colony was more than a strategic bulwark of empire, a relatively cheap way to control a distant territory: it became a tool to tackle internal social tensions and demographic decline.[19]

By situating his analysis of Roman colonies predominantly in the context of the early Republican struggle between the orders, Sigonio, who followed the Livian tradition in this respect, was able to show how Roman colonization formed a key solution for Rome's severe social problems at the time, which, once resolved, made it possible for the Romans to pursue their imperial agenda with great success.[20] In his view, the Romans used colonization not only to pursue an imperialist agenda but also to combat social instability without disturbing the status quo. For Sigonio, Roman history showed that the allocation of land to the plebs in colonies was an effective means of avoiding radical reforms such as redistribution programmes that include the transfer of land from aristocrats to the lower classes, which always ends, he argued, in 'the greatest public commotion'.[21] Colonization, according to this perspective, is framed cleverly as a practice that is attractive not only for the lower classes, who thus gain the possibility of acquiring property and political power, but also for the

[18] See Chapters 2 and 3 by Stenhouse and Rich this volume. The usage of Roman law to study social history is typical for Sigonio's overall approach: McCuaig, *Carlo Sigonio* (n 4) 124. McCuaig rightly observes that Sigonio's decision to discuss agrarian law in the chapter on colonization derives from Appian who does the same: ibid 156–57.

[19] In this, Sigonio followed late Republican Roman social theory, which regarded settler colonization a powerful antidote to imperial decadence as it created a new class of strong and morally superior citizens. Another connected line of late Republican Roman thought was predominantly concerned with freeing the city from potentially dangerous lower classes and looked at colonization as the main vehicle to achieve this goal: Evan Jewell, '(Re)moving the Masses: Colonization as Domestic Displacement in the Roman Republic' (2019) 8 Humanities 66.

[20] Arguably, Sigonio was particularly interested in the topic of patrician–plebeian conflicts as he himself was of undistinguished lineage and had experienced difficulty entering the higher echelons of socio-political life: McCuaig, *Carlo Sigonio* (n 4) 117–24. He also considered patrician power mechanisms (based on linage) an obstacle to liberty: ibid 125.

[21] Sigonio, *De antiquo iure Italiae* (n 12) 2.2, 64r: 'All agricultural laws dividing either the farmlands of enemies, the public ones, or those bought with public money, were accepted easily and without any public uproar. But a law driving rich citizens off their possessions and placing plebeians in the farmlands of noblemen—such a law has never been proposed without the greatest public commotion' (Isabelle Buhre tr). See Chapter 3 in this volume by Rich on the ingenious connection Sigonio made between agricultural acts and colonies, which according to modern scholarly opinion are very different things.

upper classes who do not have to fear social unrest and the prospect of the redistribution of their properties.[22]

In this way, Sigonio offered an elegant solution to a very old and hotly debated problem of imperial polities: their predisposition towards increasing economic inequality and consequential socio-political instability. Starting in antiquity, commentators argued that the excessive economic inequality that often accompanied imperialism resulted in social unrest and moral decay, which in turn led to civil strife and the fall of republican empires. However, much less consensus existed about how to avoid this socio-economic collapse scenario. Greek philosophers of the Platonic tradition advocated redistribution of wealth via land redistribution policies as a means to stop this process of decline, while more conservative thinkers that dominated Roman optimate intellectual circles in particular opposed such radical programmes by arguing that such popular measures resulted in social strife, demagogy, and eventually tyranny.[23] This Roman perspective remained the dominant line of thought during the sixteenth and seventeenth centuries, but it gradually lost ground as it did not offer a clear solution to the idea that imperial success came at the cost of social stability.[24]

In this changing intellectual context, Sigonio was one of the first scholars of his time to embrace the Greek positive view on Roman agrarian reform.[25] He argued that the agrarian laws and in particular the radical policies of Tiberius Gracchus were justifiable as they, in William McCuaig words, 'remedied through the high justice of ethical principles a situation of grave social iniquity'.[26] Nevertheless, Sigonio was also conscious of the dangers involved in implementing agrarian bills that enforced redistribution of landed property. By underlining the emancipating qualities of Roman colonial land division programmes, Sigonio tried to show how successful imperial powers can deal with problems of social inequality without destabilizing the fragile harmony between socio-political groupings which, once broken, could result in tyrannical rule and consequentially the loss of liberty.

[22] Machiavelli, *Discorsi* (n 8) 1.1.8 also stressed the benefits of colonization for relieving overcrowded cities and also points out that the Romans used it as a means to avoid radical land division laws (ibid 1.37.9–14). A couple of decades after Sigonio, Lipsius, *Admiranda* (n 10) 1.6.2, remarked that Roman colonies had the advantage that the best people remained in Rome, while the weak elements were removed. See also Sigonio, *De antiquo iure Italiae* (n 12) 2.2, 70.

[23] Eric Nelson, *The Greek Tradition in Republican Thought* (Cambridge University Press 2004) 49–86 (hereafter Nelson, *Greek Tradition*).

[24] Krishan Kumar 'Greece and Rome in the British Empire: Contrasting Role Models' (2010) 51 Journal of British Studies 76–101.

[25] McCuaig, *Carlo Sigonio* (n 4) 156–68.

[26] ibid 160.

Also in his discussion of who could join Roman colonies, Sigonio took care to avoid a too radical interpretation of Roman colonial social organization. Although he highlighted the plebeians' involvements in establishing colonies, and the beneficial effect this had for both the lower classes and the Roman state, he was careful to avoid the impression that these colonial landscapes were egalitarian communities; he explicitly stated that the hierarchy of classes of the city of Rome were reproduced in the colonial countryside.[27] The same is true for the procedure to select the leader(s) of the colonial land division programmes. Sigonio argued that these leaders needed to be elected by the *comitia tributa*, the more democratic voting body of Roman citizens, but he added that the *comitia curiata*, an archaic aristocratic voting body, was also crucial in this process as it provided the elected commissioners with actual power.[28] On the whole, Sigonio sketched a picture of Roman colonial practices that are emancipatory in nature, favouring lower classes, but without upsetting existing social hierarchies.

The significance of Sigonio's description of Roman colonial practices gained weight because his reconstruction differed considerably from the colonial practices of his own time, which were largely based on the Ciceronian bulwark model. Particularly important in this regard was the colonial system of the Venetian *Stato da Màr* in the Eastern Mediterranean, which, as Charles Verlinden has argued, informed the development of European colonization in the Atlantic.[29] Sigonio was a professor in Venice between 1552 and 1560, the period when he worked on his *De antiquo iure Italiae*, and the Venetian colonial experience therefore formed the direct historical context to his reconstruction of Roman colonization.[30] The colonies established by Venice, with Crete being the most important example, were mainly grounded on a system of exploitation in which landed property was handed over by the government to Venetian nobles. This colonial nobility built fortresses to protect its dominions and used serfs of local or migratory background to work the field, having to pay their lords a large percentage (one-third) of everything they produced.[31]

[27] Sigonio, *De antiquo iure Italiae* (n 12) 2.2, 70.

[28] ibid 71r.

[29] Charles Verlinden, *The Beginnings of Modern Colonization* (Cornell University Press 1970) 3–32.

[30] McCuaig, *Carlo Sigonio* (n 4) 13. For an extensive overview of Venetian imperial politics, see Benjamin Arbel, 'Venice's Maritime Empire in the Early Modern Period' in Eric Dursteller (ed), *A Companion to Venetian History, 1400–1797* (Brill 2013) 125–253. On Venetian overseas colonies specifically, see Benjamin Arbel, 'Colonie d'Oltremare' in Alberto Tenenti and Ugo Tucci (eds), *Storia di Venezia dalle origini alla caduta della Serenissima, vol. 5: Il Rinascimento. Società ed economia* (Istituto della Enciclopedia Italiana 1996) 947–85.

[31] Molly Greene, *A Shared World. Christians and Muslims in the Early Modern Mediterranean* (Princeton University Press 2002) 32; Allaire B Stallsmith, 'One Colony, Two Mother Cities: Cretan Agriculture under Venetian and Ottoman Rule' (2007) 40 Hesperia Supplements 151–71 (hereafter Stallsmith, 'One Colony, Two Mother Cities'); Sally McKee, *Uncommon Dominion. Venetian Crete*

The noble lords were responsible for the defence of the acquired territory and for the protection of Venetian interest in the region. By the sixteenth century, when hostilities with the Ottoman Empire were reactivated, it became clear that this colonial system was not functioning effectively. From the 1530s onwards, the Republic of Venice was increasingly losing colonial possessions to the Ottomans. Numerous Venetian colonies surrendered easily, as they were ruled by private families that had only loose connections with Venice and who were more inclined to negotiate expedient terms with the Ottomans, than to sacrifice everything out of loyalty to the metropolis. Colonies were unable or unwilling to muster local militia, leaving the defence of these territories to Venice, which was a very costly and in the long run unsustainable situation.[32] The waning of Venetian colonial power was explained by people like the military commander Cristoforo da Canal as a problem of moral decline. In this classical view, echoing the Roman narrative of Sallust, the Venetians, once a proud and patriot state, had grown soft by the wealth brought by empire, which led to idleness, decadence, and inertia.[33]

It is not a coincidence that in this climate of perceived Venetian imperial decline, Sigonio reconstructed a model of Roman colonial organization tailored to tackle the problems Venice was experiencing. Yet Sigonio's treaty on colonies offers neither a moralistic narrative nor an intellectual contemplation on the perfect state: it is a historical guidebook that explains how successful settler colonies could be organized in legal and practical terms. To achieve this aim, Sigonio drew on Roman agricultural law and the rather obscure texts of the Roman *agrimensores*, who provided technical information on issues such as how to create border lines and how to resolve border conflicts.[34] Although this approach might seem trivial, the clear and rational organization of landed property could be perceived as a vital instrument against aristocratic power

and the Myth of Ethnic Purity (University of Pennsylvania Press 2010). This is not to deny that in these Venetian colonies some land was also distributed to colonial settlers.

[32] Stallsmith, 'One Colony, Two Mother Cities' (n 31) 152.

[33] Canal's interpretation is quoted in Pompeo Molmenti, *La storia di Venezia nella vita privata dalle origini alla caduta* (Roux and Vavalle 1885) 196. On Canal, see Alberto Tenenti, *Cristoforo da Canal: La marine vénitienne avant Lépante* (SEVPEN 1962). For the Sallustian narrative of imperial expansion and moral decline, see Sallust, *Bellum Catilinae* 10.1–2; on its impact in early modern Europe, see Patricia J Osmond, '"Princeps Historiae Romana": Sallust in Renaissance Political Thought' (1995) 40 Memoirs of the American Academy in Rome 101–43; David Armitage, 'Empire and Liberty: A Republican Dilemma' in Martin van Gelderen and Quentin Skinner (eds), *Republicanism: a Shared European Heritage* (Cambridge University Press 2002) vol 2, 29–46; John GA Pocock, *Barbarism and Religion, vol. 3: the First Decline and Fall* (Cambridge University Press 2003) (hereafter Pocock, *First Decline and Fall*).

[34] See Chapters 2 and 3 in this volume by Stenhouse and Rich.

structures. Robust boundaries help to protect the property rights of lower classes, which otherwise would be unable to cope with formal and informal aristocratic power mechanisms that are more easily effectuated in more chaotic or indistinct situations. Sigonio's Roman colony could therefore be characterized as a well-ordered agrarian landscape concerned with protecting the property claims and political rights of a clearly defined community of citizen–farmers.[35] This colonial world he sketched was far removed from the contemporary socio-political reality in the Venetian empire, but it had already crystallized in utopian writings of theorists such as Thomas More.[36] With his detailed study of Roman colonial law and practice, Sigonio showed that there was a historical foundation for related societal models to work effectively, thus bringing the actual realization of certain aspects of such ideal states one step closer. In short, Sigonio's reconstruction of the Roman settler colony made it possible to conceive of a colonial utopia as a concrete colonial practice.

After Sigonio: The Farmer–Settler Model in Colonial Theory and Practice

In the late sixteenth century, Sigonio's analysis of Roman colonization increasingly started to make an impact not only among antiquarian scholars interested in ancient Rome but also on more topical discussions about the imperial governance of overseas territories. First published in 1560, his detailed reconstruction of the Roman colonial model was included in his massive treatise *De antiquo iure populi Romani* (1574) and soon became an authoritative reference work in humanist circles throughout Europe, especially after the Frankfurt edition of Sigonio's collected works in 1593 was published.[37] As the first comprehensive study of Roman agricultural colonization and Roman colonial law, Sigonio's analysis contributed to a gradual shift in the late humanist discourse on colonial strategies, moving from the traditional bulwark model and associated notions of centralized feudal or aristocratic territorial control, towards a farmer–settler model. By the end of the sixteenth century, settler colonies were

[35] Such an understanding of Roman colonial organization during the Republic has remained largely unchallenged in modern scholarship on Roman colonization, but see Pelgrom, 'The Roman Rural Exceptionality Thesis' (n 11); Pelgrom and Stek, 'Roman Colonization' (n 8). See also Chapter 3 in this volume by Rich for other critical notes on Sigonio's interpretation of Roman colonization in light of modern scholarship.

[36] The scholarship on More is overwhelming. For a useful interpretation in this context, see Nelson, *Greek Tradition* (n 23).

[37] On the publication process, see McCuaig, *Carlo Sigonio* (n 4) 75–77.

obviously no new invention, but their existence was generally accompanied by feudal and aristocratic power structures, most crucially in the Spanish territories in the Americas (which, tellingly, were not called 'colonies', as the language of conquest and the system of the *encomienda* did not fit the Roman colonial terminology).[38] Partly out of criticism of and competition with Spanish imperialism, the discursive trend in the last decades of the sixteenth century shifted, particularly in England, towards a colonial model that granted larger autonomy to settlers, making the land-working class coincide with the land-owning class, with the explicit aim to resolve social problems at home.

The dichotomy between the traditional, fortress-based system of colonial rule and an alternative based upon private possession of land was put on centre stage by Giovanni Botero in his hugely influential *Della ragion di stato* (1589), the groundwork of international reason-of-state literature. Pondering over the best strategies to maintain imperial dominions, Botero argued that a fortress can be a useful construction to keep a people under control, but sending out colonies (ie settlers) in the Roman way was a much more effective tool of government. Moreover, for Botero, the Roman model showed how private possession of land was crucial to create a sense of commitment to the state and that colonial land division was therefore a very effective tool to avoid social strife.[39] The work of Botero thus popularized Sigonio's academic interpretation of Roman colonization, making his analysis accessible to generations of readers and authors throughout Europe.[40] Whilst the existing scholarship has predominantly emphasized the importance of Machiavelli in this regard as the first to have drawn attention to the advantages of Roman settler colonies, Machiavelli's impact in this context should not be overstated, as the early modern discourse on colonization and its practical application, following the reconstruction of the Roman model made by Sigonio, advanced considerably from Machiavelli's impressionistic statements.[41]

The actual implementation of these (re)constructed Roman colonial principles was gradual, if ever fully realized. Yet it is clear that the intellectual discourse did affect the (attempted) organization of colonies, resulting eventually

[38] John H Elliott, *Empires of the Atlantic World. Britain and Spain in America, 1492–1830* (Yale University Press 2006) 9.

[39] Giovanni Botero, *Della ragion di stato libri dieci. Con tre libri delle cause della grandezza e magnificenza delle città* (Gioliti 1589) 160–65, 210–13.

[40] On the impact of Botero on English colonization debates, see Andrew Fitzmaurice, 'The Commercial Ideology of Colonization in Jacobean England: Robert Johnson, Giovanni Botero, and the Pursuit of Greatness' (2007) 64 The William and Mary Quarterly 791–820. See also David B Quinn, 'Renaissance Influences in English Colonization' (1976) 26 Transactions of the Royal Historical Society 73–93.

[41] See Chapters 4 and 5 in this volume by Mark Somos and Mattia Balbo.

in the concrete creation of socially motivated farmscapes. An early hybrid example hereof is the series of English colonization programmes in Ireland around 1600. After some initial and rather unsuccessful attempts to involve the Irish population in the colonization process, authors such as Thomas Smith, Edmund Spenser, and Francis Bacon advocated a plantation (ie agrarian–settler) colonial model in which English and Scottish settlers were sent to farm Irish soil.[42] Bacon, in particular, echoed Sigonio's analysis in his essay 'Of Plantations', claiming that agrarian settler colonies removed the overflow of people from Britain, which in turn would forestall internal conflict and sedition. In reality, the colonies established on for example the Munster estates did not uphold the ideals of participatory citizenship and autarky. The social and physical organization of these colonial plantations, which were owned and managed by wealthy elites, was still strongly aristocratic.[43] Nevertheless, the Munster example illustrates how colonial theories and practices became increasingly entangled in socio-economic domestic debates concerned with population politics.[44] From this perspective, agrarian colonization was not only a way to remove unwanted elements from society but it became a multifaceted instrument meant to transform perceived idle and potentially dangerous plebs into valuable citizens, while at the same time protecting aristocratic colonial interests in a cost-efficient way.

The most important contribution to this intellectual development was James Harrington's *The Commonwealth of Oceana* from 1656. Whilst Harrington has become, following John Pocock's seminal analysis of his work, a central figure in modern scholarship on Machiavellian republicanism, it is much less acknowledged that Harrington also used Sigonio to theorize the beneficial qualities of land distribution through colonization to uphold the social balance of the commonwealth.[45] In line with Sigonio's analysis, Harrington referred to the Roman example to argue that colonization allows for the distribution of 'lands

[42] Edmund Spenser, *A View of the Present State of Ireland* (William L Renwick ed, Clarendon Press 1970); Francis Bacon, 'Of Plantations' (1625) in *The Essayes or Counsels, Civill and Morall* (Michael Kiernan ed, Oxford University Press 1985). For commentary, see Jane H Ohlmeyer, 'A Laboratory of Empire?: Early Modern Ireland and English Imperialism' in Kevin Kenny (ed), *Ireland and the British Empire* (Oxford University Press 2006) 26–59 (hereafter Ohlmeyer, 'A Laboratory of Empire?'); Richard Serjeantson, 'Francis Bacon, Colonization, and the Limits of Atlanticism' conference paper (2014), <https://docplayer.net/65319781-Francis-bacon-colonization-and-the-limits-of-atlanticism.html>(cited with permission of the author).

[43] Ohlmeyer, 'A Laboratory of Empire?' (n 42) 38.

[44] For an overview of these debates, see Klaus E Knorr, *British Colonial Theories, 1570–1850* (University of Toronto Press 1944) 41–48.

[45] See John GA Pocock, *The Machiavellian Moment. Florentine Political Thought and the Atlantic Republican Tradition* (Princeton University Press 1975); and cf Pocock, *First Decline and Fall* (n 33) 276–79, 297–98. See also Nelson, *Greek Tradition* (n 23) 94–95. Sigonio is conspicuously absent from Rachel Hammersley, *James Harrington. An Intellectual Biography* (Oxford University Press 2019).

taken from enemies' without upsetting the social hierarchies in the metropolis. However, the redistribution of domestic properties, as proposed for example by the Gracchi, 'caused earthquakes', as the greedy nobility saw its privileges undermined and 'overthrew the people and the commonwealth'. Rome, in short, revealed the risks of a malfunctioning legal arrangement of land distribution: the Romans, 'through a negligence committed in their agrarian laws, let in the sink of luxury, and forfeited the inestimable treasure of liberty for themselves and posterity'.[46] Successful colonization therefore required a clear and precise agrarian law to maintain liberty and self-government at home.

In the intellectual quest for such an agrarian law, an alternative model presented itself in the Hebrew Republic, the Biblical polity that experienced a remarkable popularity in scholarly circles from the late sixteenth century onwards—a development in which Sigonio also played a major role with the publication of his *De republica Hebraeorum* from 1582.[47] The Jewish Jubilee, which set a limit to land ownership in the Land of Israel, could be considered a powerful alternative to the Roman example of agrarian property distribution. Particularly significant in this context was the interpretation of the Dutch scholar Petrus Cunaeus. His 1617 treatise on the Hebrew Republic upheld the Jewish agrarian law against that of Rome, where, despite the legal maximum of 500 *iugera* of land per person, 'the rule of law was immediately flouted by acts of deceit', with the eventual result 'that a few men were holding all of Italy and the neighbouring provinces as though these lands were their personal inheritance'.[48] Whilst Jewish land laws provided for social equality and political stability, the fate of the Roman Republic showed the dangers intrinsic to republican colonial expansion without a clear legal framework. This warning was particularly pertinent for the Dutch Republic, which had started to establish colonial outposts overseas precisely in the years Cunaeus was writing his work on the Hebrew Republic. Such a republican empire, Cunaeus implicitly

[46] James Harrington, *The Commonwealth of Oceana and A System of Politics* (John GA Pocock ed, Cambridge University Press 1992) 43–44. Harrington's reference at this passage reads: 'Sigonius De Ant. Ro.'

[47] Eric Nelson, *The Hebrew Republic. Jewish Sources and the Transformation of European Political Thought* (Harvard University Press 2011); Guido Bartolucci, *La Repubblica ebraica di Carlo Sigonio: modelli politici dell'età moderna* (Olschki 2007); Guido Bartolucci, 'The Hebrew Republic in the Political Debate of Sixteenth-Century Europe: The Struggle for Jurisdiction' in Wyger Velema and Arthur Weststeijn (eds), *Ancient Models in the Early Modern Republican Imagination* (Brill 2017) 214–33.

[48] Petrus Cunaeus, *The Hebrew Republic* (Peter Wyetzner tr, Shalem Press 2006) 1.3, 17–18. On Cunaeus, see Lea Campos Boralevi, 'Classical Foundational Myths of European Republicanism: The Jewish Commonwealth' in Van Gelderen and Skinner (eds), *Republicanism* (n 33) 247–61; and Jonathan R Ziskind, 'Petrus Cunaeus on Theocracy, Jubilee and the Latifundia' (1978) 68 The Jewish Quarterly Review 235–54.

suggested by referring to the Jewish example, could only succeed on the basis of a precise legal arrangement to distribute colonial property to farmer–settlers, with agrarian labour as the key to improving both people and land.[49]

Dutch colonial expansion, however, was not agrarian but primarily commercial in nature, as the conquest of overseas territories and the establishment of colonial outposts was driven by the commercial rationale of chartered companies for overseas trade, principally the Dutch East India Company (VOC). In this changing context, Roman agrarian law as studied by Sigonio gradually lost its appeal and became overshadowed by the significance of Roman private law, famously used by Hugo Grotius to formulate legal principles for free navigation and the seizure of commercial properties by the VOC.[50] Yet even in the Dutch colonial world, in which Grotius' principles played a foundational role, the Roman model of the semi-independent farmer–settler colony continued to set the agenda of concrete proposals for colonial government. In north-eastern Brazil, for example, conquered by the Dutch from the Portuguese in 1630, recruitment of settlers and the distribution of land in free property was deemed necessary to make the colony flourish.[51] Yet the dominance of commerce in Dutch colonial practice meant that this Sigonian discourse of agrarianism merged with the Grotian discourse of free trade. As a pamphlet from 1638 argued, the best way to attract settlers to Brazil was to 'follow the ruling of the Romans, who created their colonies mostly through *privilegia* and *immunitates*', which implied that colonists should not only receive agrarian property rights but also free trade exemptions.[52] In this way, the Sigonian and the Grotian narratives fused together in an ambiguous amalgam of the farmer–settler model adapted to the seventeenth-century world of global trade.

In practice, this attempt to reconcile ancient agrarianism with modern commercialization resulted in the development of hybrid colonial landscapes such as the colony of New Netherland in North America, where commercial settlements dominated by a fort, such as New Amsterdam, alternated with private colonial allotments (patroonships) and surrounding lands that were meant to

[49] The intellectual foundations of the Dutch 'republican empire' are explored further in Arthur Weststeijn, 'Republican Empire: Colonialism, Corruption and Commerce in the Dutch Golden Age' (2012) 26 Renaissance Studies 491–509.

[50] See Benjamin Straumann, *Roman Law in the State of Nature. The Classical Foundations of Hugo Grotius' Natural Law* (Cambridge University Press 2015) and, for the concrete colonial context, Martine van Ittersum, *Profit and Principle. Hugo Grotius, Natural Rights Theories and the Rise of Dutch Power in the East Indies, 1595–1615* (Brill 2006).

[51] Gerrit Johan van Grol, *De grondpolitiek in het West-Indisch domein der Generaliteit* (Algemeene Landsdrukkerij 1934) 57–63, 272–75.

[52] *Consideratien als dat de negotie op Brasil behoort open gestelt te worden* (1638) 10. For the context, see Arthur Weststeijn, 'Dutch Brazil and the Making of Free Trade Ideology' in Michiel van Groesen (ed), *The Legacy of Dutch Brazil* (Cambridge University Press 2014) 187–204.

be distributed to farmer–settlers from Europe. For example, when the city of Amsterdam established a new urban colony on the shores of the Delaware river in 1656, the recruitment conditions it offered to prospective colonists stated that all the lands around the city would be divided and distributed 'in free, fast and durable property', provided the colonists cultivated the land.[53] But as in Virginia, where the headright system of 1618 postulated similar conditions, settler colonization essentially failed in the Dutch world, as settlers were reluctant to cross the Atlantic in large numbers and commercial motivations dominated over Rome-inspired principles. In Dutch Brazil, and later also in Surinam, colonial territories originally intended for agrarian settlement were turned into large plantations worked by enslaved people forcefully transferred from Africa. The development of transatlantic slavery most gruesomely revealed the increasing discrepancy between colonial theory and colonial practice in the seventeenth century.

On the other side of the world, in the Dutch colony of Batavia (modern Jakarta), a colonial observer critically discussed this discrepancy in 1675 by invoking the authority of Sigonio. In a manuscript 'Advice on the Dutch colony in these Indian regions', Pieter van Hoorn, member of the VOC Council of the Indies in Batavia, argued that colonization was originally intended, following the Roman example, for the 'distribution of land and the improvement of everyone's position, as Sigonio extensively proves'.[54] Yet that ideal had never been realized in the Dutch Empire because of the commercial mindset of the VOC, which augmented the common risk threatening all colonial projects: 'the filthy desire and greed for profit at the start of colonization'. The Roman spectre of unequal distribution which troubled Sigonio, Cunaeus, and Harrington was, according to Van Hoorn, revived in the seventeenth century by the VOC, but in an even more greedy guise since 'colonies are more and better enhanced and governed by eminent and generous powers than by merchants, because they too much pursue and practice present profits'.[55] Sigonio's analysis of the Roman colonial model thus ended up in the tropics, in the wet, hot climate of Java, to

[53] Edmund B O'Callaghan (ed), *Laws and Ordinances of New Netherland, 1638–1674* (Weed, Parsons and Co 1868) 242–43. On the legal framework of patroonships, see Jaap Jacobs, 'Dutch Proprietary Manors In America: The Patroonships In New Netherland' in Louis Roper and Bertrand Van Ruymbeke (eds), *Constructing Early Modern Empires. Proprietary Ventures in the Atlantic World, 1500–1750* (Brill 2007) 301–26.

[54] National Archive, The Hague, 1.04.02, 1297 Batavia, fols 685–702: 'Copie consideratien van d'edele Pieter van Hoorn wegens de Nederlantse colonie in dese Indische gewesten', quote on fol 687. The text is partly published, but without the passages referring to Rome and Sigonio, in Jan KJ de Jonge (ed), *Opkomst van het Nederlandsch gezag over Java*, vol 3 (Martinus Nijhoff 1872) 130–47.

[55] ibid 133. For the context and further analysis of Van Hoorn's advice, see Arthur Weststeijn, 'The VOC as Company-State: Debating Seventeenth-Century Dutch Colonial Expansion' (2014) 38 Itinerario 13–34.

serve as the intellectual foundation for a critical review of the monopolistic colonial politics of the VOC.

Despite the distance in time and in space separating Sigonio's Italy from Dutch Batavia, it is not surprising that his work on Roman colonization was used as an authoritative source for criticizing the VOC. Indeed, a century after the publication of *De antiquo iure Italiae*, Sigonio was still considered the most important source for understanding the ins and outs of Roman colonization. For example, a popular Dutch overview of Roman history published in Amsterdam in 1670 directly cites Sigonio's classification of six reasons why the Romans established colonies.[56] Also in England, Sigonio continued to be read and cited. Thus, the Whig MP Walter Moyle, who extensively discussed the topic of Roman colonization in his 1698 *An Essay upon the Constitution of the Roman Government* to show why 'colonies were of excellent use to the Commonwealth', referred the reader explicitly to Sigonio, 'who has handled it with great Judgment and Accuracy'.[57] First published posthumously in 1726 and again in 1796 as *Democracy Vindicated: An Essay on the Constitution and Government of the Roman State*, Moyle's essay was one of many texts that updated Sigonio's relevance for the colonial debates of the eighteenth century.[58]

The concrete colonial experiment that arguably approached most closely the ideals of the colonial farmer–settler model in this period was Savannah, Georgia, founded in 1733 by the social reformer James Oglethorpe. Together with a group of trustees, Oglethorpe aimed to create an agrarian colonial society that, in the analysis of Tom Wilson, 'would preserve and nourish fundamental principles of the British nation . . . that were being eroded by urbanization and social disintegration'.[59] The prime target group for this utopian project were impoverished urban Britons, even ex-prisoners, who were given a new chance in life. Agrarian colonization according to strict rational and egalitarian principles was believed to transform these social outsiders into loyal and

[56] Joachim Oudaan, *Roomsche Mogentheyt, of naeuwkeurige beschryving, van de macht en heerschappy der oude Roomsche keyseren* (Daniel Baccamude 1670) 173. Sigonio's description in *De antiquo iure Italiae* (n 12) 2.2.1, 63v reads: 'The first reason was to control the original inhabitants; the second to prevent the attacks of their enemies; the third to increase the number of their own offspring; the fourth to draw people out of the city; the fifth to settle any uproar; and the sixth to grant veteran soldiers a reward' (Isabelle Buhre tr).

[57] Walter Moyle, *An Essay upon the Constitution of the Roman Government* in *Works of Walter Moyle, None of Which Were Ever before Published* (Thomas Sergeant ed, 1726) vol 1, 127–31. See Caroline Robbins, 'The "Excellent Use" of Colonies. A Note on Walter Moyle's Justification of Roman Colonies, ca. 1699' (1966) 23 The William and Mary Quarterly 620–26; Vickie B Sullivan, 'Walter Moyle's Machiavellianism, Declared and Otherwise, in *An Essay upon the Constitution of the Roman Government*' (2011) 37 History of European Ideas 120–27.

[58] For further examples, see Chapter 4 in this volume by Somos.

[59] Tom D Wilson, *The Oglethorpe Plan: Enlightenment Design in Savannah and Beyond* (University of Virginia Press 2012) 32 (hereafter Wilson, *The Oglethorpe Plan*).

productive citizens, while at the same time relieving the founding nation of excess population.[60]

Savannah's ideological founding principles, as well as their practical implementations, derived to a large extent from Roman colonial history as (re) constructed by humanist scholars such as Machiavelli and Sigonio. Apart from embracing the emancipating qualities Roman agrarian settler colonization supposedly had, Oglethorpe followed the Roman model also in practical details such as the sizes of distributed allotments. Settlers were to become freeholders and therefore received fifty acres of land per family, a recurrent amount of landed property handed to Roman colonists.[61] The maximum size of land a person could own was 500 acres, clearly reflecting the maximum amount established by the Gracchan law.[62] The general idea behind these size restrictions resonated Greco-Roman Stoic views, which suggested that allotments should be large enough to provide families with a means of subsistence but small enough to avoid the corrupting influences of wealth accumulation, which was believed to result in decadence, egoism, and idleness.[63] The same ideology also prohibited slave labour, not only because of the moral implications, but also because it would turn the colonist lazy.[64]

Also in the strict geometrical layout of both Savannah's town-plan and its hinterland, we can easily recognize Roman colonial organizational principles. The orthogonal scheme of the city clearly mirrors Roman centuriation patterns as described in the writings of the Roman land surveyors and Roman colonial town planning practices.[65] This mathematical scheme was, moreover, believed to express and stimulate order and rationalism and considered to emulate the perfect order created by God. The rational grid and egalitarian division of plots were associated with the rule of law and became a supposed symbol of civilization, separating civilized states from uncivilized ones that were unable to control the chaotic disposition of wilderness.[66]

Savannah's utopian society, however, quickly abandoned its ideological founding principles as they turned out to be ineffective in light of the harsh

[60] ibid 38.

[61] Examples of 50 *iugera*, also mentioned by Sigonio, are the allotments distributed to the colonists of Bononia and Aquileia: Livy, *Ab urbe condita*, 37.57; 40.33.

[62] Appian, *Civil Wars* 1.3; Wilson, *The Oglethorpe Plan* (n 59), 52–54. Garden plots were established at five acres.

[63] ibid 46. For the classical narrative see for example: Plato, *Laws* 737d.

[64] Wilson, *The Oglethorpe Plan* (n 59), 61; see 192–94 for the humanitarian considerations that influenced Oglethorpe's decision to prohibit slavery.

[65] ibid 55–58. See also Turpin C Bannister, 'Oglethorpe's Sources for the Savannah Plan' (1961) 20 The Journal of the Society of Architectural Historians 47–62.

[66] This view continued into the twentieth century: see for example Francis J Haverfield, *Ancient Town Planning* (Clarendon Press 1913) 14.

social and physical reality the colonists had to endure.[67] For example, the rural organization based on the principle of equality and autarky was a fiasco: the inexperienced colonial farmers could hardly make a living and complained constantly about the rationally divided and equally sized allotments. Some plots in the orthogonal grid were located in terrains unsuitable for farming such as swamps, or they were too far removed from good water resources. Farmers wanted to decide for themselves where and how much land they could cultivate. Also, the prohibition of slave labour was considered unfair as it made prices uncompetitive in regard to other nearby colonies. Eventually, the utopian colony of Savannah could only survive for about a decade because Oglethorpe and the other trustees continued to invest money in it. Only after the colony lost its semi-independent status and was transformed into a regular plantation colony, based on slave labour, did it start to prosper economically.

With the demise of Oglethorpe's ideal colony in Savannah, the farmer–settler model decisively turned out to be a Roman colonial utopia that did not match modern colonial practice. Nonetheless, Sigonio's reconstruction of Roman colonization remained an authoritative and influential source throughout the eighteenth century, both within discussions on the significance of ancient colonial models in modern contexts, for example regarding the relationship between motherland and colony in the nascent United States of America, as within scholarly debates on Roman history.[68] Moreover, the failure of the farmer–settler model in overseas colonial contexts, such as Savannah, did not discourage other attempts to initiate similar projects within the mother country. Indeed, while European colonial states in the nineteenth century gradually abandoned the idealized Roman agricultural settler model in favour of another Roman colonial model based on the idea of the civilizing mission,[69] it survived in so-called domestic colonial enterprises.[70] Increasingly, the theory that the Roman colonial settler–farmer model was a useful solution to the social problems of urban societies was adopted in social experiments at home with the objective to emancipate the urban paupers. An interesting example that encapsulates the transfer from overseas to domestic colonization at the turn of the nineteenth century are the colonies of the Dutch *Maatschappij van*

[67] Wilson, *The Oglethorpe Plan* (n 59) ch 3.

[68] See Chapters 4 and 5 in this volume by Somos and Balbo.

[69] See eg Michael Dietler, *Archaeologies of Colonialism: Consumption, Entanglement, and Violence in Ancient Mediterranean France* (University of California Press 2010) ch 1. The overseas plantation model continued for example in the Italian colonization of Libya in the opening decades of the twentieth century. For a contemporary positive British view on this, see Sir Edward J Russell, 'Agricultural Colonization in the Pontine Marshes and Libya' (1939) 94 The Geographical Journal 273–89.

[70] Barbara Arneil, *Domestic Colonies: The Turn Inward to Colony* (Oxford University Press 2017).

Weldadigheid (Society of Humanitarianism), founded in 1818 in a backward region in the Netherlands by Johannes van den Bosch.[71] Having made a military career in the Dutch colony of Batavia, Van den Bosch' objective upon his return to the Netherlands was to offer a new life to the urban poor by enrolling them into a disciplinary programme of agricultural labour based upon the Roman farmer–settler model. Also in this case, it was assumed that a project of agricultural colonization of previously uncultivated areas according to strict rational principles and schemes would have a beneficial impact on the moral of urban paupers. Moreover, their virtuous labour would bring unproductive regions into cultivation and as such enhance the value of the land considerably.[72]

More than a century later we can see the same ideology still being applied, for example, in the Fascist colonization of the Pontine Plain near Rome, and in the post-Second World War colonization of the *Mezzogiorno*, the impoverished regions of South Italy.[73] In these projects, explicitly inspired by the Roman model, agricultural colonization was believed to emancipate the urban poor while increasing the agricultural production of the nation by bringing unproductive areas into cultivation. The method to achieve this goal was found in the creation of rational and egalitarian land division systems in former swamp or woodland areas, often the former possession of aristocratic families, which were being distributed to impoverished city or village dwellers, transforming them into small proprietors. As such, these projects were also considered vital instruments to combat feudal power mechanism that were still dominating parts of southern Italy. With the partial exception of the colonization of the Pontine Plain, which after very difficult pioneer years turned out to be a modest success, most probably resulting from its profitable location close to the urban market of Rome, these social experiments failed. The rationally distributed colonial farms in the *Mezzogiorno* were quickly abandoned, as farmers preferred

[71] On Van den Bosch, see the recent biography by Angelie Sens, *De kolonieman. Johannes van den Bosch (1780–1844), volksverheffer in naam van de Koning* (Balans 2019). In these Dutch domestic colonies, land was not transferred as private property to the colonists. The idea was that they could return to 'normal' society after being disciplined in the colonies.

[72] As in the case of overseas settler colonies, these high expectations did not materialize. The living condition in the Dutch domestic colonies proved very difficult and the urban paupers did not easily transform into the ideal farmer–citizens Van den Bosh had hoped for: see Richard Paping and Vincent Tassenaar, 'Levenskansen, levensstandaard en integratie in de Koloniën van de Maatschappij van Weldadigheid' (2018) 135 Nieuwe Drentse Volksalmanak 21–48. The project was quickly abandoned and several former colonies were transformed in more regular detention centres.

[73] See Russell King, *Land Reform: The Italian Experience* (Butterworth-Heinemann 1973), and specifically on farm construction in southern Italy: Ippolita Mecca 'Borghi e paesaggi rurali della Basilicata: tipologie edilizie e tecniche costruttive' (2012) Esempi di Architettura 1–10. More examples from the interwar period are discussed in the special issue *Internal Colonization in the Age of Modern Territoriality* (2015) 3 International Journal for History, Culture and Modernity, and in Liesbeth van de Grift and Amalia Ribi Forclaz (eds), *Governing the Rural in Interwar Europe* (Routledge 2017).

to live in the old *borghi* of medieval origin, close to the bars, old churches, and palaces of the former landed aristocracy.

In contemporary Western society, the Roman agrarian colonial model has lost its appeal as a practical solution to socio-demographic problems of urbanizing societies. Still, the model remains dominant in the academic discipline of Roman studies where it continues to operate as an important explanation of Rome's imperial success.[74] The long and troublesome history of colonial implementation attempts sketched in this introductory chapter has hardly affected scholarly optimism about the success of a utopian model for which little information survives about its practical functioning in antiquity. Arguably, it is in this confidence that we can perhaps best recognize the survival of the Sigonian line of thought. Although his seminal study on Roman colonization has been surpassed by modern scholarship, especially by the great German scholars of the nineteenth century who drastically rewrote Roman colonial history, Sigonio's contention that the success of Roman Republican colonization was connected to rural reform, has endured until today.

Outline of This Volume

While this introductory chapter has given a broad and necessarily sketchy overview of the development of the farmer–settler colonial model and the role of Sigonio's seminal study of Roman colonization in this process, the next chapters of this volume explore in much greater detail Sigonio's place in the making of the legal discourse on Roman colonization.

Chapter 2 by William Stenhouse examines the work of Renaissance historians of Roman colonization before Sigonio, from Andrea Fiocchi's treatise *De potestatibus Romanis* from 1425 to Niccolò Machiavelli and Onofrio Panvinio. It shows that these earlier scholars, by thinking about Roman colonialism against the backdrop of Hapsburg power in Europe and in the New World, explored the idea of an empire that could be understood not just in terms of power (*imperium*, via the *translatio imperii*), but also in terms of territory, geographical control, and the practical administration of conquered land. Analysing the gradual rediscovery of the ancient Roman Empire and its institutions in the fifteenth and first half of the sixteenth century, Stenhouse assesses the most significant advances that Sigonio made

[74] For discussion see Pelgrom, 'The Roman Rural Exceptionality Thesis' (n 11) and Chapter 6 in this volume by Luigi Capogrossi Colognesi.

in respect to this humanist tradition. By publishing and discussing bronze fragments of the *lex agraria*, Sigonio added a crucial piece of evidence to the discourse on Roman colonial policies. Moreover, he linked historical discussions of agrarian laws and policy to historical accounts of the establishment of colonies. Previous humanist scholarship focused on the origins and status of the colonies; there were discussions of land policy, but these remained distinct from details of colonies—with the partial exception of Machiavelli, who connected the *lex agraria* with colonization. Following Livy, Machiavelli argued that the reluctance to take possession of land meant that interest in a law placing limits on land-holding and distributing land among the people remained subdued. Because he gave as much weight to Appian as to Livy, Sigonio was able to connect colonies more intimately than his predecessors with the *lex agraria*. As Stenhouse concludes, Sigonio had access to a vigorous tradition of historical discussions of Roman colonial practice that prepared the ground for an understanding of the Roman empire both as an extension of authority and as a bounded space; ground that Sigonio was to cultivate.

In Chapter 3, John Rich discusses Sigonio's view on Roman colonization within the overall structure and aims of his treatises and assesses their achievement in the light of modern scholarship. By analysing in detail the structure of Sigonio's collected work *De antiquo iure populi Romani*, Rich argues that Sigonio's innovative perspective on Roman colonial strategies was the result of his Aristotelean definition of citizenship and the connected decision to use the concept of graded *ius* to organize and analyse his source material. This lucidity of structure, together with a thorough treatment of literary and epigraphic evidence, gave Sigonio's treatises a quality unmatched by the productions of his peers and ensured that on many topics they were not surpassed until the nineteenth century. The chapter shows how Sigonio arrived at his original approach, providing a detailed overview of his studies, his close contacts with other leading academics, and the important new source material that became available at the time, most notably the Tabula Bembina. Rich argues that Sigonio's urge to systematize was one of his greatest strengths but it could also be a weakness, since it forced Sigonio to structure all the available evidence into fixed legal categories that did not always do justice to the complex and dynamic reality of Roman imperial organization. Indeed, the huge accumulation of evidence and improvement of texts since Sigonio's day has exposed many errors in his analysis, some of which resulted from Sigonio's (by our standards) uncritical acceptance of the claims and perspectives of ancient sources. But as the chapter concludes, Sigonio's work remains particularly notable for its balanced treatment of agrarian legislation and recognition of the importance of socio-economic as well as strategic factors in Roman Republican settlement programmes.

Chapter 4 by Mark Somos explores Sigonio's long-term impact by zooming in on a particular case study, turning to the nascent United States of America. By the 1740s, it was widely understood that the British imperial constitution was in urgent need of comprehensive reform. The irreconcilable patchwork of proprietary, royal, and charter colonial constitutions, the emergent historical authority of increasingly divergent local bodies of law, and the changing financial and strategic vision of the British government, together created a tremendous demand for feasible plans to sustainably recast the empire. Hundreds of proposals were hatched, circulated, and debated. Somos shows that in this intense debate, one of the most cited authorities that would-be reformers turned to was Sigonio. Perhaps more than Jean Bodin or François Hotman, Sigonio was seen as the leading comparative constitutional historian. His analyses of the Roman Empire yielded timeless lessons for metropolitan and colonial administrators alike. Most importantly, Sigonio structured his studies of Athenian, Roman, Hebrew, and medieval Italian laws and customs in a way that revealed these complex historical states' constitutional essence, making comparative analysis possible. Somos shows why American lawyers, British politicians, and merchants and soldiers with a true British–American identity, produced in the second half of the eighteenth century several reform plans for the British Empire, with particular attention to the American colonies, explicitly drawing on Sigonio's analysis of Roman colonization.

In Chapter 5, Mattia Balbo analyses the development of Roman legal colonial discourse in the eighteenth and early nineteenth century, focusing on the studies of Louis de Beaufort and Barthold Georg Niebuhr, who are generally considered to have revolutionized Roman studies by their critical approach to the literary sources. Mattia Balbo illustrates that despite their modern sceptical attitude, Beaufort and Niebuhr in fact reproduced many of Sigonio's views and differed from him only on a few issues; most notably, they both questioned, although for very different reasons, the supposed close connection between colonial law and viritane land division projects. Beaufort's attempt to disconnect Roman land distribution programmes from colonization schemes was part of a wider anti-feudal political agenda, advocating the redistribution of land to diminish aristocratic power and improve the living conditions of lower classes. In this context, Beaufort followed Montesquieu in considering the Roman practice of land division to have been crucial to the success of Roman society, which thus provided a powerful example for how modern society should progress. Niebuhr continued this interest in Roman land division policies, focusing especially on the legal definition of different types of landholding and of the personal status of the farmers. His detailed studies convincingly showed the legal differences between colonial programmes and viritane land division schemes. Moreover, he argued that this last practice was restricted only to public lands, and was not used to redistribute private properties of aristocratic landowners. Niebuhr thus softened many revolutionary aspects that previous scholars like Beaufort had ascribed to Roman popular institutions. Niebuhr's studies and interpretation of Roman agrarian and colonial history were accepted and further developed by renowned scholars such as Theodor Mommsen, giving them an almost indisputable authority that lasts until the current day. This chapter however shows that Niebuhr's reconstruction was strongly influenced by contemporary liberal political ideology and might not be as solid as is often assumed.

Chapter 6 by Luigi Capogrossi Colognesi discusses the development of the Roman colonial discourse after the pivotal studies of Niebuhr and Mommsen who revolutionized Roman studies and completely overshadowed their predecessors such as Sigonio. In line with Sigonio's approach, Capogrossi Colognesi analyses the colonization discourse especially from a legal perspective. His overview shows how this juridical outlook prospered especially in Italy, where the new sociological wave that had fundamentally changed German scholarship never really took root. Italian scholars like Ettore De Ruggiero and Plinio Fraccaro differed from Sigonio and Niebuhr in their adoption of more fluid juridical categories and sensibility for historical change. This more intuitive approach resulted in very innovative studies and crucial new insights, which however have found little support in the international academic community. The chapter shows how the marginalization of this academic tradition can be explained by the fact that in recent scholarship, Roman colonization is predominantly studied in the context of Roman imperialism or urbanism. In these more historical orientated studies there is no place for the complex legal discourse that was advanced by the Italian school and a handful of scholars from other countries. Capogrossi Colognesi argues that this scholarly divide between historical-sociological and juridical perspectives on Roman colonization is unproductive. By providing several examples of how specialized juridical insights and discussions strongly affect historical reconstructions of Roman imperial strategies and fundamentally alter our understanding of Roman colonial landscapes, the chapter shows the benefits of an integrated approach and also underlines the importance to continue the tradition started by Sigonio.

The volume ends with Chapter 7, an epilogue by Christopher Smith. Reflecting on the history of the Roman colonial discourse outlined in this book, Smith argues that it is time to depart from the strict legalistic Sigonian line of thought and the connected scholarly tradition that is almost exclusively concerned with reinterpreting the relatively late Greco-Roman sources. Instead, he advocates a more fluid and locally variable understanding of Roman Republican colonization. The colonial world in the early and mid-Republican period, he argues, may have been very different from how Livy or his contemporaries understood it to be. New intellectual models are therefore needed that may be found in the historiography of imperialism more generally. In particular, Lauren Benton's seminal work on geography and law in European imperialism offers an intellectual framework worth exploring.[75] The complex picture of partial and divided sovereignty, far removed from the classic notion of indivisible sovereignty, permits more messy and complex pictures of colonial agency that agree comfortably with recent trends in the study of Roman colonization practices.

[75] Benton, *A Search for Sovereignty* (n 1).

2

Roman Colonies and the Distribution of Land before Sigonio

William Stenhouse

How much did Carlo Sigonio's understanding of Roman colonial practice owe to the scholars who came before him? The 1560 edition of the *De antiquo iure Italiae* includes a full index of ancient authors and works discussed in the text, which runs from the predictable (Livy and Cicero) to the unexpected (the twelfth-century Byzantine grammarian John Tzetzes). Notoriously, however, sixteenth-century scholars did not usually see the need to cite their contemporaries or immediate predecessors, unless they wanted to demonstrate those writers' failings.[1] Thus, while there are plenty of references to Cicero, Columella, and others, it is not clear from Sigonio's text on colonies whether other Renaissance writers had discussed the question, and how. But we know that Sigonio was not working in isolation. He was well aware of what was going on around him, and of what people had written earlier: William McCuaig has shown clearly how Sigonio discussed issues of Roman history and the availability of books with Onofrio Panvinio (1530–68), for example, a younger contemporary, and how Sigonio honed his ideas in opposition to Nicolas de Grouchy (1510–72).[2] And in the case of colonies, for more than 100 years Renaissance historians had gathered information, and analysed how and why the Romans established these settlements. This process informed the work of Niccolò Machiavelli (1469–1527) and culminated in a long discussion by Panvinio, published in 1558. This second chapter examines the work of these historians before Sigonio to help us understand what Sigonio is likely to have read and which aspects of Sigonio's arguments and presentation would have seemed particularly acute to a contemporary audience. By thinking about

[1] On citation practices in the period, see especially Anthony Grafton, *The Footnote: A Curious History* (Harvard University Press 1997) 122–89.

[2] See William McCuaig, *Carlo Sigonio: The Changing World of the Late Renaissance* (Princeton University Press 1989) 30–33 for Panvinio and 174–250 for the controversy with de Grouchy (hereafter McCuaig, *Carlo Sigonio*).

William Stenhouse, *Roman Colonies and the Distribution of Land before Sigonio* In: *The Renaissance of Roman Colonization.* Edited by: Jeremia Pelgrom and Arthur Weststeijn, Oxford University Press (2020). © the Several Contributors.
DOI: 10.1093/oso/9780198850960.003.0002

Roman colonies and the emergence of Roman imperialism, against the backdrop of Hapsburg power in Europe and unprecedented territorial empires in the New World, these earlier scholars explored the idea of an empire that could be understood not just in terms of power (*imperium*, via the *translatio imperii*), as the Holy Roman Empire had been seen, but also in terms of territory, geographical control, and the practical administration of conquered land.[3] For many theorists of Roman colonialism in the first half of the sixteenth century, the Roman Empire still existed, under the authority of the Hapsburg Emperor, and so the rediscovery of the ancient Roman Empire and its institutions was a gradual process of historical imagination.

Humanists, Texts, and Contexts in the Fifteenth Century

Early studies of Roman colonies emerged from the humanist movement. The humanists had excavated Roman texts, tried to establish what they meant in context, and then began to write more synthetic treatments of ancient institutions. Their first contribution to the study of Roman colonization was therefore their philological expertise, providing usable texts. By the early sixteenth century, they had found many of the fundamental textual sources and made them available in easily consultable forms. These included printed editions of Livy—Niccolò Machiavelli's father Bernardo (*d* 1500) famously acquired a copy in 1476—and of speeches by Cicero, including, for example, the *Pro Balbo*, with its connection between citizenship, colonies, and Rome's power, and his fundamental speeches *De lege agraria*, in which he discussed the Italian colonies and described them as *propugnacula imperii*.[4] Such works would have been widely read, and well known even to the educated children of the elite. But the humanists had also read and published what appear today to be more recondite and technical texts. For example, in the second half of the fifteenth century, scholars at Rome rediscovered the eleventh-century manuscript of Festus, the so-called Farnesianus. Various copies exist that were made at the time, preserving the texts from pages that were subsequently destroyed, and

[3] For the persistence of the *translatio* theme in the sixteenth century, see John GA Pocock, *Barbarism and Religion, vol. 3: The First Decline and Fall* (Cambridge University Press 2003) 239–57.

[4] Cicero, *De lege agraria* 2.73. For Bernardo's Livy, see Bernardo Machiavelli, *Libro di ricordi* (Cesare Olschki ed, Le Monnier 1954) 14 and 35; Carlo Ginzburg, 'Machiavelli: L'eccezione e la regola' (2003) 38 Quaderni storici 195–213. The *Pro Balbo* and *De lege agraria* were printed together at Venice in 1471.

philologists such as Angelo Poliziano (1454–94) were able to cite it in print.[5] Humanists eagerly studied the *Noctes Atticae* of Aulus Gellius for the range of the information that the work gave about Roman customs, and imitated its miscellaneous form for their own textual research on particular passages; as a result, they would have read Gellius' famous comments in the imperial period on the increasingly blurred differences between Roman *coloniae* and *municipia*.[6] Alongside the Roman Livy, Dionysius of Halicarnassus was prized for his narratives of early Rome, and was copied widely in Latin translation in the fifteenth century, as were the texts of Strabo and Appian.[7] The humanist market attracted early printers. Aulus Gellius was printed in 1469, an epitome of Festus in 1471, Strabo and Appian in humanist Latin translations in 1472, and the first books of Dionysius, also in translation, in 1480. One further rich resource were Roman legal texts. Since the twelfth century, lawyers had tried to apply the *Digest* of Justinian to disputes in contemporary Europe, in what looks today as a determinedly ahistorical fashion. By doing so, they created a European *ius commune*, and, as a by-product, made the titles of Roman institutions and magistrates familiar to an educated public. Many educated men would have been familiar with the roles of praetors and tribunes, and with notions of personal law and Roman citizenship, even if they did not necessarily want to think about them in a historical context.

Collectively, therefore, the fifteenth-century humanists' efforts, combined with a widespread consciousness of Roman law, could provide plenty of information for anyone interested in pursuing the history of Roman colonies. The humanists' philological and legal interests, however, shaped the ways in which ideas on Roman colonial practices emerged: they were more likely to want to work out the orthography of the name for a particular site, or to establish parallels for the power of a particular magistracy, than to ponder the wider picture of Roman practice that these texts could offer collectively. But there are

5 Wouter Bracke, 'La première "édition" humaniste du *De verborum significatione* de Festus (Vat. Lat. 5958)' (1995) 25 Revue d'histoire des textes 189–215; Giovanna Mancini, 'I codici Vaticani Latini 1549 e 3369 e le pagellae perdute del Codex Farnesianus' in Fay Glinister and others (eds), *Verrius, Festus, and Paul: Lexicography, Scholarship, and Society* (BICS supplement 93) (Institute of Classical Studies 2007) 137–58, discusses the lemmata on *municeps* and *municipia*; and, in general, Peter K Marshall, 'Sex. Pompeius Festus' in Leighton D Reynolds (ed), *Texts and Transmission: A Survey of the Latin Classics* (Oxford University Press 1983) 162–64 (hereafter *Texts and Transmission*).

6 Aulus Gellius, *Noctes Atticae* 16.13; on the fifteenth-century reception of Gellius, see Anthony Grafton, 'Conflict and Harmony in the *Collegium Gellianum*' in Leofranc Holford-Strevens and Amiel Vardi (eds), *The Worlds of Aulus Gellius* (Oxford University Press 2004) 318–42, and for the manuscript tradition, see Peter K Marshall, 'Aulus Gellius' in *Texts and Transmission* (n 5) 176–80.

7 For early modern readings of Dionysius, see Gabriele Pedullà, 'Giro d'Europa. Le mille vite di Dionigi di Alicarnasso (XV–XIX secolo)' in Dionigi di Alicarnasso, *Le antichità romane* (Einaudi 2010) lix–cxlvi.

some important exceptions. In the fifteenth century, humanists began to resist using Roman law in what they saw as an anachronistic way, and started to try to contextualize familiar Roman legal texts in the same way as they did historical ones: they used the evidence of Festus or Aulus Gellius, for example, to uncover terms' original meanings, and emended passages in the *Corpus iuris civilis* with reference to other classical texts rather than legal practice.

One early pioneer in this process was Andrea Fiocchi (*c* 1400–52), who wrote a treatise *De potestatibus Romanis* (*On Roman Powers*), in around 1425. This work provided information about various magistrates and priests, including their origins and jurisdictions, and so could serve as a sort of manual for anyone interested in Roman law, history or literature.[8] For his basic organizing structure, Fiocchi followed the survey of magistrates from the rubric 'De origine iuris' at the beginning of the *Digest*, and supplemented what he found there with information from classical authors, particularly Livy.[9] By using ancient sources, and not medieval commentators, he pioneered a historicizing approach to legal questions. Furthermore, because he relied so heavily on Livy, some of his twenty-six magistracies are unusually specific, including, listed between the better-known censor and praetor, the *Triumviri coloniae deducendae* (triumvirs for the foundation of colonies, established on an ad hoc basis for that task), introduced in Livy 4.11. Fiocchi approvingly described the reasons for the creation of the magistracy, after the Romans' decision to bolster Ardea with Roman settlers as a bulwark against the Volsci, and outlined their roles for the establishment of new towns.[10] He thus gave officers responsible for colonial establishments an important place in the mechanisms of the Roman state. Fiocchi's collection was very popular, especially after it was attributed to the Roman grammarian Fenestella in the late fifteenth century and assumed to be an ancient manual, which in turn ensured the continued scholarly prominence of this magistracy.

The most important contribution to the history of colonies in the fifteenth century, though, was the *Roma triumphans* of Fiocchi's contemporary Flavio

[8] A very useful introduction to the work is Marc Laureys, 'At the Threshold of Humanist Jurisprudence: Andrea Fiocchi's *De potestatibus Romanis*' (1995) 65 Bulletin de l'Institut historique belge de Rome 25–42 (hereafter Laureys, 'At the Threshold').

[9] *Digest* 1.2.2, 13–34; see Laureys, 'At the Threshold' (n 8) 10–11.

[10] Andrea Fiocchi, *De potestibus romanorum libri II* (Plantin 1561) 2.18, 43r, referring to Livy 3.71–72 and 4.12: 'Triumviros igitur deducendæ coloniae creant: Agrippam Menenium, T. Cloelium Siculum, & M. Ebutium Helvam: nec abnuerim, hunc Magistratum alias a maioribus Romanorum creari potuisse. Cæterum ab insigniori ratione, & ingenti Pop. Rom. honestate exordiri non piguit. Pertinebat vero ad huius magistratus officium, ut & agros nouis deductis colonis dividerent, urbes designarent, ædificare volentibus areas, partirentur, commodis regionibus ciuitatem distinguerent, legibus magistratibusque sisterent, & ad speciem optimi gubernaculi Rempub. effingerent.'

Biondo. Biondo (1392–1463) wrote this ten-book survey of Roman institutions towards the end of his life, by 1459. He examined Roman religion, public institutions, the army, private institutions, and the Roman triumph. He dealt with colonies in his books on public institutions, in his section on magistrates, following his discussion of the censor's management of the Roman citizen body.[11] He therefore approached the question of colonial policy through the lens of state administration and citizenship, influenced by Fiocchi and a legalistic approach to Roman history. For Biondo, colonies were less an element of military strategy than a demonstration of effective government.[12] Biondo combined information from Livy, Cicero, and Aulus Gellius, with legal texts and other sources such as Plutarch's *Life of Gracchus*. He noted that the make-up of settlers and circumstances in which colonies were established varied, though he was less interested in giving details of all the colonies that he could find (for this he referred readers to his historical gazetteer, the *Italia illustrata*) than with distinguishing *coloniae* from *municipia* in legal terms, and *ius Latinum* from citizenship. And from his focus on citizenship, he recognized the colonies' importance in integrating Roman territory, in making new citizens, and in strengthening the state.[13]

Ironically, to modern readers, Biondo came to the right conclusion for some slightly dubious reasons. He argued that colonies were central to Roman thinking about empire and incorporation in part from his reading of the Emperor Claudius' speech, as reported by Tacitus, on including Gauls in the senate. Claudius, in Tacitus' retelling, urged the senators to accept the Gauls by reminding them of Rome's traditions of incorporating foreigners, referring to individuals, clans, and tribes. In the speech as modern editions give it, he claimed that, 'under the guise of settling our legions throughout the world, we propped up a tired empire with the addition of the strongest of the provincials.'[14] Biondo, however, read 'colonies' in place of 'legions', understandably

[11] Flavio Biondo, *De roma triumphante* (Froben 1559) 63–67, on *coloniae* and *municipia*, followed by a section on *provinciae* (hereafter Biondo, *De roma triumphante*). See, in general, Frances Muecke and Maurizio Campanelli (eds), *The Invention of Rome: Biondo Flavio's Roma triumphans and its Worlds* (Droz 2017) (hereafter *The Invention of Rome*).

[12] See Ida Gilda Mastrorosa, 'Biondo Flavio e i *Militiae romanae instituta*: Una lezione "moderna" su fondamenti e caratteri dell'impero di Rome' (2011) 2 Technai 85–103, who points out that Biondo's comments on 'romanisation', placed separately from his treatment of the army, have a decidedly modern ring, and James Hankins, 'Biondo Flavio on the Roman Republic' in *The Invention of Rome* (n 11) 101–18, esp 110–11.

[13] For example, Biondo, *De roma triumphante* (n 11) 65: 'Sed ad modos nobis redeundum est, quibus populi in civitatem Romanam accepti sunt, qui multiplices variique fuerunt, a Livioque initium est sumendum: a quo non solum qui populi & quando, sed quo etiam iure accepti sunt, facile est intelligere.'

[14] Tacitus, *Annals* 11.24.3 (*Cornelii Taciti libri qui supersunt*, vol 1 part 2: *Annales* XI–XVI (Kenneth Wellesley ed, Teubner 1986) 11), following the MS: 'tunc solida domi quies; et adversus externa floruimus, cum Transpadani in civitatem recepti, cum specie deductarum per orbem terrae legionum

given the reference to 'settling', which allowed him to underscore the importance of colonies in Rome's imperial integration. And the citizenship that they conveyed was the single largest reason for Rome's success:

> I said many things above, as I tried to show by which methods and techniques the Roman people and with it the Roman empire grew. To this end one little extract from Cicero's speech *Pro Balbo* is enough, in which these are Cicero's words: 'therefore they adopted the bravest men from all over as citizens, and preferred the virtue of low-born men to the inertia of the nobility'.[15]

For Biondo this is a strikingly forceful conclusion.

Biondo's survey became a fundamental resource for anyone interested in Roman institutions, both before it was printed in 1473, and after, right up to the time of Sigonio, and even beyond. Philological humanists used it regularly for contextual information, typically without citing it directly.[16] Biondo's account of the colonies, rather awkwardly placed among the magistrates, would therefore often have been the first port of call for anyone interested in the question of colonization, and his interests in the legal status of colonies rather than differences and variations between them, and in people and citizenship rather than

additis provincialium validissimis fesso imperio subventum est.' Biondo, *De roma triumphante* (n 11) 66 has, 'Tunc solida domi quies, & adversus externa floruimus, cum Transpadani in civitatem recepti, cum specie deductarum per orbem terrae coloniarum, additis provincialium quibusque munitionibus validissimis, fesso imperio subventum est.' (The addition of 'quibusque munitionibus' does not make any significant difference to the sense.) Having quoted the speech, Biondo drew attention to these words in analysing it: 'Quod autem Tacitum peritissime videmus dixisse, Romanos veteres illos imperii fundatores specie deductarum per orbem terrae coloniarum, additis provinciarum quibusque munitionibus validissimis fesso imperio subvenisse: libet ostensis coloniis ante oculos ponere, posteaque ipsarum coloniarum simul cum provinciis gubernationem edocere.' ('We see that Tacitus has explained most skilfully that the ancient Roman founders of the empire, under the guise of establishing colonies across the world, propped up a tired empire with the addition of each of the strongest defences of the provinces: by laying out colonies they liked to place an example before the eyes, and afterwards teach the running of those colonies together with the provinces.') The verb *deduco* ('deductarum', above) was used by Roman writers for leading an army as well as for settling a colony, as in *Triumviri coloniae deducendae*, above.

[15] Biondo, *De roma triumphante* (n 11) 66: 'Multa a nobis supra sunt dicta, dum conati sumus ostendere quibus modis & artibus & populus Romanus & simul Romanum crevit imperium: qua in re unica satisfacere potuit Ciceronis in praedicta pro Cornelio Balbo oratione particula, ubi haec sunt verba: "Itaque et cives undique fortissimos asciverunt et hominum ignobilium virtutem persaepe nobilitatis inertiae praetulerunt".' Biondo quotes Cicero, *Pro Balbo* 51; modern texts read 'itaque et civis undique fortis viros adsciverunt et hominum ignobilium virtutem persaepe nobilitatis inertiae praetulerunt'.

[16] Frances Muecke, '"Fama superstes?": Soundings in the Reception of Biondo Flavio's *Roma triumphans*' in Angelo Mazzocco and Marc Laureys (eds), *A New Sense of the Past: The Scholarship of Biondo Flavio (1392–1463)* (Leuven University Press 2016) 219–41; William Stenhouse, 'Flavio Biondo and Later Renaissance Antiquarianism' in *The Invention of Rome* (n 11) 259–73. For Bernardo's reading of Biondo, see his *Libro di ricordi* (n 4) 207.

land and its distribution, are likely to have determined scholars' sense of the colonies' importance. We know that Bernardo Machiavelli read other works by Biondo, and that Biondo would have been well known in late fifteenth-century scholarly circles in Florence. When Niccolò Machiavelli wanted information to help him think about the text of Livy, therefore, it is likely he would have turned to Biondo.

Machiavelli

> Their practice was this: as soon as war was declared, they went out with their armies to meet the enemy, and engaged quickly. When they had won, their enemies came to terms, so that their territory was not completely destroyed, and the Romans condemned them to lose land. That land they turned into private property, or assigned to a colony, which, placed on the edges of their territory, became a guard-post for Roman borders, and useful both to the colonists who took the fields, and to the Roman people, who held that guard-post without expense. This method could not be more secure, strong, or useful.[17]

As this quotation from his *Discorsi* on Livy suggests, as well as being the most famous thinker about Roman colonial policy before Sigonio, Niccolò Machiavelli was also the most forceful. Machiavelli expressed no doubt about the benefits of the Romans' policy, or about its importance for the overall arguments of his work. He stated that the colonies offered security, as effective bulkheads in enemy territory, and at a bargain price. While the Romans changed the details slightly as they went on, the basic system remained, and with it the 'usefulness and great benefit' that it brought.[18] Machiavelli compiled the *Discorsi* in 1516 and 1517, but he had held this basic view for some time. He discussed favourably Roman settlements among their enemies in his essay of 1503, 'Del modo di trattare i popoli della Valdichiana ribellati', and

[17] Niccolò Machiavelli, *Discorsi sopra la prima Deca di Tito Livio* (Mario Martelli ed, Sansoni 1971) (hereafter Machiavelli, *Discorsi*) 2.6: 'Come i Romani procedevano nel fare la guerra': 'l'uso loro era questo: subito che era scoperta la guerra, egli uscivano fuora con gli eserciti allo incontro del nimico, e subito facevano la giornata. La quale vinta, i nimici, perché non fosse guasto loro il contado affatto venivano alle condizioni ed i Romani gli condannavano in terreni: i quali terreni gli convertivano in privati commodi o gli consegnavano ad una colonia; la quale posta in su le frontiere di coloro veniva ad essere guardia de' confini romani, con utile di essi coloni, che avevano quegli campi, e con utile del publico di Roma, che sanza spesa teneva quella guardia. Né poteva questo modo essere più sicuro, o più forte, o più utile.'

[18] ibid 'l'utile e la commodità grande'.

praised the Romans' practice again in the *Prince*, of 1513, in which he used colonies as his first example from the ancient world, concluding that, 'military occupation is as useless as colonization is useful'.[19] Later, he returned to the theme: at the beginning of book two of the *Florentine Histories*, completed in 1526, he compared what the Romans had achieved with the failures of subsequent occupiers of the Italian peninsula, and argued that the abandonment of an effective policy of colonization meant that parts of Italy were now deserts. Furthermore, Machiavelli was clearly also interested in the practicalities of the Romans' method, since in the *Discorsi* he went on to ask how much land each colonist would have received.[20] His texts of Livy gave different figures, but he argued that while the exact amount varied, it must have been small: this would allow them to send enough men to maintain the outpost, and prevent those who went from living too well in comparison with those at Rome.[21] And in any case, he went on, they judged that what was important was less the amount of land, than its effective cultivation. Machiavelli here seems consciously to adopt the paternalistic tone of the Roman aristocracy.

Given its prominence and consistency across his work, Machiavelli's praise of the Romans' practice has received surprisingly little attention, at least among those scholars interested in Machiavelli's immediate context and influence.[22] One reason is likely to be that his recommendations were far from what was being practised in Italy at the time, as his comments in the *Florentine Histories* indicate; his arguments about colonies in the *Prince* precede his attack on King Louis XII of France for failing to follow the Romans' examples in securing a mixed principality. There is no easy fit between recommendation and practice

[19] Niccolò Machiavelli, 'Del modo di trattare i popoli della Valdichiana ribellati' in Niccolò Machiavelli, *Opere* vol 1 (Corrado Vivanti ed, Einaudi 1997) 22–26; Niccolò Machiavelli, *Il Principe* (Luigi Firpo ed, Einaudi 1961) ch 3: 'Da ogni parte dunque questa guardia è inutile, come quella delle colonie è utile', translation: <http://www.earlymoderntexts.com/assets/pdfs/machiavelli1532.pdf> consulted 7 July 2019.

[20] Machiavelli, *Discorsi* (n 17) 2.7: 'Quanto terreno i Romani davano per colono'.

[21] Comparing Livy 5.24 (3 7/12 *iugera*) with 4.47 (2 *iugera*).

[22] See eg Nathan Tarcov, 'Machiavelli and the Foundations of Modernity: A Reading of Chapter 3 of The Prince' in Mark Blitz and William Kristol (eds), *Educating the Prince: Essays in Honor of Harvey Mansfield* (Rowman and Littlefield 2000) 30–44, who comments on Machiavelli's claim that colonies are more faithful than garrisons: 'It is not obvious why colonists, who possess their own fields and houses in the newly acquired state, should be more faithful to the prince who sent them than would garrisons, who possess nothing in the new state and expect to go home.' Machiavelli's reading of Livy on the success of Roman colonies expressed both before and after the *Prince* explain his claim here. cf however, Mikael Hörnqvist, *Machiavelli and Empire* (Cambridge University Press 2004) 103–11. More widely, Machiavelli's views on colonization have been identified as part of his longer-term impact: see eg David Armitage, *The Ideological Origins of the British Empire* (Cambridge University Press 2004) 125–45. Clearly, another influential text on colonization from this period is Thomas More's *Utopia*. More uses the Latin term *colonia*: see, in translation, Thomas More, *Utopia* (Clarence Miller tr, 2nd edn, Yale University Press 2014) 66–67. Because, however, More's colonies are established on unused land, probably in a deliberate rejection of the Roman model, I do not discuss them here.

as there is in the case of Cesare Borgia, for example. But as Gabriele Pedullà, one of the few contemporary writers to take seriously Machiavelli's arguments about colonies, has shown, in his discussions Machiavelli was indebted less to contemporary practice, than to long-standing Renaissance humanist discussions of Roman texts, legal theory, and governing practice, and especially to Biondo.[23] Pedullà argues that lying behind Machiavelli's argument for the strategic importance of colonies was his knowledge of Biondo's connection of colonies with citizenship, and his argument that Rome's inclusivity led to her success.[24] But whereas Biondo included his discussion of colonies in his section on the magistrates who administered them, Machiavelli places his argument unambiguously in a discussion of military tactics.

Humanists, Texts, and Contexts in the Sixteenth Century

Machiavelli complained at the beginning of the *Discorsi* that whereas artists and poets had taken the examples of antiquity and successfully imitated them in their own work, contemporary politicians had failed to put into practice the precepts taught by ancient history. He composed his *Discorsi* to show how the lessons of Livy could be applied.[25] We can see his comments as a reflection on ancient historical studies up to this point, in which humanists were usually more interested in explaining Roman texts in Roman terms than in drawing explicit lessons from them for the present. On colonization, Machiavelli did have some sixteenth-century readers: in his 1533 praise of the Portuguese empire, João de Barros (*c* 1496–1570) proposed that the Portuguese establish settlements as the Romans did; more explicitly, in his *De sapientia* (1544) Girolamo Cardano (1501–76) engaged with Machiavelli, and recommended mixing indigenous people and conquerors in newly acquired territory, rather than establishing colonies.[26] But despite Machiavelli's arguments, most

[23] Gabriele Pedullà, '"Concedere la civiltà a' forestieri". Roma, Venezia e la crisi del modello municipale di res publica nei *Discorsi* di Machiavelli' (2003) 25–26 Storica 105–73 (hereafter Pedullà, '"Concedere la civiltà a' forestieri"'). This article is adapted in Gabriele Pedullà, *Machiavelli in Tumult: The* Discourses on Livy *and the Origins of Political Conflictualism* (Cambridge University Press 2018). As Pedullà notes, he owes a debt to a brief comment on the importance of Machiavelli's understanding of Roman policy by Arnaldo Momigliano, 'Camillus and Concord' (1942) 36 Classical Quarterly 111–20.

[24] Pedullà, '"Concedere la civiltà a' forestieri"' (n 23) 117–22.

[25] Machiavelli, *Discorsi* (n 17) 1 pref: 'Nondimanco, nello ordinare le republiche, nel mantenere li stati, nel governare e' regni, nello ordinare la milizia ed amministrare la guerra, nel iudicare e' sudditi, nello accrescere l'imperio, non si truova principe né republica che agli esempli delli antiqui ricorra.'

[26] See Giuseppe Marcocci, 'Machiavelli, la religione dei romani e l'impero portoghese' (2008) 41–42 Storica 35–68; Lorenzo Bianchi, 'Machiavelli e Cardano. Note su naturalismo e fortuna' in Lorenzo

scholars continued as before. Sixteenth-century historians developed fuller pictures of the procedures involved in colonial settlement, and compiled better documentation of its spread, without the sort of calls to arms that Machiavelli formulated. Sigonio's *De antiquo iure Italiae* is a good example of this: after the dedication to the pope and praise of the city of Rome, he carefully documented the legal statuses and arrangements of Italy in antiquity. In twenty-first-century terms, he proceeded as a historian and not a political scientist. McCuaig has shown in a slightly different context Sigonio's cautious reluctance to deal directly with contemporary political debates; he recommended to Panvinio in a letter advising him to stay clear even of an academic dispute, 'let's learn to live, and not stir up wasps' nests, and let's talk in our own way'.[27] So Machiavelli's approach is something of a red herring if we want to understand the origins of Sigonio's *De antiquo iure Italiae* (although with one important exception, as we shall see). Subsequent readers, including Thomas Smith and then James Harrington, were to yoke Sigonio's insights to Machiavelli's willingness to apply Roman exempla to the world around them.[28]

Early sixteenth-century writers of philological and contextual miscellanies regularly betrayed an unacknowledged debt to Biondo: when they highlighted how knowing about colonies helped in the understanding of other texts, for example, they often followed Biondo's interest in defining and categorizing the *colonia* as a particular type of settlement. Alessandro d'Alessandro (1461–1523), for example, in his regularly reprinted *Genialium dierum libri sex* (1522), examined colonization in a discussion of a passage from Juvenal (5.170–173), where the poet made reference to his addressee having his head shaved, and so

Bianchi and Alberto Postigliola (eds), *Dopo Machiavelli/Après Machiavel* (Liguori 2008) 53–73, citing Girolamo Cardano, *De sapientia* (Iohannes Petreius 1544) 137: 'Quod si novum regnum bellica virtute vel successione antiquo adiungatur, quatuor modis absque seditione retinetur: vel coloniis in locum deductis, quod Romani facere solebant: vel habitatione principis, ut cum Turcarum princeps in Graeciam sedem suam transtulit: vel mixtione populorum, quod Romani cum Sabinis & Hetruscis fecerunt. Neque enim hoc adeo servile est ut habitatio, nec tam crudele ut coloniae deductae; in quibus quod optimum est ac tutissimum, antiquos habitatores delere; hoc autem inhumanum est.'

[27] Quoted in McCuaig, *Carlo Sigonio* (n 2) 17: 'impariamo a vivere et non stucchiamo i vespai, et parliamo . . . a nostro modo'. McCuaig concludes: 'the complete exclusion from [Roman studies] of factors touching current religious or national disputes afforded a freedom of thought and expression that was vanishing from the discussion of even remote episodes of the Christian centuries under the pressure of religious controversy'. See now Guido Bartolucci, 'Carlo Sigonio and the "Respublica Hebraeorum": A Re-evaluation' (2008) 3 Hebraic Political Studies 19–59, who shows that by turning to ancient Israel in 1582 Sigonio did engage with contemporary politics.

[28] For Smith's plans for Ireland, strongly influenced by Roman models, see Richard Simpson, 'Sir Thomas Smith (1513–77). An Overview of his Life and Works' in Andrew Burnett and Richard Simpson (eds), *Roman Coins. Money, and Society in Elizabethan England: Sir Thomas Smith's* On the Wages of the Roman Footsoldier (The American Numismatic Society 2017) 1–71; more generally, see DB Quinn, 'Renaissance Influences in English Colonization' (1976) 26 Transactions of the Royal Historical Society 73–93.

being treated as a slave; d'Alessandro managed to use this as a springboard for discussing the types of legal freedom in the Roman world, and their origins in settlements and colonies on the Italian peninsula.[29] In his notes on the *Digest*, Guillaume Budé (1467–1540) discussed colonies in his notes to a passage where Ulpian distinguished doing business in a *colonia* and in a *municipium*. Budé corrected what the medieval commentator Accursius had to say on this passage (he had said that a *colonia* was a villa), and gave his readers etymologies of the term *coloniae*, as well as the passage from Aulus Gellius on the difference between *colonia* and *municipium*, Cicero's *propugnacula imperii*, and other quotations from Suetonius and Caesar.[30] Another legal scholar, Andrea Alciato (1492–1550), discussed the difference between *colonia* and *municipium* in his extended commentary on the meaning of legal terms, the *De verborum significatione*. In his definition of *municipes*, he started with a brief account of *coloniae*, saying that veterans were settled in them, and also addressed, albeit briefly, the practical issues colonies might raise: he said that veterans received two *iugera* of land 'so that they could survive old age', and said that the reason for settling colonies was either a shortage of cities, or 'a punishment imposed on old farmers deserving ill of the republic'.[31]

Alciato's brief comments here perhaps owe something to his awareness of new texts that were to prove relevant to the discussion of colonies. In 1515, Beatus Rhenanus found a manuscript of Velleius Paterculus in the abbey of Murbach, which he published early in 1521. The manuscript was unusually corrupt, and difficult to read, which meant that humanists could dispute the proper names, in particular, in the text.[32] But Velleius' chronological list of colonies was clear enough to become a central part of scholarly discussions, and its place in his narrative suggested their importance to Roman mentalities. Alciato also knew of work on the texts of the *agrimensores*, which humanists at Rome

[29] Alessandro d'Alessandro, *Genialium dierum libri vi* (De Vascosan 1549) 4.10, 530–45, entitled 'Locus ex Iuvenale declaratur, quotuplex apud veteres libertatis genus fuerit, qualiterque civitas amittebatur vel dabatur'.

[30] Guillaume Budé, *Annotationes priores et posteriores . . . in Pandectas* (De Vascosan 1556) 259r–259v, on *Digest* 50.1.27.1 (Ulpian, 'Si quis negotia sua non in colonia, sed in municipio semper agit').

[31] Andrea Alciato, *De verborum significatione* (Gryphius 1530) 247, on *Digest* 50.16.228 (Paulus, '*Municipes* intellegendi sunt et qui in eodem municipio nati sunt'): 'Coloniae erant, in quas cives Romani habitatum deducati erant, agerque eis assignatus: solebant autem deduci veterani, & pro diutinorum laborum mercede, unde senectutem tolerarent, iugera bina accipiebant. Causa deductionis erat, vel infrequentia urbium, vel poena, qua veteres Coloni male de Republica meriti, mulctabantur.'

[32] Velleius Paterculus, *Historiae Romanae duo volumina* (Froben 1520 [recte 1521]); see LD Reynolds, 'Velleius Paterculus' in *Texts and Transmission* (n 5) 431–33 and Lorenzo Calvelli, 'Novità sulla fortuna del Codex unicus di Velleio Paterculo' (2016) 58 Rivista di cultura classica e medioevale 357–72. Rhenanus had worked from a copy of the manuscript made for him; when Johannes Albert Burer saw the proofs at Froben's printing shop, and compared them with the original manuscript, he added ten pages of errata to the end of the book (sig G–Gv for the passage on colonies from book 1).

in the early sixteenth century had started to examine in depth.[33] These treatises on land surveying, collected together in late antiquity, were discovered in three separate classes of manuscript in this period.[34] Each version included different texts. Humanists were especially interested in the details of measurements and in the illustrated treatises, which seemed to show how the Romans surveyed and saw the world. Some tried to imitate those illustrations in their own representations of Rome; in his *Antiquae Urbis Romae cum regionibus Simulachrum* (*Facsimile of Ancient Rome with its regions*, 1527), Fabio Calvo reversed the usual argument that colonies were made in the image of Rome, and produced a reconstruction of early Rome that looks very like a Roman colony illustrated in the *agrimensores*.[35]

These compilations also included many other details relevant to the study of colonization in theory and practice. Among them were the *De conditionibus agrorum* attributed to Siculus Flaccus, with its discussion of why colonies were made, the fragmentary Lex Mamilia Roscia Peducaea Alliena Fabia on creating colonies, and the *liber regionum* or *liber coloniarum* (also known to the humanists as the *liber de coloniis*, and attributed by them to Frontinus), with its list of settlements. Because of their technical nature, the varied texts, and the problems involved in rendering the illustrations, humanists found it difficult to find publishers willing to attempt to print these works. Johannes Sichard included three treatises particularly relevant to Roman law from a manuscript he found in Fulda in his 1528 Basle edition of the Theodosian Code (at great personal expense, as he complained in the introduction).[36] Then in 1554 Adrien Turnèbe published many more texts from a collection that he and

[33] Annalisa Belloni, *L'Alciato e il diritto pubblico romano: I Vat. Lat. 6216, 6271, 7071* (Biblioteca Apostolica Vaticana 2016) vol 2, 690–711 (hereafter Belloni, *L'Alciato*).

[34] MD Reeve, 'Agrimensores' in *Texts and Transmission* (n 5) 1–6; Lucio Toneatto, *Codices artis mensoriae. I manoscritti degi antichi opuscoli latini d'agrimensura* (V-XIX sec.) (Centro italiano di studi sull'alto medioevo 1994-95) vol 1, 55–75 and vol 3, 1232–34 (hereafter Toneatto, *Codices artis mensoriae*); and for a useful edition and account of the contents, Brian Campbell, *The Writings of the Roman Land Surveyors: Introduction, Text, Translation and Commentary* (Institute of Classical Studies 2000) xxi–xliv. For interests in these texts in sixteenth-century Rome, see Ingrid Rowland, *The Culture of the High Renaissance: Ancients and Moderns in Sixteenth-Century Rome* (Cambridge University Press 1998) 135–39.

[35] Philip Jacks, 'The *Simulachrum* of Fabio Calvo: A View of Roman Architecture all'antica in 1527' (1990) 72 Art Bulletin 453–81; See also Bianca de Divitiis, Fulvio Lenzo, and Lorenzo Miletti (eds), *Ambrogio Leone's* De Nola, *Venice 1514* (Brill 2018) , which shows that Leone's 1514 illustrations of the *municipium* of Nola, apparently indebted to the *agrimensores*, were a significant influence on Calvo.

[36] *Codicis Theodosiani Libri XVI* (Johannes Sichardus ed, Henricus Petrus 1528) sig α3v. The texts were Volusius Maecianus' *De asse*, and the work on land disputes attributed to Frontinus, with the commentary attributed to Aggenius Urbicus. Sichard refers to comparing the Fulda manuscript with a manuscript in Strasbourg, which included a little more 'de limitis prorsis, & transversis' (ibid fol. 174v). See Toneatto, *Codices artis mensoriae* (n 34) vol 1, 56–57 and 63–64.

Pierre Galland had found at the monastery of Saint Bertin, near Saint-Omer.[37] Turnèbe's edition included Siculus Flaccus and the Lex Mamilia: its publication meant, for example, that Louis le Caron included the *lex* in his 1555 edition of Ulrich Zasius' compilation of Roman *leges*, which became a standard reference work, as did François Hotman in his similar collection of 1557.[38] Despite being known in Florence and Rome much earlier, the *liber regionum* was not printed until 1563, when Paolo Manuzio took the text from a copy in Rome of the Arcerianus manuscript, and published it as a small pamphlet, perhaps encouraged by the success of Sigonio's *De antiquo iure Italiae* and the issues that it had raised (when completing his *De antiquo iure Italiae*, Sigonio had written from Venice to Panvinio in May 1560, asking for a copy of the text, which Panvinio had previously cited).[39] To come back to Alciato: he had access to one manuscript of the *agrimensores*, which included schematic plans of the allocation of land in colonies; for that reason, maybe, he was attentive to the practicalities of distributing land as well as to the legal issues involved in defining *coloniae* and their citizens' rights.

Local Histories and the Analysis of Empire

Alciato was also aware of one other trend affecting the interpretation of Roman colonization: the rise of local historical writing in the former Roman Empire. Although they were willing to criticize details, Renaissance scholars did not attempt to replace the narratives of Livy or Tacitus by writing new histories of the Roman world centred on Rome: the ancients still had too much authority. Writing town histories, or regional histories, though, was a different matter. Humanists on the Italian peninsula and beyond saw writing accounts of their native places as ways of promoting and understanding where they lived.

[37] *De agrorum conditionibus, & constitutionibus limitum* (Turnèbe 1554). Turnèbe had found the manuscript, the so-called Gudianus, ten years earlier. See Toneatto, *Codices artis mensoriae* (n 34) vol 1, 64. For an early response to the work, comparing it with another manuscript, see Lucio Toneatto, 'Dalla biblioteca privata del giurista Jean Matal (Metellus Sequanus, 1510 ca.-1597): una copia annotata della 'princeps' turnebiana dei Gromatici (Codici d'agrimensura perduti o non identificati. Notizie e dati filologici, II)' (2004) 32 Index: Quaderni camerati di studi romanistici 123–58.

[38] Ulrich Zasius, *Catalogus legum antiquarum* (Guillaume Cavellat 1555) 143v–45r (herafter Zasius, *Catalogus*); François Hotman, *De legibus populi romani liber* (Episcopius 1557) 46–47. For an edition and translation of the Lex Mamilia, see *Roman Statutes* (MH Crawford ed, Institute of Classical Studies 1996) vol 2, 763–67 (argued to be part of a Lex Iulia agraria of 59 BCE).

[39] *Sex. Ivlii Frontini de coloniis libellus* [1563]; see Lucio Toneatto, 'L'editio princeps del "Liber regionum I"' (1983) 1 Dialoghi di archeologia 87–95 and Lucio Toneatto, 'Ancora sull'editio princeps del "Liber regionum I"' (1985) 3 Dialoghi di archeologia 125–29. For Sigonio's letter, see Carlo Sigonio, *Opera Omnia* (Argelati 1732-37) vol 6, 1013–14 (hereafter Sigonio, *Opera omnia*).

Evidence from the Roman period was potentially prestigious, including any testimony for towns' statuses in the period. Alciato wrote a history of Milan himself, which praised the native Galli and documented their resistance to the Roman invaders, before dealing with the town's transformation under Rome.[40] Following Livy he recorded the foundation of Piacenza and Cremona as colonies to the south-east of Milan, and the consequent hostility of the Gauls, angered at the seizure of their land; he went on to argue tendentiously that a colony of veterans who had fought in Germany had been settled in what was now Monza, in Milanese territory, on the basis of an inscription that he had found there.[41] He attacked Marcus Claudius Marcellus' removal of citizenship from the colonists installed by Caesar at Como, which he described as 'a terrible example', and later distinguished the rights of *coloniae* from other settlements within Roman territory.[42]

A more extensive and developed example of this interest in Roman colonies from a local perspective is Jean Poldo d'Albenas' history of Nîmes, which he finished in 1557, just before Sigonio's *De antique iure Italiae*.[43] Poldo was clearly interested in what being a Roman colony meant in practice. Early on in his work, he briefly surveyed the spread of the Romans in Gallia Narbonensis, and discussed the establishment of Narbonne for the tenth legion as the 'lookout for the Romans, their defence, and fortress', citing the Theodosian Code, Cicero, and others.[44] When dealing with the foundation of Nîmes itself as a colony, he discussed *ius Latinum*, the development of *ius Italicum*, and the rights of colonies, citing the jurists Paul and Ulpian, Velleius Paterculus, and Suetonius, but also d'Alessandro, Budé, and Alciato.[45] Then when discussing the city's coins, he examined the best-known coin from Nîmes, which featured on the obverse a crocodile chained to a palm tree, with the legend COL NEM above. He argued that these letters referred not to Nîmes itself (the Latin for which was 'Nemausus') but to a colony established in Egypt, after the Roman conquest,

[40] See Andrea Alciato, *Rerum patriae libri IIII* (Bidelli 1625) 66–67 (hereafter Alciato, *Rerum patriae*) for his praise of the Galli. Alciato worked on Milanese history throughout his life, but this work was only published long after his death: see Belloni, *L'Alciato* (n 33).

[41] Alciato, *Rerum patriae* (n 40) 50–51 and 76–77. His inscription recorded a 'civium Romanorum Moguntiaci curator', and he assumed that this man and others had fought at Mainz (Moguntiacum), and then named their new settlement Moguntiacum in memory of their service there. See Belloni, *L'Alciato* (n 33) vol 1, 325, 405–07.

[42] Alciato, *Rerum patriae* (n 40) 80–81 ('Quarum illa ad praesentem historiam attinet, quod Marcellus Consul in Novocomensi Decurione pessimo exemplo fecit') and 88. See Belloni, *L'Alciato* (n 33) vol 1, 172.

[43] Jean Poldo d'Albenas, *Discours historiale de l'antique et illustre cite de Nismes* (Roville 1559). The privilege in the work is dated 1557; some copies are dated to 1560.

[44] ibid 7: 'la centinele des Romains, defense, & forteresse'.

[45] ibid 31–33.

by Roman subjects from Nîmes. This, he argued, was a great honour, and not one that he could pass over in silence. (Poldo's argument is tendentious: scholarly consensus now sees the image and legend as a reference to the settlement of soldiers from the Egyptian campaign in the colony at Nîmes.) Poldo moved on to reflect about colonies more generally.[46] He presented them as part of a general strategy on the part of the Romans to settle conquered territory, citing Appian and Dionysius of Halicarnassus in particular; he then came back to the question of colonies' legal status, again distinguishing the Latin rights of Nîmes from those which came with full Roman citizenship, and discussing the benefits of the latter.[47] And having done that, he also decided to address what many of his predecessors had done before, the differences between *coloniae* and *municipia*, before concluding that his putative colony in Egypt could have enjoyed Latin rights, but because it came from Nîmes, not full citizenship.[48] At this point, Poldo revealed one reason why he was so interested in Nîmes as a Roman colony and then mother-city: he saw contemporary parallels. When Louis XI took Arras in 1477, Poldo wrote, he expelled the inhabitants and made a new city, settling loyal subjects from 'good French towns': these included people from Nîmes. Among others, nearly the whole Robert family was sent, which he described as 'one of the honourable houses of the city'.[49] The loyal inhabitants of Nîmes could be relied upon in the present day, just as they were in antiquity. Then, taking a line reminiscent of Machiavelli in the *Prince*, Poldo concluded that had the French kings done the same in Geneva, Milan, Naples, and other Italian cities, they would not have spent so much in reconquering them, or suffered the shame of losing them.

By attempting civic or regional history, therefore, writers like Poldo thought about how Roman colonization, and the Roman empire that emerged, worked at a local level. They were usually more interested in evidence for provincial administration once the territory was settled, but also addressed questions about

[46] ibid 99: 'En ceste numisme estoit faict mention de la Colonie de Nismes, qui estoit honneur tresgrand aux habitans, ce que nous ne pouvons bonnement passer par silence, ayant desir d'escrire un peu des Colonies, & choses y appertenans.' See also ibid 104: 'En quoy aussi lon peut voir, de quelle grande, & singuliere confidence les Romains honnoroyent nos maieurs.'

[47] ibid 99–103.

[48] ibid 103–104.

[49] ibid 104: 'Et ie croy, que meu ou de ceste memoire, ou pour le moins de pareille recommendation de fidelité le Roy Louys xi du nom, ayant pris Arras en l'an M.cccclxxvii y envoya comme colonies des habitans de Nismes, exilant, & bannissant, comme dit nostre histoire Françoise, les habitans d'Arras, & y faisant ville neufve, la repeuplant de gens de tous estats d'aucunes bonnes villes Françoise, & le plus de Normandie, qui ne s'y tindrent guieres, envoyant ceux d'Arras demeurer es extremités du Royaume de France. Et entre autres, dont nous ayons particuliere memoire en nostre cité, y fut envoyee toute presque la famille des Roberts, qui eft l'une des honnorables maisons de la ville, ainsi que i'ay veu par leurs particulieres memoires, & que de ce encor noz vieillars ont souvenance l'auoir entendu de leurs peres.'

colonies' origins. Poldo also pondered contemporary parallels. A good example of how this approach could then affect scholars' understanding of Rome as a whole is the work of Wolfgang Lazius, who worked in the Hapsburg court in Vienna as official historian to Emperor Ferdinand I around the middle of the century. Lazius explored ways of making sense of the region in which he lived: he designed historical maps, composed a history of Vienna and its hinterland, and then attempted to write an account of the Germanic invasions at the end of the Roman period.[50] In 1551 he also published a voluminous commentary in twelve books on the Roman state in the provinces, the *Commentarii reipublicae romanae*.[51] He built on the work of previous historians of Rome, and of local historians in German-speaking lands, to try to document how and where the Romans ruled, in as much detail as possible: he reviewed magistrates and the army in depth, but also games and festivals, religion, honours, and clothing. His final book dealt with colonies. The fact that he placed this last already gives some idea of his approach: he saw colonies less as part of the strategy of Roman conquest, than what the Romans left behind.

Lazius divided the book on colonies into two parts, first looking at colonies in general terms, and then by giving specific evidence for Roman settlements across the northern frontier of the empire. The second part is much more extensive, detailing inscriptions and written sources, and offering potted histories of some sites to the present, whereas the first gives a better idea of Lazius' overall conception of colonization. Like his predecessors, he began by defining Roman settlements in legal terms and addressing whether their inhabitants had Roman citizenship, referring to Livy for evidence about sites on the Italian peninsula, quoting Tacitus' Claudius (he has 'legions', rather than 'colonies', suggesting that Biondo was not his primary source), and citing various other narrative and legal sources.[52] These included Urbicus from the *agrimensores*, for example, on the allocation of land to veterans. Then he considered social ranks and societies within colonies, and evidence for farms in the countryside. The result is a survey of the extent of Roman territory, and a demonstration of consistent phenomena across towns (in the second part, the inscriptions he cites, mostly gravestones with details of individuals' careers, do a good job of showing how magistrates' titles and offices were the same from place to place),

[50] See Walter Goffart, *Historical Atlases: The First Three Hundred Years* (Chicago University Press 2003) 61–66.

[51] The full title of the work, *Twelve books of commentaries on the Roman state established in foreign provinces won in war*, gives a better idea of its approach: *Commentariorum Reipublicae Romanae illius, in exteris provinciis, bello acquisitis, constitutae, libri duodecim* (Oporinus 1551).

[52] ibid 1046–54.

but not much of an analysis of colonization as a phenomenon. Lazius later wrote an account of the history of Greek states, with similar results: he outlines which city is a colony of which mother-city, without stepping back to analyse the process as a whole.[53]

Lazius wrote quickly, and in many ways he was a prisoner of his sources, taking the Roman line and talking in Roman terms, without making many direct comparisons with the present. He differs in approach, for example, from a predecessor called Johannes Turmair (known as Aventinus), whose *Seven Books on the Deeds of the Bavarians* (*Rerum Boiorum libri septem*) took a notably hostile line to the Roman conquest, stressing the destruction that the Romans caused while acknowledging the peace that followed. He said that local leaders were taken to Rome and savaged by beasts to provide a 'most cruel spectacle and bloody pleasure' for the people, or killed in prison—something, rumour had it, the contemporary Turks also did. But the Romans were not exactly like Turks. They settled colonies, he wrote, which they filled with Roman and Italian colonists, and they paid stipends to the soldiers, 'in the same way as to priests today'.[54] Aventinus seems to suggest that the settlers were almost like missionaries for the state (his sympathies were with the new religious reformers, which probably explains his tone). Beatus Rhenanus, another German-speaking historian, and the editor of Velleius, whom Lazius used extensively, was more measured in his assessment of the Romans, though not uniformly positive. When he composed the inscription for a new statue of Munatius Plancus in Basle, who was to be celebrated as the founder of the Roman colony on the site, he noted that Plancus had dispersed the original inhabitants of the area, but was to be celebrated for his love of virtue and moderation toward the enemy.[55] Lazius did not adopt the tone of Turmair or Rhenanus. And while he did not hold back from drawing wider conclusions from his work—in fact, in both the Roman and Greek histories he invited the Hapsburg Emperor to raise an army and take back those areas whose classical

[53] Wolfgang Lazius, *Commentariorum rerum Graecarum libri II* (Raphael Hoffalter 1558).

[54] Johannes Turmair, *Annalium Boiorum libri septem* (Weissenhorn 1554) 96: 'Romani victores superiores regiones in formam provinciae redegerunt, Colonias deduxerunt, Romanis, Italicis colonis oppleverunt. . . Praedia stipendaria (Parrochias vocabant) militibus, quemadmodum nostro aevo sacerdotibus, assignata sunt. . . Nobilitas, principes, sacerdotes (ne reliqueretur materia bellandi) aut occisi, aut captivi Romam cum uxoribus, liberis abducti, cathenis collo, manibusque colligati, triumphati sunt. Deinde partim leonibus, apris, & huiusmodi bestiis in circo, harenave obiecti, Ro. populo crudelisimum spectaculum, sanguinariamque praebuere voluptatem: pars in carcere necati, sublatique sunt: quemadmodum nostro aevo Turcas factitare fama est.'

[55] Beatus Rhenanus, *Briefwechsel* (Adalbert Horawitz and Karl Hartfelder eds, Teubner 1886) 622–23: 'L. Munatio Planco . . . S. P. Q. Basiliensis tametsi Alemannorum transducti coloni subactis ac depulsis Rauricis, amore tamen virtutis quae etiam in hoste venerationem meretur . . . culpa temporum prorsus abolitam memriam postliminio renovarunt.'

past he studied, but which were now oppressed by Ottoman hands—his arguments for the contemporary relevance of what he was doing were a long way from the specificity of Machiavelli.

What Lazius does illustrate, however, very effectively, is the geographical extent of Rome. His Rome was a contiguous territory, with frontiers (he talks about outlining the borders (*limites*) of the empire in the subtitle to his work, and McCuaig deemed him a pioneer of *limes* studies).[56] He was by no means the first to outline the extent of the Roman Empire. For example, Petrus Apianus and Bartolomaeus Amantius had organized their 1534 inscription collection geographically, beginning in Spain, and moving eastwards through the former empire, to Greece, Asia Minor, and then back west along the southern shore of the Mediterranean. They were closely connected to Charles V's imperial court—they dedicated the work to their patron, Raymund Fugger, whom they described as his councillor—and called Charles 'Romanorum Imperator Augustus'.[57] As a result, their readers were invited to parallel the ancient Roman Empire with Charles' domain, in spatial terms.[58] It seems reasonable to see here the influence of Hapsburg possessions in Europe, and of information about territorial empire in the New World, affecting how scholars of the Roman world thought about the Roman Empire. As we have seen, humanist writers on the Italian peninsula approached colonies primarily in terms of powers and categories: they were interested in who had *imperium* as magistrates, and what rights citizens and inhabitants of various settlements had. This accords with most medieval thinking about empire, where emperors were defined by the authority (*imperium*) that they had rather than the territory that they controlled.[59] This thinking lay behind the concept of *translatio imperii*. As ideas of what exactly an empire was changed in the early sixteenth century, so historians wrote about the Roman world in changed ways, which in turn affected how they wrote about colonies. As we shall see, this is one way of explaining Sigonio's focus on land as well as power in Roman colonial practice.

Sigonio's most direct influence in thinking about Roman practice was not Lazius, however, but Panvinio.[60] Panvinio was younger than Sigonio, but the pair clearly saw themselves as colleagues, and letters between the two show

[56] McCuaig, *Carlo Sigonio* (n 2) 58 n170.

[57] Petrus Apianus and Bartolomaeus Amantius, *Inscriptiones sacrosanctae vetustatis non illae quidem Romanae, sed totius fere orbis* (Apianus 1534) sig [A2i]v.

[58] Martin Ott, *Die Entdeckung des Altertums: Der Umgang mit der römischen Vergangenheit Süddeutschlands im 16. Jahrhundert* (Lassleben 2002) 179.

[59] Although cf eg Marsilius of Padua, *Writings on the Empire* (Cary Nederman ed, Cambridge University Press 1993) 66.

[60] See also Chapter 3 in this volume by John Rich.

that Sigonio asked Panvinio for information about developments at Rome, after they had collaborated together in Venice. Rome in the 1550s was a hotbed of antiquarian research, as scholars gathered and discussed material and textual evidence for the ancient world. Sigonio benefited from information about coins and inscriptions, and new versions of ancient texts, such as Antonio Agustín's impressive new edition of Festus, published in 1559. As we have seen, in 1560 Sigonio asked Panvinio for information about a text of the *liber regionum*; in 1558, when he was working on the *De antiquo iure Italiae*, he wrote discussing his problems about getting evidence for inhabitants of colonies voting at Rome; and later that same year he pondered Panvinio's interpretation of the *ius Italicum*.[61] Sigonio asked for Panvinio's advice because Panvinio had recently completed his *Three books of Commentaries on the Roman State* (*Reipublicae Romanae Commentariorum libri tres*), dedicated to the Hapsburg Emperor Ferdinand I (who could be a more appropriate dedicatee, Panvinio pointed out, than the Roman emperor?).[62] This long work rather awkwardly documented Rome's institutions while providing a historical account of the growth of the state, all backed up by large quantities of the evidence that his Roman colleagues were assembling (Panvinio took the opportunity to include various primary sources in what we would call documentary appendices). Panvinio divided his material into one book for the city of Rome, one for what he called the *civitas Romana*, covering the constitution of the republic, and then one for the Roman empire. Ostensibly, then, he followed a roughly chronological path, charting the rise of the city-state, but in practice, as he acknowledged, he progressed 'more in the manner of a commentary than a history'.[63] Thus much of his evidence for the city of Rome dates from late antiquity, including his edition of the fifth-century *De reditu suo* by Rutilius Claudius Namatianus, whereas he deals with colonies in book three. Panvinio documented the Roman conquest of the Italian peninsula, and dealt with the various legal categories taken on by their allies and subjects, before turning to colonies.

Panvinio saw colonization as an archetypal element of Roman expansion: it was a practice begun by Romulus, he wrote, 'in order to stabilize

[61] Sigonio, *Opera omnia* (n 39) vol 6, 1001, 1003, 1013–14. When the *De antiquo iure Italiae* was completed in 1560, Sigonio alerted Panvinio to the fact that his interpretations sometimes differed: ibid 1011: 'Sono discordante da voi in alcune cose.'

[62] Onofrio Panvinio, *Reipublicae Romanae Commentariorum libri tres* (Valgrisi 1558) sig a4v: 'In quibus mihi cogitationibus versanti, Maiestatem tuam huius potissimum operis patronum deligendam esse existimavi. Quod cur facerem multas omnino causas habui: quarum praecipua, quod imperii Romani breviarium, non nisi imperatori Romano dicari oportere duxi.'

[63] ibid 292.

the Roman Empire'.[64] Colonies were organized on the model of Rome, with Roman magistrates and laws—a claim which he qualified in a long discussion of the *ius Latinum*, prefectures, and citizenship law, again dealing in legal categories.[65] Only then did Panvinio present a list of colonies. He began with those he could place in chronological order, from Romulus' Caenina (Ciano), mentioned in Dionysius of Halicarnassus, to number 98, Capua Iulia Felix, established by Julius Caesar. He added thirty more, which he argued were established by Caesar or Augustus, but which he could not pin down more precisely, and three established in the reign of Claudius. He then gave twenty-one further examples, which he could not place chronologically at all. For some entries in this final category, he only had the evidence of inscriptions mentioning a colony that were found in particular towns, so their inclusion seems forced, but also suggests to his readers the lengths to which he had gone to establish an exhaustive list.[66] For each entry, Panvinio gave quotations from his best sources (usually Dionysius, Livy, or Velleius Paterculus) and references to other authors or inscriptions that mention the sites (authors such as Pliny or Strabo, who were not writing narrative histories). Where his sources disagreed, he quoted them without going further. For example, he had information from Velleius and the *liber coloniarum* for a colony called Nepet, Colonia Nepensis, or Nepis, and because Velleius offered a date for its foundation, he placed it twenty-first in his list. But he added that Festus recorded that it was a *municipium sui iuris*.[67] Having given the details, Panvinio then went on to list *municipia*, and prefectures. What Panvinio gave his readers, therefore, was less an analysis of colonization than an updated version of the sorts of lists in Velleius Paterculus or the *liber coloniarum*, documenting the existence of colonies as a phenomenon, but not pondering the practicalities involved in their creation or their exact place in Roman strategies, except to point out that they helped strengthen the empire. Like Lazius, Panvinio followed his Roman sources, and was more concerned to document than explain. It is not hard to see, then, why Sigonio was not concerned about duplicating his friend's work. Panvinio

[64] ibid 693: 'quo imperium Romanum stabilirent'.

[65] ibid 694–702.

[66] For example ibid 752: 'Colonia Tolentinum. Tolentini vetus inscriptio haec adhuc extat: MAVORTI. ET.GENIO.COLONIAE'.

[67] ibid 710. See also eg his entry for number 40, Cosa (716), which he noted that Cicero called a *municipium* in his *In Verrem*, numbers 58, Vulturnum, and 59, Linternum (724), which Festus calls *praefecturae*, and number 85, Ferento (732), where his only evidence is from the *liber coloniarum*, and he notes that Livy refers to the Ferentine people asked for Latins enrolled in Roman colonies to be made citizens.

built on the legalistic and textual traditions of the humanists without going beyond them.[68]

Conclusion: Sigonio and Previous Discussions of Colonies

The most significant advances that Sigonio made in respect to this tradition can be summarized as follows. First, by printing and discussing bronze fragments of the *lex agraria*, Sigonio added to the ancient evidence for colonial policies. This is on the one hand not just surprising—he went down the same route humanists had been following for many years—but also striking, in that he was the first to try to integrate the fragments in discussions of Roman history, but did so away from Rome, and so at a distance from the antiquarian discussions of his time. Although he did not engage with material evidence to the extent of Panvinio, or of another colleague, the legal scholar Antonio Agustín (who was subsequently to produce a fuller analysis of the fragments), this shows at the very least Sigonio's comfort with inscribed evidence.[69] Second, as McCuaig showed, by taking an Aristotelian social perspective on Roman constitutional developments, Sigonio was able both to distance himself from the Roman sources with which he worked, and to create the sort of workable structure for the discussion of Roman institutions that Panvinio lacked. And third, most importantly for the discussion of colonization, Sigonio linked historical discussions of agrarian laws and policy to historical accounts of the establishment of colonies, which is worth documenting in more detail.

Previously, as we have seen, the humanists focused on the origins and status of the colonies; only Alciato, to a small extent, and Machiavelli, much more directly, thought more about the practical implications of the allocation of land. There were discussions of land policy, but these remained distinct from details of colonies. Biondo, for example, included brief comments on agrarian laws in a discussion of different types of law and actions made by the senate, highlighting their prominence: 'We have kept the *lex agraria* for

[68] See McCuaig, *Carlo Sigonio* (n 2) 33: 'The example of Panvinio's disorganization, in fact, may have inspired [Sigonio] to order his own work more effectively than he would otherwise have done.'

[69] In his 1560 *De antiquo iure Italiae* Sigonio initially used the version of one fragment printed in a 1521 collection of inscriptions, and added details of others in the 1568 *De antiquo iure provinciarum*: see Andrew W Lintott, 'The So-Called Tabula Bembina and the Humanists: A Chapter Rewritten in the Renaissance Discovery of Classical Epigraphy' (1983) 61 Athenaeum 201–14; for the text and edition, with details of other later sixteenth-century editions, *Roman Statutes* (n 38) vol 1, 39–63 and 113–80.

the final position, because there are many full books about it, and it seems to be a conflagration for the city of Rome, rather than a law.'[70] He then gave a short history of laws on land redistribution, noting Spurius Cassius (Livy 4.41), Tiberius Gracchus, and the proposed legislation of Gaius Licinius (Livy 6.35).[71] As Biondo's comments suggest, the *lex agraria* was well known as an incendiary political move to fifteenth century readers, from Cicero, Livy, and perhaps Plutarch's *Life of Gracchus*; he might have thought it did not require much further analysis. *Leges agrariae* appeared in the standard account of the history of Roman law, and in Zasius' compilation; Paolo Manuzio, whose work Sigonio used, gave a detailed, chronological account of the persistence of agrarian laws in his *De legibus* (*On the laws*) of 1557; the question of whether to have a *lex agraria* became a school exercise.[72] In an address to Pope Clement VII of 1524, Battista Casali rejected the idea of having an agrarian law for sixteenth-century Campania, based in part on ancient Roman precedent.[73] Machiavelli, again, is something of an outlier. He addressed agrarian law in the first book of his *Discorsi*, which dealt with constitutional rather than military issues, ostensibly separate from his discussion of colonies. He attacked the law not so much on principle, as for the disruption it caused to the state.[74] But almost incidentally, he here connected the *lex agraria* with colonization: he pointed out that despite the desire that lands taken from the enemy should be distributed among the Roman people, Livy claimed that it was difficult to persuade the plebs to form the colony at Antium. Following Livy, Machiavelli argued that the reluctance to take possession of land meant that interest in a law placing limits on land-holding and distributing land among the people remained subdued.[75] As McCuaig showed, it was because he gave as much weight to Appian as to Livy that

[70] Biondo, *De roma triumphante* (n 11) 90: 'Legem agrariam ultimo servavimus loco, quia de ea multi pleni sunt libri, & incendium magis urbi Romae quam lex fuisse videtur.'

[71] ibid 91. He also mentions a Lex Curii, perhaps a misinterpretation of Columella 1.3.10, who records that Manius Curius Dentatus declined the extra land offered him by the people as a reward.

[72] Aymar du Rivail, *Civilis historiae iuris, sive in XII. tab. leges commentarii* (Schoeffer 1527) 16, 116, 152, 195–97; Zasius, *Catalogus* (n 38) 10v–23r; Paolo Manuzio, *Antiquitatum romanarum liber de legibus* (Bernard Turrisan 1557) 96–100 (hereafter Manuzio, *De legibus*); Aonio Paleario et al., *ΘΕΣΙΣ positio, sive constitutio causae, et distributio patrium actionis pro lege agraria* (Moschenius 1557).

[73] Battista Casali, *In legem agrariam pro communi utilitate, et ecclesiastica libertate tuenda, ad Clementem VII Pont. Max. oratio* (De Henricis and Perusinus 1524). See Giampiero Carocci, 'Problemi agrari del Lazio nel "500"' (1959) 1 *Studi storici* 3–23.

[74] Machiavelli, *Discorsi* (n 17) 1.37: 'Quali scandoli partorì in Roma la legge agraria: e come fare una legge in una republica, che riguardi assai indietro, e sia contro a una consuetudine antica della città, è scandolosissimo.' See Ronald T Ridley, '*Leges agrariae*: Myths Ancient and Modern' (2000) 95 Classical Philology 459–67.

[75] Machiavelli, *Discorsi* (n 17) 1.37: 'Dove Tito Livio usa un termine notabile, dicendo che con difficultà si trovò in Roma chi desse il nome per ire in detta colonia: tanto era quella plebe più pronta a volere desiderare le cose in Roma, che a possederle in Anzio.'

Sigonio was able to connect colonies more intimately than his predecessors with the *lex agraria*, but he might also have read Machiavelli.

When he wrote the *De antiquo iure Italiae*, therefore, Sigonio had access to a vigorous tradition of historical discussions of Roman colonial practice. Humanists had explored the sources for colonization and subjected them to some analysis. They had thought about colonies on a local level, and started to see them as part of Roman policy from a provincial perspective. And Sigonio's friend Panvinio had compiled and digested much of this material. Machiavelli, who was able to take a critical attitude to the humanists' work, had tried to apply their lessons to contemporary policy. In doing so, he had made a striking historical argument for the centrality of colonies to Roman success, and started to think about the practicalities of land distribution. All these scholars worked against the backdrop of new European territorial empires, which would have been particularly vivid for those, like Lazius, who were involved with the Hapsburg court. As they did so, they prepared the ground for an understanding of the Roman empire both as an extension of authority and as a bounded space, ground that Sigonio was to cultivate.

3

The Mommsen of the Renaissance

Sigonio, the *De antiquo iure populi Romani*, and Roman Republican Colonization

John Rich[*]

Carlo Sigonio's three linked treatises on the 'ancient *ius*' of Roman citizens, Italy, and the provinces, which he eventually brought together in a single volume as *De antiquo iure populi Romani*, have been widely recognized as the greatest single contribution by a Renaissance humanist to the study of the institutions of the Roman Republic and its empire. A number of Sigonio's contemporaries in the mid-sixteenth century produced work in this field which marked a great advance on their predecessors, both in depth of treatment and in the range of sources (both literary and non-literary) which they were able to exploit. Sigonio's treatises, however, were outstanding in their scope and acumen, and in the analytic power with which they were organized and argued. Jakob Bernays, in a review of the first edition of Theodor Mommsen's *Römisches Staatsrecht*, singled out Sigonio and the eighteenth-century scholar Louis de Beaufort as the only writers on Roman institutions worthy to be regarded as Mommsen's precursors, and Arnaldo Momigliano approved this judgement.[1] The comparison with Mommsen is singularly apt, for both the impact and the character of their works. Sigonio's treatises remained pre-eminent until the nineteenth century, while the dominance of Mommsen's *Staatsrecht* continues to this day. Both writers showed not only a peerless mastery of their

[*] I am grateful to Federico Santangelo, William Stenhouse, and the editors for commenting on earlier drafts of this chapter.

[1] Jakob Bernays, 'Die Behandlung des römischen Staatsrechts bis auf Theodor Mommsen' in *Gesammelte Abhandlungen* (Hertz 1885) vol 2, 255–75; Arnaldo Momigliano, 'Review of E. Meyer, *Römischer Staat und Staatsgedanke*' (1949) 39 Journal of Roman Studies 155–57. See also Ronald T Ridley, *Gibbon's Complement: Louis de Beaufort* (Istituto Veneto di Scienze, Lettere ed Arti 1986) 153–55 (hereafter Ridley, *Gibbon's Complement*); William McCuaig, *Carlo Sigonio. The Changing World of the Late Renaissance* (Princeton University Press 1989) 182–83 (hereafter McCuaig, *Carlo Sigonio*); Wilfried Nippel, 'Das *Staatsrecht* in der Diskussion—von 1871 bis heute' in Wilfried Nippel and Berndt Seidensticker (eds), *Theodor Mommsens langer Schatten: Das römische Staatsrecht als bleibende Herausforderung für die Forschung* (Olms 2005) 9–60, esp 27–30 (hereafter Nippel, 'Das *Staatsrecht* in der Diskussion').

John Rich, *The Mommsen of the Renaissance* In: *The Renaissance of Roman Colonization*. Edited by: Jeremia Pelgrom and Arthur Weststeijn, Oxford University Press (2020). © the Several Contributors.
DOI: 10.1093/oso/9780198850960.003.0003

subject matter but also a juridical focus and a resulting determination to fit their material into a rigorous theoretical framework and draw inferences for Roman principles and practice from that framework (with not always happy results).

Sigonio's career and works have been admirably studied by William McCuaig. However, the two erudite and densely argued chapters which McCuaig devotes to the *De antiquo iure populi Romani* do not offer an overview of the work as a whole but instead provide close studies of selected aspects, namely Sigonio's treatment of Roman social structures and of the late Republican developments over land and court reform and the extension of the citizenship, and his dispute with Nicolas de Grouchy over magistracy, *imperium*, and the assemblies, and its later reception. This chapter therefore seeks to analyse the overall structure and aims of Sigonio's treatises and assess their achievement in the light of modern scholarship.[2] Introductory remarks on Sigonio's works and approach will be followed by examination of each of the three treatises. The concluding section of the chapter will then provide closer consideration of Sigonio's treatment of the topics of colonization and agrarian legislation. Sigonio's contribution on these themes was to be of crucial importance for their subsequent study, but it can only be adequately understood in its overall context in the three linked treatises.

Sigonio's Works and Approach

Sigonio was born in Modena in 1522 or 1523 and educated there and in Bologna and Pavia. He began his career as a scholar and teacher at Modena, but moved to Venice in 1552 on his appointment to the lectureship in the Scuola di San Marco. In 1560 he was appointed to the chair of humanity at Padua, but his time there was overshadowed by a bitter quarrel with his predecessor Francesco Robertello who had been reappointed at the university. In 1563 he escaped to a professorship at Bologna, which he retained until his death in 1584.[3]

[2] For another assessment see Ridley, *Gibbon's Complement* (n 1) 157–67. See also the brief remarks of Andrew W Lintott, *The Constitution of the Roman Republic* (Oxford Unversity Press 1999) 244–46 (hereafter Lintott, *Constitution*); John GA Pocock, *Barbarism and Religion, vol. 3: the First Decline and Fall* (Cambridge University Press 2003) 276–79; Christopher Smith, *The Roman Clan: The* Gens *from Ancient Ideology to Modern Anthropology* (Oxford University Press 2006) 66–71 (hereafter Smith, *The Roman Clan*); Jeremia Pelgrom and Tesse D Stek, 'Roman Colonization under the Republic: Historiographical Contextualization of a Paradigm' in Tesse D Stek and Jeremia Pelgrom (eds), *Roman Republican Colonization. New Perspectives from Archaeology and Ancient History* (Palombi 2014) 10–41, at 16–17 (hereafter Pelgrom and Stek, 'Roman Colonization under the Republic').

[3] For a full account of Sigonio's career see McCuaig, *Carlo Sigonio* (n 1) 3–95.

Sigonio's first major projects, which made his scholarly name, were his editions with commentary of Livy and of the consular and triumphal *Fasti*, published in successive versions over the years 1550–59.[4] These related undertakings, both of lasting importance, were prompted by the discovery in the Roman Forum in 1546–47 of extensive fragments of an inscribed list of consuls and triumphs, which were then installed in the Palazzo dei Conservatori on the Capitol and so became known as the *Fasti Capitolini*.[5] During the same period Sigonio also produced a disquisition on Roman names and an edition of the fragments of Cicero, which was the first published collection exclusively devoted to literary fragments preserved by citation.[6]

In 1560 Sigonio produced the first two of his three linked treatises, *De antiquo iure ciuium Romanorum libri II* and *De antiquo iure Italiae libri III*, each published in Venice by Giordano Ziletti. At the time, Sigonio had hopes of securing a post at Rome, and sought to advance his claim by dedicating the first work to the new pope, Pius IV, and the second to 'the Roman senate and people'. The first dedication appears to have misfired but the Roman civic authorities responded to the second on 12 October 1560 by honouring Sigonio with Roman citizenship and requesting the pope to appoint him to teach at Rome. By then, however, he had accepted the chair at Padua.[7]

In the second treatise, Sigonio had promised a third, on the provinces, but other preoccupations intervened.[8] His output in the following years included revised editions of the first two treatises (1562–63) and a study of the political institutions of another ancient state, a pioneering work on the Athenian constitution (*De republica Atheniensium libri IIII*, 1564). In 1562 Sigonio also

[4] McCuaig, ibid 346–56 gives a complete listing of Sigonio's publications. McCuaig accepts the attribution to Sigonio of the *Iudicium de historicis qui res Romanas scripserunt*, first published in 1604, but Jean-Louis Ferrary, *Onofrio Panvinio et les antiquités romaines* (École française de Rome 1996) 42, 214 (hereafter Ferrary, *Onofrio Panvinio*), shows that the work should be ascribed to Panvinio.

[5] On the early debates over the *Fasti Capitolini* and the editions by Marliani, Sigonio, Robertello, and Panvinio see William McCuaig, 'The Fasti Capitolini and the Study of Roman Chronology in the Sixteenth Century' (1991) 79 Athenaeum 141–59; William Stenhouse, *Reading Inscriptions and Writing Ancient History: Historical Scholarship in the Late Renaissance* (Institute of Classical Studies 2005) 103–12 (hereafter Stenhouse, *Reading Inscriptions*).

[6] Anna Carlotta Dionisotti, 'On Fragments in Classical Scholarship' in Glenn W Most (ed), *Collecting Fragments—Fragmente sammeln* (Vandenhoeck & Ruprecht 1997) 1–33. Sigonio may also have inspired the first collection of the fragments of the Roman historians by his pupil (and later adversary) Antonio Riccoboni, published first in 1568 and in an expanded second edition in 1579: Mark P Pobjoy and John W Rich, 'From Riccoboni to Roth: Early Editions of the Fragments of the Roman Historians' in Tim J Cornell and others, *The Fragments of the Roman Historians* (Oxford University Press 2013) vol 1, 652–60.

[7] On the dedications and Sigonio's manoeuvrings for appointment at Rome and Padua see McCuaig, *Carlo Sigonio* (n 1) 39–43. McCuaig's claim that the second dedication 'made no impression on these aldermen' overlooks the citizenship grant, for which see Ferdinand Gregorovius, 'Alcuni cenni storici sulla cittadinanza romana' (1876–77) 274 Atti della R. Accademia dei Lincei 342 (I thank William Stenhouse for this reference.)

[8] Sigonio had planned to write on the provinces as early as 1556: McCuaig, *Carlo Sigonio* (n 1) 30.

attacked his enemy Francesco Robertello in two volumes of vicious polemic, much of which he devoted to a scathing but well-merited critique of a brief disquisition on the Roman provinces (*De prouinciis Romanorum et earum distributione atque administratione*), which Robortello had published in 1559.[9] Sigonio took the opportunity there to outline how he thought the subject should be handled, but it was not this feud but his dispute with Grouchy which eventually prompted him to compose his own promised work on the provinces. In 1565 Grouchy published a response to the disagreements with his work on the Roman assemblies which Sigonio had expressed in the *De antiquo iure ciuium Romanorum*. In 1566 Sigonio published the first of his ripostes to Grouchy, and in 1567 he completed his trilogy with the publication (again by Ziletti) of *De antiquo iure prouinciarum libri II*.[10]

In 1574 Sigonio finally brought his three treatises together in the single-volume *De antiquo iure populi Romani libri XI*, published at Bologna by a new press which he had helped to found, the Societas Typographiae Bononiensis. In this edition the three treatises retained their separate identities but underwent substantial revision and reorganization. The *De antiquo iure prouinciarum* now acquired a third book, not restricted to the provinces: this was a revised version of a work separately published in 1569, and presented Sigonio's definitive statement of his dispute with Grouchy. The volume closes with a new three-book treatise on the Roman courts (*De iudiciis*), already promised in the original edition of the *De antiquo iure prouinciarum*, which greatly expands the treatment of the topic previously included in chapter 2.18 of the *De antiquo iure ciuium Romanorum*.

This publication completed Sigonio's work on the Roman Republic, and in fact from 1568 on he had been mainly occupied with the diachronic studies of later periods which were the principal products of his later years: a commissioned history of Bologna (1571) was followed by two major works, annalistically organized histories of respectively the kingdom of Italy (1574) and the later Roman Empire in the West (1578).[11] Sigonio did, however, write one

[9] Carlo Sigonio, *Disputationes Patauinae aduersus Franciscum Robortellum* (Percacino 1562) 1.11v-22v, 2.33r–44r, criticizing Francesco Robortello, *De uita et uictu populi Romani sub impp. Caess. Augg. tomus primus . . . Disputationes nouem, de prouinciis Romanorum et earum distributione atque administratione, etc.* (Benati 1559) 117r–123v.

[10] Sigonio speaks of his delight in returning to Roman studies after a five-year interval in a letter to Panvinio of 21 February 1567: Carlo Sigonio, *Opera Omnia* (Argelati 1732-1737) vol 6, 1023 (hereafter Sigonio, *Opera omnia*); McCuaig, *Carlo Sigonio* (n 1) 56–57.

[11] cf Arnaldo Momigliano, 'Ancient History and the Antiquarian' (1950) 13 Journal of the Warburg Institute 293 (perhaps unintentionally dismissive in tone): 'Sigonio, who did mere antiquarian work when concerned with classical Roman and Greek history, wrote ordinary medieval history.' On the problematic character of Momigliano's conception of 'antiquarianism' see Stenhouse, *Reading Inscriptions* (n 5) 16–18; Ingo Herklotz, 'Arnaldo Momigliano's "Ancient History and the Antiquarian": A Critical

more ground-breaking synchronic study of ancient political institutions, on the Hebrew state (*De republica Hebraeorum libri VII*, 1582).[12]

The three treatises collected in *De antiquo iure populi Romani* deal with different groups within the Roman empire but share a common theme, defined by their titles, namely the 'ancient *ius*' applicable to those groups. The term *antiquum* ('ancient') denotes Sigonio's chosen time frame, namely the period before the emperors, or, as he puts it at one point, when 'the Roman people' was 'free, or not yet wholly oppressed by slavery' (*populus Romanus liber aut nondum omnino seruitute oppressus*).[13] He throughout explicitly refrains from treating developments occurring under the emperors. At several points in the final treatise on the provinces he promises a further work dealing with the provinces in the imperial period, and in letters to his friend Onofrio Panvinio he envisaged including Rome and Italy as well in this work, but in the event nothing came of these plans.[14]

Sigonio here uses *ius* in what the *Oxford Latin Dictionary* defines as the word's twelfth sense: 'position or standing in respect of the law (esp. as regards the enjoyment or exercise of rights)'. In his usage the term covers not only the rights enjoyed by the members of the relevant group but also their obligations, for example for military service or taxation. Rendering it into English is thus sometimes problematic: 'right' will often serve, but sometimes a term like 'status' may be more appropriate, and it will often be safest to retain the Latin original.[15]

In the combined 1574 edition of the three treatises, the first opens with a new sentence designed to show how they were coordinated:

Review' in Peter N Miller (ed), *Momigliano and Antiquarianism: Foundations of the Modern Cultural Sciences* (Toronto University Press 2007) 127–53.

[12] For this work see Guido Bartolucci, 'Carlo Sigonio and the "Respublica Hebraeorum": A Re-evaluation' (2008) 3 Hebraic Political Studies 19–59.

[13] Carlo Sigonio, *De antiquo iure ciuium Romanorum* 1.18 in *De antiquo iure populi Romani libri undecim* (Societas Typographiae Bononiensis 1574) 332 (hereafter Sigonio, *De antiquo iure ciuium*). Sigonio's treatises are usually cited below first by book and section number and then (except where otherwise indicated) by the pagination of the combined 1574 edition.

[14] For his promised work on the provinces under the emperors, see Carlo Sigonio, *De antiquo iure prouinciarum* 1.2, 5, 12, 18 in *De antiquo iure populi Romani libri undecim* (Societas Typographiae Bononiensis 1574) 290, 298, 323, 332 (hereafter Sigonio, *De antiquo iure prouinciarum*). For his comprehensive project, see the letters to Panvinio from 1 February and 21 February and 5 November 1567: Sigonio, *Opera omnia* (n 10) vol 6, 1023, 1026. See McCuaig, *Carlo Sigonio* (n 1) 57–58; Ferrary, *Onofrio Panvinio* (n 4) 165–66.

[15] McCuaig, *Carlo Sigonio* (n 1) is sometimes too loose in indicating the scope of Sigonio's term, eg 124: 'Sigonio gave his work a juridical title, *De antiquo iure ciuium Romanorum*, but in fact emphasized what we call social history. . . The *antiquum ius* of the Romans in Sigonio's title means the complex of their institutions.'

> Of those who received *iura* from the same free and victorious Roman people, there were, if we attend carefully, four grades: the first of Roman citizens, the second of Latins, the third of Italici, and the fourth of provincials, and of these the Roman citizenship was more prestigious and valuable than the *ius Latii*, Latinity than the Italic *ius*, and the Italic than the provincial.[16]

The sentence thus identifies a hierarchy of four grades of *ius* among the free inhabitants of the Roman empire under the Republic, with the Roman citizens enjoying the most favourable *ius* and the provincials the least favourable. Although this passage is an addition, the conception was not new: similar statements had already appeared at the start of the second and third treatises in their first editions.[17] Thus, as the treatise titles indicate, the different grades of *ius* provided the overall organizing principle for Sigonio's whole project.

By opting to structure his work around this theme, Sigonio was making a radical departure which found no followers. Most humanist studies of Roman antiquities were organized topically, by institutions and the aspects of Roman life. Biondo Flavio, the pioneer in this field, followed his three-book *Roma instaurata* on the buildings and topography of ancient Rome (completed in 1446) with the ten-book *Roma triumphans* (completed in 1459), which dealt successively with Roman religion, government (loosely subdivided by magistrates, assemblies, and laws), military organization, private life, and the triumph. Sigonio's contemporaries brought new standards of accuracy and detail to such studies, but their contributions mainly dealt with single institutions: thus treatises on the assemblies and the senate were published by respectively Grouchy and Jan Zamoyski, and several scholars published works listing the Roman laws. One of these, Paolo Manuzio, envisaged his *De legibus* (1557) as the sixth of ten planned books on Roman antiquities, organized on topical and institutional lines, of which the others were to deal successively with the city, citizenship, religion, the senate, the assemblies, the magistracies, the courts, and two unknown subjects. His treatise on the laws was the only one to be published in Manuzio's lifetime, although his draft accounts of citizenship, the senate, and the assemblies were published posthumously by his son Aldo. Manuzio appears to have abandoned the project around 1560, perhaps

[16] Carlo Sigonio, *De antiquo iure populi Romani libri undecim* (Societas Typographiae Bononiensis 1574) 2–3 (hereafter Sigonio, *De antiquo iure populi Romani*): 'eorum, qui iura a populo Romano uictore eodem ac libero acceperunt, quattuor, si diligenter attendimus, quasi gradus fuerunt: unus ciuium Romanorum, alter Latinorum, tertius Italicorum, provincialium quartus, ex quibus ut iure Latii ciuitas Romana, sic Italico Latinitas, et Italicum provinciali honestius et commodius fuit.'

[17] Carlo Sigonio, *De antiquo iure Italiae libri III* (Giordano Ziletti 1560) 4v; Sigonio, *De antiquo iure prouinciarum libri II* (Giordano Ziletti 1567) 1 = Sigonio, *De antiquo iure populi Romani* (n 16) 151, 286.

because he felt that Sigonio's treatises had made it redundant.[18] In the event, it was left to Johann Rossfeld (Rosinus) to provide the first comprehensive account of Roman antiquities since Biondo. His *Romanarum antiquitatum libri X*, first published in Basel in 1583 and often republished, particularly with the additions of Thomas Dempster, followed the established topical and institutional pattern, covering successively the Roman city and people, religion and festivals, assemblies, magistrates, laws and courts, and military organization.[19] The influence of these humanist models proved long-lasting: comparable structures were still adopted by Louis de Beaufort in his *La République Romaine* (1766) and in the great nineteenth-century multi-volume handbook of Roman antiquities by Wilhelm Adolf Becker and Joachim Marquardt. However, Mommsen, in replacing Becker's account of the Roman 'constitution' (*Staatsverfassung*) for the revised edition of the handbook, opted for a juridical focus, devoting his treatise to what he termed 'Roman public law' (*Römisches Staatsrecht*).[20]

Sigonio himself conformed to his predecessors' institutional pattern in his works on the political systems of the Athenians and the Hebrews, but for his Roman treatises he opted instead for the novel theme of the graded *iura*. How he came to settle on this *ius*-centred approach is unknown.[21] In the new

[18] On Manuzio's project see Ferrary, *Onofrio Panvinio* (n 4) 229–37; Jean-Louis Ferrary, 'Rome et Venise dans la pensée politique et chez les antiquaires du XVIe siècle: à propos des *Antiquitates Romanae* de Paul Manuce' (1997) Comptes Rendus de l'Academie des Inscriptions et Belles-Lettres 491–514 (hereafter Ferrary, 'Rome et Venise'). Manuzio's departure for Rome in 1561 to become printer to the papacy may have been another factor in his abandonment of this project.

[19] On the humanist tradition of writing on Roman antiquities from Biondo to Rosinus see Angelo Mazzocco, 'Biondo Flavio and the Antiquarian Tradition' in Richard J Schoeck (ed), *Acta Conventus Neo-Latini Bononiensis: Proceedings of the Fourth International Congress of Neo-Latin Studies* (University Centre at Binghamton 1985) 123–36; Angelo Mazzocco, 'A Reconsideration of Renaissance Antiquarianism in light of Biondo Flavio's *Ars Antiquaria*' (2014–15) 59/60 Memoirs of the American Academy in Rome 121–59; Ingo Herklotz, *Cassiano dal Pozzo und die Archäologie des 17. Jahrhunderts* (Himer 1999) 242–48 (hereafter Herklotz, *Cassiano dal Pozzo*); Frances Muecke, '*Fama superstes*? Soundings in the Reception of Biondo Flavio's *Roma triumphans*' in Angelo Mazzocco and Marc Laureys (eds), *A New Sense of the Past: The Scholarship of Biondo Flavio (1392–1463)* (Leuven University Press 2016) 219–41; Duncan Macrae, '*Diligentissimus investigator antiquitatis*? "Antiquarianism" and Historical Evidence between Republican Rome and the Early Modern Republic of Letters' in Kaj Sandberg and Christopher J Smith (eds), Omnium annalium monumenta. *Historical Writing and Historical Explanation in Republican Rome* (Brill 2017) 137–56; William Stenhouse, 'Flavio Biondo and Later Renaissance Antiquarianism' in Frances Muecke and Maurizio Campanelli (eds), *The Invention of Rome: Biondo Flavio's* Roma triumphans *and its Worlds* (Droz 2017) 259–73. See also Chapter 2 in this volume by William Stenhouse.

[20] The first edition of Becker and Marquardt's *Handbuch der Römischen Alterthümer, nach den Quellen bearbeitet* was published between 1843 and 1856. On Mommsen's decision to take 'public law' as his subject and its implications for the character of his work see Yan Thomas, *Mommsen et l'"isolierung' du droit (Rome, l'Allemagne et l'État)* (De Boccard 1984); Nippel, 'Das *Staatsrecht* in der Diskussion' (n 1), and 'The Structure and Legacy of Mommsen's Staatsrecht' in Jean-Louis Ferrary and John Scheid (eds), *Il princeps romano: autocrate o magistrato?* (IUSS Press 2015) 35–53.

[21] Sigonio had evidently not yet settled on the *ius*-based structure in 1556, when, in the dedication of his *Fasti* commentary, he alluded to projected treatises on Roman families and provinces: Carlo Sigonio,

opening paragraph which he composed for the 1574 edition, Sigonio expresses the hope that his work will be of value not only for Roman letters but also for civil jurisprudence, and jurists are likely to have been among his target readership from the outset.[22] However he came by it, Sigonio's choice of theme conferred great structural advantages in both thematic flexibility and analytic power, as will be shown in more detail in the following sections.

Whereas his predecessors had mostly focused on the city of Rome and its civic institutions, Sigonio's choice of theme gave him the scope to write at length on Italy and the provinces as well as on Rome itself. Using and adapting an Aristotelian model, he opened each treatise by defining the groups holding the grade or grades of *ius* in question and analysing the components of their *ius*, but his theme also enabled him to pass on to other related aspects, such as (in the first treatise) divisions within the citizen body with implications for *iura* and (in the second) the *iura* enjoyed not just by particular peoples, but also particular categories of communities. In this way he was able to work in discussions of numerous relevant institutions and historical developments, usually with appropriate succinctness, but sometimes permitting himself more expansive digressions. It was thus that, along with many other topics, he was able to include extensive treatment of both agrarian legislation (in the first two treatises) and colonization (in the second and third).

Whereas other Renaissance writings on Roman institutions were largely descriptive, Sigonio's decision to structure his work around the graded *iura* obliged him to write analytically and develop an argued case throughout. Although his conception of the *iura* was, as we shall see, in some ways flawed, notably in respect of *ius Italicum*, his thematic choice nonetheless helped him to produce a work which was altogether superior to those of his peers in rigour of argument and analysis.

Although a doughty controversialist, Sigonio also maintained cordial dealings, chiefly by correspondence, with numerous scholars, both in Italy and beyond. He was on terms of warm mutual respect with Fulvio Orsini, Antonio Agustín, and others in the group of scholars active at Rome and associated with

In fastos Romanos ac triumphos Romanos commentarius (Paolo Manuzio 1556) 3r (hereafter Sigonio, *In fastos*). However, by late 1558 he was at work on *De antiquo iure ciuium Romanorum* and *De antiquo iure Italiae*, as is shown by references in his letters to Panvinio: Sigonio, *Opera omnia* (n 10) vol 6, 100–103 and Panvinio's published allusion: Onofrio Panvinio, *Reipublicae Romanae Commentariorum libri tres* (Valgrisi 1558) 952 (hereafter Panvinio, *Reipublicae Romanae*). cf McCuaig, *Carlo Sigonio* (n 1) 30–33.

[22] Sigonio, *De antiquo iure populi romani* (n 16) 3: 'haec autem iura . . . uisa res est digna, in qua illustranda omnem meam operam atque industriam collocarem, non solum ut iis litteris, unde praeclara haec monumenta sumuntur, sed etiam ut civili ipse disciplinae, ad quam haec omnia tamquam ad finem ultimum referuntur, opis aliquid atque adiumenti afferrem.'

the Farnese cardinals.[23] Among this group, Sigonio's closest ties were with the Augustinian friar Onofrio Panvinio (1530–68), an expert on both Roman antiquities and ecclesiastical history and one of the leading epigraphists of the day.[24] Like Sigonio, Panvinio produced an edition of the *Fasti*. The publication of unauthorized and unsatisfactory versions of this and another work in 1557 led Panvinio to spend the period October 1557 to September 1558 in Venice preparing revised versions and supervising their publication. During this time he was evidently in close contact with Sigonio, and after his departure they kept up frequent correspondence. The numerous surviving letters from Sigonio to Panvinio show the high esteem in which Sigonio held him, and make frequent reference to the treatises *De antiquo iure*, reporting progress, discussing problems, and, after publication, keenly seeking Panvinio's opinion of them.

During his stay in Venice Panvinio completed a further work on Roman antiquities, *Reipublicae Romanae commentariorum libri tres* (1558), whose three books treat respectively the city of Rome, the constitution, and the Roman empire. The second and third books thus cover much of the same ground as Sigonio's three treatises, although (unlike him) extending treatment to the imperial period. Like Sigonio, Panvinio opted for an unconventional structure, but with much less success, particularly in the second book in which a chronological narrative of Roman history is interrupted by lengthy institutional digressions: an extended treatment of Roman priesthoods thus appears under Numa, of tribes under Servius Tullius, and so on. Panvinio lacked Sigonio's analytic power and for most topics his treatment is much thinner, while much of the *Commentarii* is taken up with listings. Nonetheless, the work presents a remarkable collection of material, particularly epigraphic. At its close, Panvinio acknowledges that he had benefited substantially from the advice of Sigonio, who, he tells us, was working on his books on the ancient *ius* of Roman citizens and Italy when he was completing the *Commentarii* in Venice.[25] There is indeed much agreement between the *Commentarii* and Sigonio's treatises. McCuaig envisages the debt as all on Panvinio's side, but Sigonio in his turn

[23] On the Farnese circle of scholars see Michael H Crawford (ed) *Antonio Agustín between Renaissance and Counter-Reform* (The Warburg Institute 1993); Herklotz, *Cassiano dal Pozzo* (n 19) 214–25; and on Sigonio's relations with them see Pierre de Nolhac, *La bibliothèque de Fulvio Orsini* (Bouillon & Vieweg 1887) 72–74; McCuaig, *Carlo Sigonio* (n 1) 31. Letters from Sigonio to Orsini are published in Pierre de Nolhac, 'Piero Vettori et Carlo Sigonio. Correspondance avec Fulvio Orsini' (1889) 10 Studi e documenti di storia e diritto 138–49.

[24] On Panvinio see Davide A Perini, *Onofrio Panvinio e le sue opere* (Propaganda Fide 1899); Ferrary, *Onofrio Panvinio* (n 4); Jean-Louis Ferrary, 'Onofrio Panvinio' in Colette Nativel (ed), *Centuriae Latinae: Cent une figures humanistes . . . offertes à Jacques Chomarat* (Droz 1997) 595–99; and Chapter 2 in this volume by Stenhouse.

[25] Panvinio, *Reipublicae Romanae* (n 21) 951–52.

is likely to have owed much to his friend's work. Sigonio, as we shall see, acknowledged Panvinio's assistance with epigraphic material, and in a letter he credits Panvinio with inspiring him to write his first treatise and to complete his second when interest in Greek problems was distracting him.[26] Towards the end of his short life, Panvinio drafted ambitious outlines for a comprehensive work on Roman antiquities in first sixty and later a hundred volumes. By contrast with the *Commentarii*, these sketches envisage a more conventional structure by topics and institutions, and Sigonio is followed closely on the subjects for which his treatises now provided the most authoritative treatment.[27]

Another scholar with whom Sigonio formed a close relationship during his time in Venice was the great Venetian humanist and printer Paolo Manuzio (1512–74), whose press published Sigonio's editions of Livy and the *Fasti* in 1555–56. Sigonio was well aware of Manuzio's projected work on Roman antiquities: in the early editions of the *De antiquo iure ciuium Romanorum*, he referred his readers to Manuzio's long promised treatise on the magistracies for further information on that topic.[28] The work which was closest in subject matter to Sigonio's treatises was Manuzio's *De civitate Romana* (as noted above, this was only published posthumously, in 1585, but it was probably composed in the period 1558–60, when Sigonio was working on his first two treatises). Manuzio's unrevised and chaotically structured work is much inferior to Sigonio's, but there is a good deal of agreement between them. Thus here, as with Panvinio, there may have been mutual influence, but in this case the debt was mainly on Manuzio's side.

Sigonio's treatises show a remarkable command of all the relevant ancient literature available to him. In this regard he and his contemporaries were in a significantly better position than earlier humanists. They could draw on previously unavailable Latin works, such as Velleius Paterculus (discovered 1515, published 1520) and Books 41–45 of Livy (discovered 1527, published 1531), and improved texts, like those published for the *Digest* by Lelio Torelli in 1553 and for Festus by Agustín, with Sigonio's assistance, in 1559.[29] The

[26] Letters of December 1559 to February 1560: Sigonio, *Opera omnia* (n 10) vol 6, 1008–11, esp 27 January: 'Faccio à vostro senno. Sono intorno all'Italia. Ho lasciato gli Archonti: in effetto voi foste causa ch'io fornissi quel *De iure ciuium*, et sarete ancora di questo.' cf Ferrary, *Onofrio Panvinio* (n 4) 158 n78 and McCuaig, *Carlo Sigonio* (n 1) 32–33.

[27] On Panvinio's debt to Sigonio here and in the earlier *Commentarii* see Ferrary, *Onofrio Panvinio* (n 4) 148–61.

[28] Sigonio, *De antiquo iure ciuium Romanorum libri II* (Giordano Ziletti 1560) 140; omitted in the edition of 1574 (n 13) 88.

[29] See Douglas J Osler, 'Humanist Philology and the Text of Justinian's *Digest*', in Paul J du Plessis and John Cairns (eds), *Reassessing Legal Humanism and its Claims:* Petere Fontes? (Edinburgh Unversity Press 2016) 41–58; Anthony Grafton, *Joseph Scaliger. A Study in the History of Scholarship, vol. 1: Textual Criticism and Exegesis* (Oxford University Press 1983) 140–44; McCuaig, *Carlo Sigonio* (n 1) 33.

Greek historians of Rome, previously only available in Latin translation, had now been published in the original Greek: Polybius in 1530, Dionysius in 1546, Cassius Dio in 1548, Appian in 1551, and Dio's epitomator Zonaras in 1557. Sigonio thus had access to most of the relevant literary works available to us, albeit in texts which were still often defective by comparison with modern editions. However, some significant works had not yet come to light, including the Constantinian Excerpts, our chief source for the parts of the Greek historians not directly transmitted, which were only discovered from the later sixteenth century on, and works found only in the nineteenth century such as Gaius' *Institutes* and the palimpsest preserving much of Cicero's *De re publica*.

Sigonio usually tries to harmonize discrepancies between his sources, but on occasion is willing to challenge even sources he regards as authoritative, like Asconius, Dionysius or Appian.[30] He can move fluidly from quotation to paraphrase, and the italics introduced in the 1574 edition to identify quotations can mislead. Occasionally he contrives to bolster his argument by misquotation.[31] Like all his contemporaries, Sigonio accepted without question the traditional account of early Roman history from Romulus on.

One surprising flaw in Sigonio's treatises is his acceptance of the notorious forgeries of Annius of Viterbo. Annius' *Commentaria super opera diversorum auctorum de antiquitatibus loquentium* (1498) presented and commented on invented texts which he attributed to various ancient writers, including the early Roman historians Fabius Pictor, Cato, and Sempronius (in fact Sempronius Tuditanus).[32] By Sigonio's time Annius' forgeries had long been recognized by well-informed scholars, but Sigonio doggedly insisted on using their evidence. He was criticized for doing so by Agustín in a detailed critique of the *De antiquo iure civium Romanorum* forwarded by Panvinio, but Sigonio responded that, while not accepting their attribution to Fabius, Cato, and Sempronius, he regarded the texts as ancient and more valuable than some

[30] Sigonio, *De antiquo iure ciuium* (n 13) 1.3, 2.12, 10–11 (Asconius, in fact Pseudo-Asconius), 121–22 (Dionysius). For Appian, see Sigonio, *De antiquo iure Italiae* 1.21, 2.15 in Sigonio, *De antiquo iure populi Romani libri undecim* (Societas Typographiae Bononiensis 1574) 197, 257 (hereafter Sigonio, *De antiquo iure Italiae*); McCuaig, *Carlo Sigonio* (n 1) 144, 151–52.

[31] For example, Sigonio, *De antiquo iure Italiae* (n 30) 1.1, 151, where Claudius' reference, in Tacitus' version of his speech on the Gallic senators, to the extension of magistracies successively to plebeians, Latins, and other Italians (*Annales* 11.24.7: *plebei magistratus post patricios, Latini post plebeios, ceterarum Italiae gentium post Latinos*), is misleadingly adduced as support for Sigonio's conception of the four grades of *iura*, and a final phrase (*exterorum post Italos*) is slipped in without Tacitus' authority.

[32] On Annius' forgeries see Christopher R Ligota, 'Annius of Viterbo and Historical Method' (1987) 50 Journal of the Warburg and Courtauld Institutes 44–56; Anthony Grafton, *Defenders of the Text* (Harvard University Press 1991) 76–103; Walter Stephens, 'When Pope Noah Ruled the Etruscans: Annius of Viterbo and his Forged *Antiquities*' (2004) 119 Modern Language Notes 201–23 (hereafter Stephens, 'When Pope Noah Ruled'); Stenhouse, *Reading Inscriptions* (n 5) 75–79.

other generally accepted sources.[33] He continued to use this material in the *De antiquo iure Italiae*, and retained almost all the citations unchanged in the combined 1574 publication. After citing one of the spurious fragments of Cato's 'epitomes of Italian origins' as support for the claim (convenient for a scholar writing in Venice) that the domain of the ancient Veneti had extended to Istria, he defiantly adds that 'to these epitomes I attribute such authority as is rightly attributed to uncorrupted ancient records'.[34] Sigonio's weakness for forgeries was to betray him in his final years, when his reputation was stained by his attempt to pass off a spurious *Consolatio* as a genuine work of Cicero.[35]

By Sigonio's day, non-literary evidence was yielding great advances in knowledge, both through new discoveries, of which the *Fasti Capitolini* were the most notable, and the increased intensity and sophistication of their study.[36] Sigonio himself was not a collector of inscriptions, and depends mainly in his treatises on literary evidence. However, as was to be expected from an editor of the *Fasti*, he shows keen awareness in the treatises of inscriptions' value as historical evidence.[37] Sigonio's self-imposed restriction to the Republican period limited the range of epigraphic material on which he was able to draw, and later finds hugely increased the available evidence, of which the municipal laws, discovered from the eighteenth century on, are just one group.[38] Nonetheless, besides frequent reference to the *Fasti*, Sigonio deploys inscriptions as evidence for the civic institutions of colonies and for the distribution of tribes across post-Social War Italy, in the latter case with effusive acknowledgement to Panvinio for supplying the

[33] See the letter to Panvinio from 15 June 1560 in Sigonio, *Opera omnia* (n 10) vol 6, 1015: 'respondeo me Pictoris, Sempronii, et Catonis nomina non probare; ueterum tamen commentariorum aliquot esse fragmenta existimare; et quidem aliquanto locupletiora quam Orosii, Eutropii, et Rufi, et aliorum quorundam, quibus uulgo auctoritatem tribuimus'. On Agustín's critique (which has not survived, but was accompanied by warm overall praise) and on Sigonio's response see McCuaig, *Carlo Sigonio* (n 1) 42. Agustín's contempt for Annius' literary and epigraphic forgeries is vividly displayed in his posthumous *Dialogos de medallas, inscriciones y otras antiguedadas* (Felipe Mey 1587) 439, 448; see Stephens, 'When Pope Noah Ruled' (n 32) 206–09.

[34] Sigonio, *De antiquo iure Italiae* (n 30) 1.25, 211: 'quibus epitomis tantam ego tribuo auctoritatem, quanta incorruptis ueteribus monumentis merito tribuenda est'. Sigonio's other citations of Annian texts: ibid 1.9, 1.16, 1.17, 3.6; *De antiquo iure ciuium* (n 13) 1.2–1.3. A further citation in the 1560 edition of *De antiquo iure Italiae* (1.24, 56r) was omitted in the 1574 edition.

[35] See McCuaig, *Carlo Sigonio* (n 1) 291–344.

[36] See especially Stenhouse, *Reading Inscriptions* (n 5).

[37] Coin evidence is mentioned at *De antiquo iure ciuium* (n 13) 1.6, 33, coins showing that the tribune responsible for the *Lex Porcia de provocatione* was a Porcius Laeca; and *De antiquo iure Italiae* (n 29) 2.2: 227, military standards or ploughs on coin types as evidence for colony foundation. The first instance is a revision made at Agustín's suggestion: cf Sigonio, *Opera omnia* (n 10), vol 6, 1016. Sigonio had earlier made extensive use of the coin collection of the Venetian patrician Andrea Loredan for his editions of Livy and the *Fasti*: McCuaig, *Carlo Sigonio* (n 1) 15.

[38] On the discovery of the municipal laws see Jean-Louis Ferrary, *Recherches sur les lois comitiales et sur le droit public romain* (Pavia University Press 2012) 291–342 (hereafter Ferrary, *Recherches*).

material,[39] and at various points in the treatises he reproduces the full text of several inscribed laws or decrees.

In both his first and subsequent editions, Sigonio quotes the two fragments which Agustín was later to identify as from the *Lex Cornelia de XX quaestoribus* as evidence for scribes and magistrates' assistants, and the *Lex Antonia de Termessibus* to illustrate the status of free cities in the provinces.[40] These two texts had been discovered together at Rome *c* 1528; Sigonio's was the first publication of the *Lex Cornelia* and the second of the *Lex Antonia*.[41] In his 1574 edition, Sigonio also included a Latin text of the *Senatus Consultum de Asclepiade*.[42] This inscription had been discovered at Rome in 1570, when it was acquired by Orsini, and was first published by Vettori in 1571. Sigonio inserted it somewhat awkwardly at the end of the first chapter of the *De antiquo iure prouinciarum* as evidence for individuals of favoured status in the provinces, omitting the better preserved Greek text, but using it to provide the first reconstitution of the missing sections of the Latin.[43]

Sigonio's most notable epigraphic achievement concerned the agrarian and *repetundae* laws preserved on the fragmentary bronze tablet now generally known as the Tabula Bembina.[44] The tablet had passed from the collection of the Dukes of Urbino to that of Pietro Bembo in Padua in the early sixteenth century; some fragments were subsequently dispersed, and the remainder were acquired by Orsini in 1575. One of these fragments (now known as A) had been published in Giacomo Mazzocchi's *Epigrammata antiqua urbis Romae* (1521), and in his first edition Sigonio observed that, since the fragment showed that the agrarian law removed a *vectigal*, it should be identified with the third post-Gracchan law reported by Appian in *Civil Wars* 1.27.[45] During his time in Padua in 1560–63, Sigonio was able to study the fragments still remaining in Padua, and this bore fruit in the combined 1574 edition, in which

[39] Sigonio, *De antiquo iure Italiae* (n 30) 2.4, 3.3, 232-33, 270–72.

[40] Sigonio, *De antiquo iure ciuium* (n 13) 2.9, 2.15; Sigonio, *De antiquo iure prouinciarum* (n 14) 1.10. See Michael H Crawford, *Roman Statutes* (Institute of Classical Studies 1996) nos 14 and 19 (hereafter Crawford, *Roman Statutes*).

[41] See further Ferrary, *Recherches* (n 38) 3–42; McCuaig, *Carlo Sigonio* (n 1) 150–51.

[42] Robert K Sherk, *Roman Documents from the Greek East.* Senatus Consulta *and* Epistulae *to the Age of Augustus* (Johns Hopkins Press 1969) no 22.

[43] Sigonio, *De antiquo iure prouinciarum* (n 14) 288–89. See further Andrea Raggi, 'Senatus consultum de Asclepiade Clazomenio sociisque' (2001) 135 Zeitschrift für Papyrologie und Epigraphik 73–116.

[44] Crawford, *Roman Statutes* (n 40) nos 1–2.

[45] See the 1560 edition of *De antiquo iure Italiae* 2.2, 67v. In a letter of 17 February 1560, Sigonio had unsuccessfully requested a better text from Panvinio: Sigonio, *Opera omnia* (n 10) vol 6, 1011–12.

he published texts of these fragments (now known as Aa, Ab, Ba, and Bb) with his supplements, and used them to inform his revised discussions of agrarian and *repetundae* laws.[46] Although Sigonio's texts were soon superseded by the more complete version, incorporating further fragments, published by Orsini in 1583, he had nonetheless made an important contribution.

The outstanding quality of Sigonio's treatises was recognized from their first publication, for example by the French jurist François Baudouin who the following year gave them a warm encomium in his treatise on historiography and its value for jurisprudence.[47] The subsequent decline in original research in this field meant that they long retained their status as the pre-eminent treatment of their subject matter, and in particular of the Roman Republic's government of Italy and the provinces. Rosinus' work on Roman *antiquitates* was an essentially derivative compilation and drew heavily on Sigonio's treatises, with fulsome acknowledgement. Even Beaufort, writing two centuries after Sigonio, used him as his chief authority on relevant topics, with repeated acknowledgement.[48] As we shall see, it was only when critical study of Roman history and institutions gathered pace in the early nineteenth century that some of Sigonio's core contentions came to be challenged. The great handbooks of the middle and later nineteenth century synthesized this then recent research but still owed a debt to Sigonio's pioneering achievement. Whereas Mommsen offered no bibliographical overviews, Marquardt did so in his *Römische Staatsverwaltung*. The relevant treatise by Sigonio heads each of his bibliographies on the organization of pre-Social War Italy, colonies and *municipia*, and provincial government, always as the only contribution before the eighteenth and in some cases the nineteenth century.[49]

[46] Sigonio, *De antiquo iure populi romani* (n 16) 220–21, 525–26, with inserted sheets. See further Andrew W Lintott 'The So-Called Tabula Bembina and the Humanists' (1983) 51 Athenaeum 201–14; McCuaig, *Carlo Sigonio* (n 1) 160–68. Sigonio identified the *repetundae* law, now held by most scholars to be Gracchan, with the later *Lex Servilia Glauciae*.

[47] François Baudouin, *De institutione historiae universae et eius cum iurisprudentiae coniunctione* προλεγομένων *libri II* (André Wechel 1561) 111–12: 'nuper legebam perlubenter nouos de antiquo iure ciuium Romanorum et Italiae commentarios doctissimi hominis Caroli Sigonii, qui de historia Romana praeclare meritus est'. On Baudouin's work see Donald R Kelley, *Foundations of Modern Historical Scholarship: Language, Law and History in the French Renaissance* (Columbia University Press 1970) 117–41; Anthony Grafton, *What Was History? The Art of History in Early Modern Europe* (Cambridge University Press 2007) 62–122.

[48] McCuaig, *Carlo Sigonio* (n 1) 220–21 and see Chapters 4 and 5 in this volume by Mark Somos and Mattia Balbo.

[49] Joachim Marquardt, *Römische Staatsverwaltung* (Hirzel 1881) 21n12, 92n6, 241n1, 497n1 (hereafter Marquardt, *Staatsverwaltung*).

De antiquo iure ciuium Romanorum

Sigonio devotes the first book of his first treatise, on the ancient *ius* of Roman citizens, first to providing a definition of Roman citizenship (1.1–1.4) and then to an exposition of the citizens' *ius*, that is, their rights and obligations (1.5–1.21). In tackling the definition, Sigonio explicitly takes Aristotle as his model, adapting for Roman conditions the definition of the citizen which Aristotle had given in the opening chapter of the third book of his *Politics* (1274b32–1275b21).[50]

Before proceeding to his definition, Sigonio first gives a brief sketch of Roman constitutional development in terms of Aristotle's doctrine of constitutional types and the superiority of the mixed constitution, and the application of such conceptions to Rome by Polybius (not here named) and by Cicero in the *De re publica*. A fuller presentation of this interpretation of Roman development had already been given in the preface to Sigonio's commentary on the *Fasti*.[51] He now summarizes the sequence as follows:

> First kings held the state, then a tyrant; after he had been expelled from the city, a faction of a few patricians took over, who denied the *plebs* all access to office and exercized such unrestrained domination over them, that they did not become tranquil until, by stirring up seditions in the city, they secured a share in the magistracies and the whole state. Then indeed was achieved that blending (*temperatio*) of the state which Cicero's Scipio praised to the heavens. This was shaken by the Gracchi as tribunes and wholly overthrown by others, so that the whole state came into the hands of the *plebs*. Relying on their support, C. Caesar did not hesitate to seize the ruinous domination of one man.[52]

[50] Sigonio refers to Aristotle in *De antiquo iure ciuium* (n 13) 1.1, 1.17–1.18, 2.18, 2.21, 2–3, 83, 134, 143. On Sigonio's debt to Aristotle see McCuaig, *Carlo Sigonio* (n 1) 97–98, 129–36, 151–53 (152: 'an outstanding example of the creative Aristotelianism of the late Renaissance').

[51] Sigonio, *In fastos* (n 21) 3–5. Panvinio had taken the same view, evidently following Sigonio: *Reipublicae Romanae* (n 21) 366–67.

[52] Sigonio, *De antiquo iure ciuium* (n 13) 1.1, 3–4: 'Primum enim reges rempublicam tenuerunt, tum tyrannus: quo urbe pulso paucorum patriciorum inuasit factio. qui cum in plebem omni honorum aditu interdicto impotentius dominarentur, eandem eo deduxerunt, ut non ante seditionibus in urbe agitandis conquieuerit, quam et ipsa in partem magistratuum et totius reipublicae uenerit. Tum uero inducta est illa, quam Scipio apud Ciceronem laudibus in caelum extulit, reipublicae temperatio, qua deinde per Gracchos tribunos plebis temptata, per reliquos omnes labefactata, ad plebem summa reipublicae recidit. Cuius tandem opibus fretus C. Caesar perditum unius dominatum inuadere non dubitauit.'

The *Fasti* preface shows that Sigonio regarded the process of extending full participation to the plebs as only completed by the Lex Hortensia of 287 BCE, which was passed after the last of the plebeian 'secessions' and gave the decrees of the plebeian assembly the force of law, and held that the constitution remained well blended from the passage of that law and the ensuing Pyrrhic War until the Third Punic War (149–146 BCE) and the subsequent tribunates of the Gracchi.

Sigonio now goes on to insist that, for his definition of citizenship, account must be taken only of the period between the plebs' achievement of full participation and the accession of the emperors:

> Accordingly, in seeking here to discover what a Roman citizen with full rights is, we shall leave aside the earlier constitution of the kings or patricians in investigating the definition of a Roman citizen, and focus our entire discussion on the constitution which was introduced when offices were opened to the *plebs*, especially after the Tarentine [ie Pyrrhic] War, and which was not afterwards changed until the emperors administered everything at their whim.[53]

These conceptions reflect Sigonio's political attitudes: his hostility to the rule of the emperors is in the tradition of civic humanism and his strongly negative view of the Gracchi and their successors is conventional. However, his disapproval of patrician dominance in the early Republic and sympathy with the plebeian struggle against it is more original, and striking in a work produced in patrician-ruled Venice. The resulting insights not only played a crucial role in shaping Sigonio's treatise, but also had lasting importance for the study of the Roman Republic: no earlier writer had recognized to the same extent the importance of the plebeians' achievement of full access to office and political participation, or drawn attention to the period 287–133 BCE as the time of greatest political stability, a periodization which still shapes much current interpretation.[54]

[53] ibid 1.1, 4: 'Quocirca nos, qui ciuem Romanum qui optimo iure ciuis sit, hoc loco quaerimus, primam illam uel regum uel patriciorum rempublicam in ciuis Romanae definitione investiganda relinquemus, ad eam uero quae aequatis cum plebe maxime post bellum Tarentinum honoribus est inducta, nec post, nisi imperatoribus omnia ex libidine administrantibus, commutata, omnem nostram hanc disputationem accommodabimus.'

[54] On the originality of Sigonio's view of Republican constitutional development see McCuaig, *Carlo Sigonio* (n 1) 129–33; Ferrary, 'Rome et Venise' (n 18) 511–13 (noting the contrast with other Venetian writing); Lintott, *Constitution* (n 2) 245. For a provocative recent discussion of Republican periodization, see Harriet I Flower, *Roman Republics* (Princeton University Press 2010), and the review by John W Rich (2012) 102 Journal of Roman Studies 306–07.

In this instance, the limits of Sigonio's knowledge were actually to his advantage. His knowledge of Cicero's lost *De re publica* was based solely on the references to and quotations from it in Cicero's other works and in later writers, which he had collected and discussed in his pioneering collection of Cicero's fragments. These testimonia and fragments were sufficient to show that Cicero had presented Scipio Aemilianus as claiming that the Roman constitution was both mixed and the best possible. Sigonio alludes to one of these testimonia, from Cicero's later *De legibus*, in his reference (cited above) to Scipio's praise for 'the blending of the state'.[55] The evidence available to Sigonio did not, however, give any indication of when Cicero's Scipio claimed that the Roman constitution had reached perfect blending. The discovery in 1819 of a palimpsest preserving much of the *De re publica* showed that the historical survey in its second book dated its achievement much earlier than Sigonio would have expected, to the overthrow of the Decemvirate in 449 BCE.

After this brief historical survey Sigonio passes to the definition itself, which he gives as follows:

> A Roman citizen with full rights is in my view a man having residence (*domicilium*), a tribe (*tribus*), and eligibility for offices (*honores*).. . We accept this definition the more readily, because it is not too far from the definition of a citizen handed down by Aristotle. For just as he distinguished the full and complete citizen by eligibility to hold offices, so we define the same by residence, tribe and offices.[56]

Sigonio's divergence from Aristotle is rather greater than he acknowledges here, since Aristotle in fact specified two requirements, participation in judgement (κρίσις) and in office (ἀρχή), or, as he puts it later, 'in deliberative and judicial office'.[57] As we shall see, Sigonio later explains that he has omitted the judicial

[55] Cicero, *De Legibus* 3.12: 'haec est enim quam Scipio laudat in libris et quam maxime probat temperationem rei publicae', cited at Carlo Sigonio, *Fragmenta Ciceronis, variis in locis dispersa* (Giordano Ziletti 1559) 41v (editors now insert *sex* [Powell] or *illis* [Turnebus] before *libris*). For Sigonio's general remarks on the structure and argument of the *De republica* see ibid 32r–35r.

[56] Sigonio, *De antiquo iure ciuium* (n 13) 1.1, 4–5: 'Is mihi demum optima lege ciuis Romanus uidetur, qui domicilium, qui tribum, qui honorum potestatem sit adeptus. . . Huic autem definitioni eo libentius assentimus, quod ab Aristotelis definitione ciuis tradita non longe recedit. Ut enim ille ciuem plenum et perfectum honorum gerendorum potestate descripsit, sic nos eundem domicilio, tribu et honoribus definimus.'

[57] Aristotle, *Politics* 3.1, 1275a22–3: πολίτης δ' ἁπλῶς οὐδενὶ τῶν ἄλλων ὁρίζεται μᾶλλον ἢ τῷ μετέχειν κρίσεως καὶ ἀρχῆς,1275b18–20: ᾧ γὰρ ἐξουσία κοινωνεῖν ἀρχῆς βουλευτικῆς καὶ κριτικῆς, πολίτην ἤδη λέγομεν εἶναι ταύτης τῆς πόλεως. On Aristotle's definition of citizenship and its problems see Claude Mossé, 'La conception du citoyen dans la *Politique* d'Aristote' (1967) 6 Eirene 17–21; Curtis Johnson, 'Who is Aristotle's citizen?' (1984) 29 Phronesis 73–90; Dorothea Frede, 'Citizenship in Aristotle's *Politics*' in Richard Kraut and Steven Skultety (eds), *Aristotle's Politics: Critical Essays*

criterion as inapplicable to the Roman case. Aristotle had rejected residence as a criterion since it was also held by slaves and resident aliens. Although acknowledging that it was not a sufficient condition of citizenship, Sigonio nonetheless includes residence as a requirement, and adds the further requirement of membership in a tribe.

Having set out his definition in *De antiquo iure ciuium Romanorum* 1.1, Sigonio then goes on to clarify his residence and tribe requirements with chapters on 'the city and territory of Rome', *urbs agerue Romanus* (1.2), and on the tribes and the associated divisions by *curiae*, *classes*, and centuries (1.3–1.4), drawing for his discussion of the thirty-five local tribes on the epigraphic researches of Panvinio and other contemporaries.[58]

All full Roman citizens certainly belonged to a tribe, but Sigonio's other two requirements for citizenship are problematic. The importance he attached to the breaking of the patrician monopoly of office led him to follow Aristotle in making office-holding a criterion, although this carried the corollary (unwarranted in our sources' usage) that the plebeians lacked full citizenship before the monopoly was broken and that freedmen (who were normally ineligible for office) continued to do so afterwards. This stipulation also brought him into conflict with the political realities, since Roman magistrates and priests were normally well to do and drawn from the equestrian order. Sigonio does address this difficulty at a later point, when he insists that craftsmen, shopkeepers, and the like were not only able to vote but also to hold office, adducing the tales of men like Varro, Rupilius, and Scaurus who were said to have reached the consulship from modest beginnings.[59] However, if there is any substance in such stories, those concerned will have made their fortunes before aspiring to office.

(Rowman & Littlefield 2005) 167–84; David J Riesbeck, *Aristotle on Political Community* (Cambridge University Press 2016).

[58] On Renaissance research on the local tribes see Giovanni Forni, 'Tribù romane e problemi connessi dal Biondo Flavio al Mommsen' in *Studi di storia antica in memoria di Luca de Regibus* (Istituto di storia antica 1969) 17–90; Stenhouse, *Reading Inscriptions* (n 5) 6–11; Ginette Vagenheim, 'La critique épigraphique au XVIe siècle: Ottavio Pantagato, Paolo Manuzio, Onofrio Panvinio, Antonio Agustín et Pirro Ligorio: à propos des tribus romaines' (2012) 86 Aevum 949–68. Panvinio's and Sigonio's lists are accurate except for the substitution of the spurious Veientina for Camilia (attested only from inscriptions unavailable to them).

[59] Sigonio, *De antiquo iure ciuium* (n 13) 2.12, 123. McCuaig, *Carlo Sigonio* (n 1) 134 overlooks this passage when interpreting Sigonio as meaning merely that 'the equestrian and senatorial orders . . . and the higher magistracies were accessible with a rise (to which there was no juridical barrier) in socioeconomic status'. Sigonio elsewhere acknowledges that senators were normally drawn from the *equites*: *De antiquo iure ciuium* (n 13) 2.2, 95; for this expectation see Claude Nicolet, 'Le cens sénatorial sous la République et sous Auguste' (1976) 66 Journal of Roman Studies 20–38. On senatorial wealth see Israël Shatzman, *Senatorial Wealth and Roman Politics* (Latomus 1975), and on the dubious exemplary tales of senators of modest means see William V Harris, *War and Imperialism in Republican Rome 327–70 BC* (Clarendon Press 1979) 66, 264–65.

Sigonio would have done better to lay more stress on the vote rather than eligibility for office as a minimum requirement for full citizenship, and this would have been consistent with Aristotle, who counts assembly membership as an office for the purposes of his definition.[60]

From the fourth century BCE on various Italian communities were incorporated in the Roman citizen body as *municipia*, retaining their own civic identities. In some cases (generally near Rome) they received Roman citizenship with the vote; the remainder initially received citizenship without the vote (*sine suffragio*), but were subsequently granted it. Modern scholars hold that those communities who received the vote had Roman citizenship with full rights (*optimo iure*).[61] Sigonio, however, asserted repeatedly in this and the following treatise that their citizens lacked the residence requirement for full Roman citizenship unless they moved to Rome; those who remained in their home town ranked as *municipes*, not *ingenui ciues Romani* ('native Roman citizens'), and were excluded from the *curiae* and the cults of the city of Rome.[62]

This doctrine is a good example of how Sigonio could be led astray by his theoretical constructions. It is true that the *municipia* retained their own cults, and their citizens may well not have been included in the Roman *curiae*.[63] However, as Sigonio himself acknowledged, the political role of the *curiae* dwindled to a few vestiges, with the Roman people represented in the curiate assembly just by lictors, and many attended their festivals who did not know to which *curia* they belonged.[64] Sigonio appealed for support to Cicero's use of the phrase *ingenuus ciuis Romanus*, but no contrast with *municipes* is intended there and,

[60] Aristotle, *Politics* 1275a26–9.

[61] On *ciues sine suffragio* see Henrik Mouritsen, 'The *civitas sine suffragio*: Ancient Concepts and Modern Ideology' (2007) 56 Historia 141–58; James Tan, 'The *dilectus-tributum* System and the Settlement of Fourth Century Italy' in Jeremy Armstrong and Michael P Fronda (eds), *Romans at War: Soldiers, Citizens and Society in the Roman Republic* (Routledge 2020) 52–75. On *municipia* of both kinds see Adrian N Sherwin White, *The Roman Citizenship* (2nd edn, Clarendon Press 1973) 38–73 (hereafter Sherwin White, *Citizenship*); Hartmut Galsterer, *Herrschaft und Verwaltung im republikanischen Italien. Die Beziehungen Roms zu den Italischen Gemeinden vom Latinerfrieden 338 v. Chr. bis zum Bundesgenossenkrieg 91 v. Chr.* (CH Beck 1976) 64–84; Michel H Humbert, Municipium e Civitas sine suffragio. *L'organization de la conquête jusqu'à la guerre sociale* (École française de Rome 1978); Edward H Bispham, *From Asculum to Actium. The Municipalization of Italy from the Social War to Augustus* (Oxford University Press 2007) (hereafter Bispham, *From Asculum to Actium*). Sherwin White and others suppose that the term *municipium* was originally used only of communities incorporated without the vote and speak of pre-Social War towns which had been granted citizenship with the vote as *oppida ciuium Romanorum*.

[62] Sigonio, *De antiquo iure ciuium* (n 13) 1.1, 1.4, 1.8, 4–5, 20, 46; *De antiquo iure Italiae* (n 30) 2.7, 244. Panvinio too held that *municipes* were excluded from the *curiae* and city cults: *Reipublicae Romanae* (n 20) 690–92.

[63] Festus 146L; Smith, *The Roman Clan* (n 2) 228–29.

[64] Sigonio, *De antiquo iure ciuium* (n 13) 20, 82. See Cicero, *De lege agraria* 2.31; Ovid, *Fasti* 2.531–2.532; Plutarch, *Moralia* 285D. In general on the *curiae* see Smith, *The Roman Clan* (n 2) 184–234.

as elsewhere in conjunction with *ciuis*, *ingenuus* means just 'freeborn'.[65] As Sigonio recognized, the term *ager Romanus* had a fluid usage, referring sometimes just to the area in the immediate vicinity of Rome and sometimes to all of Italy occupied by Roman citizens. There is no reason to suppose that in the latter sense it excluded the territory of *municipia* with the vote.[66]

Having dealt with his definition of Roman citizenship and its implications, Sigonio was free to move on to the (on the whole safer) ground of the citizens' *ius*. After an introductory discussion of the sources of their *ius*, rightly stressing the role of custom as well as statute, he devotes the rest of his first book to an itemized exposition of the various components of the *ius*, accompanied by discussions of the relevant institutions, most of them admirably succinct and well-informed (*De antiquo iure ciuium Romanorum* 1.6–1.21).

Sigonio begins with an excellent analysis of the various ways by which the Roman people's *libertas* was secured, with its components identified as freedom from personal slavery, from kingship or tyranny (finally subverted by Augustus), and from oppression by overmighty magistrates or by creditors, and electoral freedom guaranteed by the ballot laws.[67] Sigonio next passes to *gens* membership, and this provides him with the opportunity for a detailed discussion of the patricians, tracing how the plebeians came to share in all but a few of their privileges and reasserting the radical view of the origins of the patriciate which he had first presented in 1555 in his commentary on Livy and in the treatise on Roman names which he appended to his commentary on the *Fasti*.[68] Hostile as ever to the patricians, he rejects Dionysius' preferred view that Romulus created them by selecting those who were outstanding in birth, virtue and wealth, which other Renaissance scholars accepted without question. In its place, Sigonio opts for the alternative view mentioned by Dionysius and some other sources, that the original patricians were simply those who, unlike the other settlers at Romulus' foundation, could name their fathers.[69]

[65] Sigonio, *De antiquo iure ciuium* (n 13) 4. See Cicero, *Brutus* 261; cf Sallust, *Bellum Catilinae* 61.5; Gaius, *Institutiones* 3.56 (not known to Sigonio).

[66] Sigonio, *De antiquo iure ciuium* (n 13) 7–9. On the term *ager Romanus* and its multiple signification see now Daniel J Gargola, *The Shape of the Roman Order: The Republic and its Spaces* (University of North Carolina Press 2017) 140–49 (hereafter Gargola, *The Shape of the Roman Order*).

[67] Sigonio, *De antiquo iure ciuium* (n 13) 1.6, 25–38. cf Lintott's praise for this section, *Constitution* (n 2) 246: 'it is doubtful whether modern discussions have improved on its fundamentals'. For modern treatments see Chaim Wirszubski, *Libertas as a Political Idea at Rome during the Late Republic and Early Principate* (Cambridge University Press 1950); Peter A Brunt, *The Fall of the Roman Republic and Related Essays* (Clarendon Press 1988) 281–350; Valentina Arena, *Libertas and the Practice of Politics in the Late Roman Republic* (Cambridge University Press 2012).

[68] Sigonio, *De antiquo iure ciuium* (n 13) 1.7, 38–43; McCuaig, *Carlo Sigonio* (n 1) 140–43.

[69] Patricians originating as those able to name their fathers: Livy 10.8.10 (anti-patrician speech of P. Decius Mus); Dionysius of Halicarnassus 2.8.3; Plutarch, *Romulus* 13.3, *Moralia* 278d; cf Cincius, *ap.* Festus 277L. On Sigonio's view of the origins of the patriciate see McCuaig, *Carlo Sigonio* (n 1) 137–44;

Whereas for his contemporaries *gentilitas* was an aristocratic quality, Sigonio did not doubt that all freeborn Roman citizens belonged to *gentes* and so had *gentilitas*: although the first plebeians could not name their fathers, subsequent generations could do so and so belonged to plebeian *gentes*.[70]

Next come discussions of Roman citizens' participation in cult at Rome, both public and private (1.8), and of their rights under private law (1.9–1.13), which (for no good reason) Sigonio regards as the proper meaning of the term *ius Quiritium*. From these he passes to their public obligations and rights: first, their duties to register at the census (1.14), perform military service (1.15) and pay direct and indirect taxes (1.16), and then their right to vote in the assemblies (1.17) and eligibility for office (*honores*, 1.18–1.21).

Sigonio subdivides offices into those which concern the gods, priesthoods (1.19), and those dealing with human affairs. For the latter we might have expected a single chapter on magistracies, but instead we get two, the first on *magistratus* (1.20), dealing with the magistrates' powers in relation to domestic matters, for which he regarded *potestas* as the appropriate term, and the second on *imperia* (1.21), treating their role in army command. The rationale for this division was that Sigonio regarded the term *imperium* as properly applying only to military command, and held that this power was conferred on consuls, praetors, or dictators, between their entry into office and departure from the city for their province, by the passage of the *lex curiata* mentioned in several sources. This view of *imperium* and of the *lex curiata* conflicted with the position taken by Grouchy in his very thorough treatise on the Roman assemblies (*De comitiis Romanorum libri III*, 1555). Already in his first edition, Sigonio, while referring his reader to Grouchy's work for further detail after his own brief treatment of the assemblies, entered into polemic with him on these issues, and, as we have seen, an extensive controversy followed, with Sigonio repeatedly refining his position up to his final summation in the combined 1574 edition of his treatises.[71] These issues have remained controversial up to the

Smith, *The Roman Clan* (n 2) 67–70. For contemporary acceptance of Dionysius' preferred view see eg Panvinio, *Reipublicae Romanae* (n 21) 297; Paolo Manuzio, *Antiquitatum Romanarum Paulli Mannuccii liber de ciuitate Romana* (Bartholomaeus Grassus 1585) 3–4 (hereafter Manuzio, *De ciuitate Romana*).

[70] On the aristocratic conception of *gentilitas* and its application to Rome by Budé in his 1508 commentary on the *Digest* see McCuaig, *Carlo Sigonio* (n 1) 119–24.

[71] On Sigonio's controversy with Grouchy see ibid 202–19; William MCuaig, 'Sigonio and Grouchy: Roman Studies in the Sixteenth Century' (1986) 74 Athenaeum 147–83; Frederik J Vervaet, *The High Command in the Roman Republic. The Principle of the* summum imperium auspiciumque *from 509 to 19 BCE* (Steiner 2014) 300–51. In his revised statements Sigonio did concede some use of the term *imperium* in relation to magistrates' civil functions: *De antiquo iure ciuium* (n 13) 87, 89–90; McCuaig, *Carlo Sigonio* (n 1) 211.

present day. Sigonio's view of the *lex curiata* as empowering the recipient to exercise *imperium* in military command still has many supporters, but almost all scholars have taken the term *imperium* itself as designating the totality of its holders' powers, civil as well as military. Recently, however, Fred Drogula, although unaware of his Renaissance predecessor, has advocated a view of *imperium* very similar to Sigonio's.[72]

In the early editions of the *De antiquo iure ciuium Romanorum*, Sigonio closed its first book with a further chapter on the triumph as 'the greatest of all the *honores* conferred by the vote or enthusiasm of the citizens'.[73] Here he may perhaps have been influenced by the culminating position which Biondo had allotted to the triumph in his survey of Roman antiquities. However, the triumph could not be regarded as an office (ἀρχή) in Aristotelian terms, and in the combined 1574 edition Sigonio wisely transferred this topic to the *De antiquo iure prouinciarum* (2.10).

Having devoted his first book to defining Roman citizenship and analysing the *ius* enjoyed by all citizens, Sigonio turns in the second to divisions within the Roman citizen body, of which he identifies three: by *ordines*, *imagines*, and factions. A fourth division, between patricians and plebeians, is passed over, since Sigonio had already dealt with it in the first book, showing that from the time of the Pyrrhic War the distinction retained little political importance, and, as he now points out, some patricians became so impoverished that they belonged to the lowest *ordo*.[74]

It is not immediately apparent what the three divisions have to do with Sigonio's overall subject, the *ius* of Roman citizens.[75] However, as he proceeds, the connection is made clear: some *iura* were distributed in accordance with his first two divisions, with the favoured groupings enjoying rights not open to their fellow citizens. A further theme is flagged up from the start:

> These divisions not only embraced the whole citizen body, but also by their strength and energy stirred up almost all the seditions from which the republic suffered, brought with them all the upheavals in the public order

[72] Fred K Drogula, '*Imperium*, *potestas* and the *pomerium* in the Roman Republic' (2007) 56 Historia 419–52; Fred K Drogula, *Commanders and Command in the Roman Republic and Early Empire* (The University of North Carolina Press Chapel 2015), and see the review by John W Rich (2016) 106 Journal of Roman Studies 279–80.

[73] Sigonio, *De antiquo iure ciuium Romanorum libri II* (Giordano Ziletti 1560) 1.22, 144: 'honorum, qui aut suffragio aut studio ciuium deferrentur, omnium amplissimus.'

[74] Sigonio, *De antiquo iure ciuium* (n 13) 2.5, 108.

[75] cf McCuaig, *Carlo Sigonio* (n 1) 152, claiming that 'by the end Aristotle and the polis have to an extent receded from view'. Sigonio does, however, continue to cite Aristotle in this book (above n 50).

and communal life, and finally destroyed the most successful republic itself for ever.[76]

Sigonio devotes the bulk of the book to the division by what he regards as the three *ordines* (2.1–2.19): the senators, the *equites*, and the rest of the citizen body, the plebs, with this word now used in a different sense than in the patrician/plebeian polarity. This conception of the three orders seems to have been pioneered by Manuzio: Sigonio in the first (1555) edition of his treatise on Roman names referred to a forthcoming treatment of the topic by Manuzio in a work *De familiis*, of which nothing more is heard, and Manuzio expounds it briefly in his *De ciuitate Romana*.[77] In one respect, their conception oversimplifies, since, although those outside the senate and the equestrian order were referred to collectively as the plebs, ancient sources do not normally speak of them as a single *ordo*. However, in drawing attention to its stratification by *ordines*, Manuzio and Sigonio had highlighted a crucially important aspect of Roman Republican society, and Sigonio's full treatment was long to remain definitive.[78]

Sigonio's careful discussions of the senatorial and equestrian orders (2.2–2.3) focus mainly on the complex issues relating to their membership, paying due attention both to the wealth requirement for each order and the censors' role in selection. Sigonio was troubled by the apparently inconsistent evidence on whether an *eques* could retain this status after appointment to the senate.[79] The problem was to be resolved by the discovery of the palimpsest of Cicero's *De re publica*, which revealed that a tribunician law passed in or shortly before 129 obliged senators to give up their equestrian status.

After a chapter on the *publicani* appended to his treatment of the *equites* (2.4), Sigonio moves on to a remarkably extensive treatment of the plebs

[76] Sigonio, *De antiquo iure ciuium* (n 13) 2.1, 91: 'Quae divisiones non solum uniuersam ciuitatem amplexae sunt, sed etiam pro uiribus neruisque suis omnes prope seditiones quibus respublica laborauit excitarunt, omnesque publici status communisque uitae perturbationes secum traxerunt, ac demum rempublicam ipsam florentissimam in perpetuum perdiderunt.'

[77] Manuzio, *De ciuitate Romana* (n 69) 4–10, 57. On Sigonio's reference to Manuzio's projected *De familiis*, presumably planned as one of the books of his projected work on Roman antiquities (above at n 18), see McCuaig, *Carlo Sigonio* (n 1) 143. The reference is omitted from the 1556 and 1559 editions of the *De nominibus Romanorum*, and in his 1556 commentary on the *Fasti* Sigonio himself announced his intention to write *de familiis*. Panvinio's discussion of the divisions by *ordines* and factions clearly reflects Sigonio's influence: Panvinio, *Reipublicae Romanae* (n 21) 299–301.

[78] For an evaluation of Sigonio's treatment and its influence, and in particular the application of his model to French society by Loyseau (1610) see McCuaig, *Carlo Sigonio* (n 1) 113–14, 147–53, 237–43. For modern discussions of the Roman *ordines* see Benjamin Cohen, 'La notion *d'ordo* dans la Rome antique' (1975) Bulletin de l'Association Guillaume Budé 259–82; Claude Nicolet (ed), *Des ordres à Rome* (Université de Paris I 1984); Ferrary, *Recherches* (n 38) 593–623.

[79] Sigonio, *De antiquo iure ciuium* (n 13) 99–102; cf McCuaig, *Carlo Sigonio* (n 1) 148.

(2.5–2.15). On the rural plebs he largely follows the sources' idealizing (2.6), but he paints a vivid portrait of the diversity of the urban plebs, drawing on a wealth of literary sources and, as we have seen, on an epigraphic law. His chapters include treatments of scribes (2.9) and other attendants of the magistrates (2.15), traders (2.10), bankers (2.11), and craftsmen (2.12). As McCuaig observes, this 'may be a landmark in the historiography of social history'.[80]

After this lengthy description of the *ordines* and the part they played in the state, Sigonio adds a chapter on the censors' marks of censure (*notae*), by which a man might be removed from his *ordo* (2.16), and then passes to the *iura ordinum*, that is, the rights enjoyed exclusively by one or both of the higher *ordines* (2.17–2.19). He identifies two such rights in particular: the right to serve as judges (*iudices*) and privileged seating at the theatre. As he explains, service as *iudices* was confined to senators down to 123 BCE, when Gaius Gracchus transferred it to the *equites*, and thereafter eligibility was hotly disputed and frequently changed, while separate seating at the theatre was introduced for senators in 194 BCE and for the *equites* in 67 BCE. In his first version, Sigonio's chapter on the courts (2.18) provided a lengthy attempt at a comprehensive treatment of the topic, but, as we have seen, in the final, combined edition of his treatises, most of this material was transferred to the new treatise devoted to this subject, retaining at this point just the account of judicial eligibility itself.[81] In each version, his discussion opens with another reference to Aristotle, at last acknowledging and explaining the omission from his definition of citizenship of the judicial requirement which for Aristotle had been one of his two defining criteria. As Sigonio points out, accepting this principle for the Roman Republic would entail the absurd conclusion that only senators were citizens down to 123 BCE and for the following years only *equites*.[82]

Sigonio's two other divisions within the citizen body are accorded just one chapter each. The first of these concerns *nobilitas* and is linked to the right to an *imago*, that is, to have displayed at the family home a wax mask taken from one's

[80] McCuaig, *Carlo Sigonio* (n 1) 149.

[81] Sigonio, *De antiquo iure ciuium* (n 13) 133–38.

[82] ibid 134: 'Quare in constituendo Romano ciue non omnibus in partibus Aristotelicam definitionem ciuis traditam possumus sequi. Ille enim ciuem magistratibus et iudiciis circumscripsit, quod iudicia et omnibus ciuibus committi, suffragio mandari aeque ac magistratus ipsos posse censuit, nos aliam rationem in legendis iudicibus, aliam in deferendis [magistratibus Romae initam inuenimus]. Itaque si ciuem statuerimus eum, qui iudicia habeat, graui illo incommodo urgebimur, ut usque ad sexcentesimum tricesimum ab urbe condita annum senatores solos ciues, quia soli iudicarunt, fuisse concludamus, deinde uero una cum iudiciis ciuitatem a senatoribus ad solos equites esse translatam dicamus, quo quid potest dici peruersius?' The words *magistratibus Romae initam inuenimus*, present in the 1560 edition, are omitted in the 1574 edition by printer's error. Sigonio here seems to overlook that he has identified as a defining requirement for citizenship not the right to elect magistrates, but eligibility for office.

face, to remain there in perpetuity to the glory of the individual and his family and be worn at family funerals.[83] Sigonio draws on two passages of Cicero to show that only holders of curule magistracies had this right.[84] He then adduces further texts to show that descendants of those who had held these offices and so handed on their *imago* were known as *nobiles*, and men who were the first in their family to hold such office were known as 'new men' (*noui homines*). Possession of family *imagines* thus constituted another *ius* which, like judicial service and front seats at the theatre, was enjoyed only by a favoured section of the citizen body, and Sigonio goes on to make the over-schematic claim that all citizens not ranking as *nobiles* or *noui homines* were classed as *ignobiles* (a term of opprobrium which might of course be applied to 'new men' as well).

Despite this blemish, Sigonio here made a contribution of lasting importance.[85] Earlier writers such as Guillaume Budé had misunderstood the Roman concept of *nobilitas*.[86] Sigonio recognized clearly that nobility in the Roman Republic was based on office-holding, and the importance which he attached to the breaking of the patrician monopoly of office enabled him to perceive that, after it had been broken, a new patricio-plebeian nobility emerged, whose members enjoyed substantial electoral advantage. Sigonio's view of *nobilitas* and the right to *imagines* was adopted by almost all subsequent writers up to the great nineteenth century handbooks, and, although here, as elsewhere, he makes no reference to Sigonio, Mommsen's classic statements on the subject in essence adopt Sigonio's conception.[87] The full significance of Sigonio's insight was, however, not brought out until Matthias Gelzer published his groundbreaking study of the Roman nobility in 1912 (again with no reference to Sigonio). Since then, the *nobiles* have been one of the dominant (and latterly contentious) themes of Roman Republican studies. Modern research has made some modifications to Sigonio's conception, demonstrating that, although the tenure of not only the consulship, but also the praetorship and aedileship (plebeian as well as curule) entitled a man to pass on his *imago* to his descendants, the term *nobilis* was normally applied only to men with consular ancestors.[88]

[83] ibid 2.20, 139–42.
[84] Cicero, *Verrines* 2.5.36; *Pro Rabirio Postumo* 16.
[85] Sigonio had already outlined his view of *nobilitas* in his 1555 treatise on Roman names: McCuaig, *Carlo Sigonio* (n 1) 142–43.
[86] ibid 121–22.
[87] Theodor Mommsen, *Römisches Staatsrecht* (3rd edn, Hirsel 1887) vol 1, 442–47, vol 3, 461–65 (hereafter Mommsen, *Staatsrecht*).
[88] Matthias Gelzer, *The Roman Nobility* (R Seager tr, Blackwell 1969) 27–40; David R Shackleton Bailey, 'Nobiles and Novi reconsidered' (1986) 107 American Journal of Philology 255–60, refuting the objections of Peter A Brunt, '*Nobilitas* and *novitas*' (1982) 72 Journal of Roman Studies 1–17. Plebeian aediles entitled to pass on their *imago*: Lily R Taylor, 'Cicero's Aedileship' (1939) 60 American Journal of Philology 194–202.

However, in its essentials, Sigonio's view still holds: once patrician exclusivity was ended, a patricio-plebeian nobility emerged, based on office holding, and *nobilitas* and *imagines* were closely linked in Roman discourse.[89]

Sigonio's final division is between *optimates* and *populares*, the product in his view of 'depraved party spirit' (*praua . . . partium studia*).[90] There is no differentiation of *iura* here, but the topic picks up the other theme announced at the start of his second book, that divisions within the citizen body had served to undermine and eventually destroy the republic, and with it the citizens' *antiquum ius*. At various points in the course of the book Sigonio had drawn attention to the destabilizing effects of the divisions he was analysing, pointing out opposition between the *equites* and the other orders, the greed of the *publicani* and its political consequences, the urban plebs' support for the 'sedition' of Saturninus, conflict over debt, the role of the 'forum mob' (*turba forensis*), and the long-running dispute over judicial service initiated by the turbulent Gaius Gracchus.[91] He had also shown some sympathy for agrarian legislation, to be repeated (as we shall see) in the *De antiquo iure Italiae*.[92] Here, however, as at the outset, Sigonio's stance on developments from the Gracchi on is staunchly optimate. Moreover, his readiness to accept not only his sources' testimony, but also their standpoint here leads him astray: his characterization of the *optimates* and *populares* is largely drawn from the notoriously partisan version presented by Cicero in the *Pro Sestio* 96–135. Sallust's very different viewpoint could have supplied a corrective, but Sigonio cites him here just for his denunciation of Catiline.

Despite this disappointing final chapter, the *De antiquo iure ciuium Romanorum* is overall a remarkable success. Although there are some misapprehensions and the Aristotelian model for his definition led him into some overschematism, Sigonio's structuring of the treatise around the citizens' *iura* enabled him to present what for its day constituted a rich and superbly well-documented portrait of what Claude Nicolet was to term the *métier* of the citizen in the Roman Republic, covering both what the citizens had in common and what divided them.

[89] Sigonio's achievement here is rightly applauded by McCuaig, *Carlo Sigonio* (n 1) 145–47. The few other recent writers who note his contribution have been unfairly critical, blaming Sigonio as the creator of a legalistic chimera, a supposed *ius imaginum*: see eg Harriet I Flower, *Ancestor Masks and Aristocratic Power in Roman Culture* (Clarendon Press 1999) 53–54. Sigonio in fact speaks only of a *ius imaginis*, and his wording does not seriously misrepresent Cicero's statements. Against the view that Cicero was referring to a general right of magistrates to have their statue or portrait set up in public places, see Flower, *Ancestor Masks*, 53–59.

[90] Sigonio, *De antiquo iure ciuium* (n 13) 2.21, 142–46.

[91] ibid 2.3–2.4, 2.7, 2.11, 2.13, 2.18, 99, 107, 110, 118–20, 123–24, 134–37.

[92] ibid 1.16, 80.

De antiquo iure Italiae

In a letter to Panvinio dated 31 August 1560, Sigonio writes: 'My *Italia* is finished, except for the dedication: the subject matter is difficult, more than I thought at the outset.'[93] His misgivings were well founded. The work's topic is complex, and much remains problematic and controversial even today. In its lucidity of structure and depth of treatment, Sigonio's synthesis was a huge advance on what went before, and its influence was accordingly long-lasting, but it does have numerous flaws, many of them arising, as before, from his determination to classify and systematize.[94]

The *De antiquo iure Italiae* has one more book than its predecessor, with the third book dealing with Italy after the Social War and the resulting extension of citizenship to all of Italy up to the Po. The first two books treat the organization and *iura* of Italy before that war, and their structure is modelled on that of the *De antiquo iure ciuium Romanorum*. In the earlier treatise Sigonio devoted the first book to defining who the Roman citizens were and then expounding their *iura*, and in the corresponding book of this work he addresses the same questions for the peoples of Italy who, in his conception, held the three progressively inferior grades of *ius*. In each treatise the second book is devoted to a different, but related topic: in the earlier treatise it dealt with divisions within the Roman citizen body and their consequences for *iura*; here its subject is the division of pre-Social War Italy not by peoples but by the various types of communities (*ciuitates*), each of which enjoyed their own *ius*. Since Aristotle had concerned himself just with the individual *polis*, he could no longer be of direct assistance, but Sigonio continued to follow the methodology for which Aristotle had provided the model.

Sigonio opens the first book with an introductory chapter whose topics include the varying usage of the word *Italia* and the character of Roman treaties.[95] He then devotes the rest of the book to successive treatment of his three groupings for the peoples of pre-Social War Italy, namely the Latins (1.2–1.7), the *Italici* (1.8–1.21), and the province of Cisalpine Gaul (1.22–1.26). As in the earlier treatise, he envisages these accounts as proceeding from definition to *iura*. Thus he introduces his discussion of the Latins as follows:

[93] Sigonio, *Opera omnia* (n 10) vol 6, 1019: 'La mia *Italia* è finita, se non che *de consecrando agitur*. E' una difficil materia, più che non credetti da principio.'

[94] Ferrary's evaluation of the *De antiquo iure Italiae* is just: *Recherches* (n 38) 293n6: 'la qualité remarquable de cet ouvrage (malgré quelques grosses erreurs . . .) explique l'influence qu'il conservera jusqu'au XIXe siècle.'

[95] Sigonio, *De antiquo iure Italiae* (n 30) 1.1, 149–55.

> As in the book in which I revealed the *iura* of the Roman citizens, I derived the whole treatment from the definition of a Roman citizen, it seems to me necessary to follow the same procedure here, so that, starting from the definition of the Latins, I may arrive at an explanation of their *iura*. Thus just as we described the Roman citizens as free men, inhabitants of the Roman city and territory, who had a tribe and the right (*ius*) to offices, so now we define the Latins as dwellers in Latium, treaty-allies of the Roman people, who had been granted the Latin Right (*ius Latii*).[96]

A similar statement opens Sigonio's account of the *Italici*:

> As, however, we defined the Latins as dwellers in Latium, treaty-allies of the Roman people, who had been granted the Latin Right, so we consider that the *Italici* can be conveniently defined as inhabitants of the rest of Italy up to the Rubicon, treaty-allies of the Roman people, who had been endowed with the Italic Right (*ius Italicum*).[97]

Sigonio envisages all the settlements by which these peoples came under Roman rule as treaties (*foedera*) and these treaties as the source of their *iura*, and so regards himself as obliged to give an account both of the treaties and of the wars which preceded them. As he explains at the outset:

> Since . . . all the Latins' *ius* comes from their treaty (*foedus*), and some traces of the treaty itself may be, so to speak, detected from the victory won and the peace granted, I shall accordingly briefly expound the wars and defeats incurred on each side, so that I may the more readily discover the individual peoples' treaties. I shall follow this practice not only for the Latins, but also for the *Italici* and *prouincia Gallia*, so that, by proceeding from a description of their territory (*ager*) to the wars, from the wars to the treaties, and from the treaties to the *iura*, our discourse may provide a continuous explanation of the *ius* of each of the peoples.[98]

[96] ibid 1.2, 156: 'Quod autem eo libro feci, in quo ciuium Romanorum iura aperui, ut omnem disputationem ex ciuis Romani definitione deriuarem, idem hoc loco mihi faciendum esse censeo, ut a Latinorum definitione profectus ad eorum iura explicanda perueniam. Itaque ut tum ciues Romanos homines liberos, urbis agrique Romani habitatores, qui cum tribu ius honorum haberent, diximus, sic nunc Latinos Latii incolas, populi Romani foederatos, iure Latii donatos definimus.'

[97] ibid 1.8, 171: 'Ut autem Latinos Latii incolas, populi Romani foederatos, iure Latii donatos definiuimus, sic Italicos, reliquae ad Rubiconem Italiae habitatores, populi Romani foederatos, iure Italico praeditos commode definiri posse censemus.'

[98] ibid 1.2, 156: 'Quoniam . . . ius eorum omne e foedere proficiscitur, foedus autem ex uictoria parta et pace concessa quaedam quasi per uestigia indagatur: propterea, ut commodius foedera singulorum populorum inueniam, bella quoque et clades ultroque citroque illatas, paucis exponam. atque hoc non

Despite his promise of brevity, Sigonio in fact devotes a large portion of this book to summarizing the often numerous wars between the individual peoples and the Romans reported by the ancient sources: thus over a third of the book is occupied by his account of the territories, wars, and treaties of the peoples he classes as *Italici*, beginning with the Etruscans and ending with the Samnites.[99] By contrast with the first treatise, where the analysis of Roman citizens' *ius* took up the greater part of the first book, here Sigonio devotes just a single chapter to each of his three inferior categories of *iura* (1.4 on *ius Latii*, 1.21 on *ius Italicum*, 1.25 on the *ius* of *prouincia Gallia*).

In broad terms Sigonio's grading is sound enough: provincial communities (unless specially privileged) had a less favourable status than those of pre-Social War Italy, and among the latter those with the Latin Right had further advantages. His terminology, however, is flawed. *Ius Latii* did indeed evolve in pre-Social War Italy, and was later extended as a privileged status to the provinces. However, the term *ius prouinciale* is Sigonio's own coinage, and his view of *ius Italicum* as having undergone the same evolution as *ius Latii* is a fundamental misconception, which, after having long been generally accepted, was finally exploded by Friedrich von Savigny.[100] *Ius Italicum* was in fact a privilege granted by the emperors to certain communities (mostly citizen colonies) in the provinces, giving them the same advantages (chiefly exemption from direct taxes) then enjoyed by the towns of Italy, and thus had no connection whatever with the status of the pre-Social War Italian allies.[101]

We saw above that Sigonio was led astray in his previous treatise by his insistence on residence as a criterion for citizenship, and it contributed to further confusion here in his treatment of the Latins. In the definition cited above he specifies the Latins as 'dwellers in Latium' (*Latii incolae*). After correctly noting the fluidity of the sources' terminology in relation to the Latin allies, he goes on to explain that he is using Latium as a geographical term in the extended sense, attested in various ancient writers, denoting the region from the Tiber to the Liris, and so counts as its inhabitants not just the ethnic Latins, but also the neighbouring peoples to the south, including the Volsci, Aequi, and Hernici,

in Latinis solum, sed in Italicis etiam, et Gallia provincia institutum tuebor, ut ab agri descriptione exorsus ad bella, a bellis ad foedera, a foederibus ad iura singulorum populorum explananda nostra continenter oratio delabatur.'

[99] ibid 1.9–20, 171–95.

[100] Friedrich C von Savigny, 'Über das *ius Italicum*' in *Vermischte Schriften* (Veit 1850) vol 1, 29–80, an expanded version of a paper first published in 1818. For Sigonio's view of the evolution of *ius Italicum* see especially *De antiquo iure Italiae* (n 30) 195–96.

[101] On *ius Italicum* see Sherwin White, *Citizenship* (n 61); 275–77, 316–22; Thomas H Watkins, '*Coloniae* and *ius Italicum* in the Early Empire' (1983) 78 Classical Journal 319–36.

and he maintains this regional conception throughout his detailed exposition of the Latin Right and its holders in the first book.[102] Sigonio conveys the impression that most of the inhabitants of the region from the Tiber to the Liris held *ius Latii*, retaining it from the treaties said to have been made in the early fifth century by Spurius Cassius, and that these were the main holders of *ius Latii* in pre-Social War Italy. This is a completely misleading picture. In reality, most communities in the region from the Tiber to the Liris had been incorporated into the Roman citizen body (with or without the vote) by the end of the fourth century BCE; the only non-colonial communities in the region which retained their status unchanged after the warfare of the later fourth century BCE were the Latin towns Tibur and Praeneste and various Hernican towns; and the chief holders of *ius Latii* were the Latin colonies, some in the extended Latium but many others across Italy. Here, as elsewhere in his treatises, Sigonio takes surprisingly little account of Latin colonies, a flaw to which we shall revert below.

Sigonio shows insufficient awareness as well of the extension of the Roman citizen body across central Italy, which played such a crucial part in the establishment of Roman control in the fourth and third centuries. This partly results from the work's structure: since Roman citizens had been dealt with in the previous treatise, they lay outside the scope of the first book of the *De antiquo iure Italiae*, but were dealt with in the section on *municipia* in the second book (with listing of individual grants at 2.9). Further factors were Sigonio's misunderstanding of *praefecturae*, discussed below, and his belief, based on a false reading in Livy, that the grant of Roman citizenship without the vote to the important city of Capua in 338 BCE was made not to the whole citizen body (known as Campani), but just to their cavalry.[103]

Sigonio was also in error in his conception of northern Italy as organized as a province with inferior status to the rest of the peninsula. Magistrates (usually consuls) were indeed regularly deployed there for military purposes from the late third century BCE, but it was only in the last years of the Republic that Gallia Cisalpina formed a separate administrative province, marked off from the rest of Italy by an Arno-Rubicon boundary. This arrangement, which was terminated in 42 BCE, had probably been put in place in the 80s.[104] It therefore

102 Sigonio, *De antiquo iure Italiae* (n 30) 1.2–1.3, 155–57.

103 ibid 178, 243, 248; so also Panvinio, *Reipublicae Romanae* (n 21) 760. Modern texts of Livy 8.14.10 read *Campanis equitum honoris causa . . . ciuitas sine suffragio data*, but Sigonio's and other Renaissance editions read *equitibus* instead of *equitum*. With the true reading, Livy is in agreement with Velleius 1.14.3 (except on the date).

104 Umberto Laffi, 'La provincia della Gallia Cisalpina' (1992) 80 Athenaeum 5–23, with earlier bibliography.

did not impair the status of the region's inhabitants, since, as Sigonio later acknowledges, after the Social War those living south of the Po all received full Roman citizenship and the Transpadani were granted Latin status (advanced to full citizenship in 49 BCE).[105]

Sigonio documents the military obligations of the Latins and other Italian allies to Rome well, but wrongly claims that they also paid tax to Rome.[106] In support of this view, he first argues that, if Roman citizens had to pay taxes, the peoples of inferior status could not have been exempt, and then adduces various texts, of which none prove his point and one is another false reading.[107] Sigonio was right that the Italian allies had a fiscal liability, but (unlike the provincials) they did not discharge it directly to the Roman authorities, but instead provided pay and equipment for the contingents they contributed to Roman forces, and Livy's references to their contributing *stipendium* relate to this obligation.[108]

As to the Latins' privileges, still a vexed question today, Sigonio accords them just two, a limited right to vote at Rome and the right to the Roman citizenship itself for their magistrates (the latter now generally regarded as a relatively late accretion).[109] He insists that the Latins cannot have enjoyed any of the private rights of Roman citizens, disregarding the evidence which has led many scholars to conclude that they had *commercium* with Roman citizens and some to accord them *conubium* as well, and also passes over the right to gain Roman citizenship by migrating to Rome attested by Livy.[110]

[105] Sigonio, *De antiquo iure Italiae* (n 30) 3.2.

[106] ibid 163–64, 195–97.

[107] ibid 163 takes Livy 8.8.3 as calling the Latins *stipendiarii*, on the basis of the manuscript reading (*clipeis antea Romanis usi sunt, dein, postquam stipendiarii facti sunt, scuta pro clipeis fecere*), but the early correction to *Romani* is clearly correct and adopted in all modern editions. cf Stephen P Oakley, *A Commentary on Livy Books VI–X. Vol. 2: Books VII–VIII* (Clarendon Press 1998) 466.

[108] Polybius 6.21.5; Livy 27.9.2, 13; 35.16.3; Mommsen, *Staatsrecht* (n 87) vol 3, 681–82; Claude Nicolet, 'Le *stipendium* des alliés Italiens avant la Guerre Sociale' (1978) 46 Papers of the British School at Rome 1–11; Saskia T Roselaar, *Italy's Economic Revolution: Integration and Economy in Republican Italy* (Oxford University Press 2019) 53–54 (hereafter Roselaar, *Italy's Economic Revolution*). The requirements imposed in 204 on the twelve Latin colonies which had refused the levy were exceptional punitive measures (Livy 29.15.9).

[109] Sigonio, *De antiquo iure Italiae* (n 30) 161–66.

[110] Livy 41.8.9, cited by Sigonio only as evidence for allied eagerness for Roman citizenship: ibid 3.1, 259. On these issues Panvinio, *Reipublicae Romanae* (n 21) 689–90, 697–98 provides a superior treatment, mentioning the *ius migrandi* and Cicero's evidence (*Pro Balbo* 53–54) for Latins acquiring citizenship through prosecution, and accepting a Latin right of *commercium*. For recent debates over the Latins' rights see David Kremer, *Ius Latinum. Le concept de droit latin sous la république et l'empire* (De Boccard 2006); Kremer, 'À propos d'une tentative récente de déconstruction des privilèges latins et en particulier du *ius migrandi*' (2014) 102 Athenaeum 226–37; Altay Coşkun, *Bürgerrechtsentzug oder Fremdenausweisung? Studien zu den Rechten von Latinern und weiteren Fremden sowie zum Bürgerrechtswechsel in der römischen Republik (5. bis frühes 1 Jh. v. Chr.)* (Steiner 2009) (hereafter Coşkun, *Bürgerrechtsentzug oder Fremdenausweisung?*); Coşkun, 'The Latins and Their Legal Status in the Context of the Cultural and Political Integration of Pre- and Early Roman Italy' (2016) 98 Klio 526–69; Saskia T Roselaar, 'The Concept of *commercium* in the Roman Republic' (2012) 66 Phoenix

Among the most enduring features of this part of his work has been the doctrine, worked out much more thoroughly by Sigonio than in any earlier treatment, that the Romans' relationship with all her Italian allies rested on treaties (*foedera*). This conception has remained largely unchallenged in later scholarship. Although a different view was adopted by Barthold Georg Niebuhr, the classic later nineteenth-century treatments by Karl Julius Beloch, Marquardt, and Mommsen all took the treaty status of the Italian allies for granted.[111] Beloch indeed denied that the status of the Latin colonies rested on a treaty, and this point (which Sigonio did not directly consider) has remained controversial.[112] With this exception, the allies' treaty status has continued to be generally accepted almost to the present day. This orthodoxy, however, deserves to be questioned. In the regions conquered by the Romans by 265 BCE, their allies (excluding the Latin colonies) appear to have numbered at least 125 autonomous states, but treaties of alliance likely to have endured until the Social War are attested securely for only fourteen of these states, and with varying degrees of plausibility for a further nine. No doubt there were quite a number more which happen to have left no record. However, this evidence does not entitle us to conclude that all the Italian allies had treaties, and in my view further considerations make it more likely that in Italy, as later in the provinces, the Romans concluded treaties only with selected communities, and many others, having come over to the Romans by *deditio* (surrender) or capture, were retained in treaty-less alliance and regarded by the Romans as in their *dicio*, liable to do their bidding.[113]

For the second book of the *De antiquo iure Italiae*, Sigonio turns, as we have seen, from the peoples of pre-Roman Italy to the *ciuitates*. At several points he stresses the difficulty of the material.[114] After a short introductory chapter,

381–413 (hereafter Roselaar, 'The Concept of *commercium*'); Roselaar, 'The Concept of *conubium* in the Roman Republic' in Paul du Plessis (ed), *New Frontiers: Law and Society in the Roman World* (Edinburgh Universty Press 2013) 102–22; Michel H Tarpin, 'Strangers in Paradise. Latins (and Other Non-Romans) in Colonial Context: A Short Story of Territorial Complexity' in Tesse D Stek and Jeremia Pelgrom (eds), *Roman Republican Colonization: New Perspectives from Archaeology and Ancient History* (Quasar 2014) 161–91; Roselaar, *Italy's Economic Revolution* (n 108) 128–32.

[111] Barthold G Niebuhr, *Römische Geschichte* (Reimer 1828-32) vol 3, 611–41, 726–27 (hereafter Niebuhr, *Römische Geschichte*); Karl Julius Beloch, *Der italische Bund unter Roms Hegemonie* (Teubner 1880) 158–77, 194–224; Marquardt, *Staatsverwaltung* (n 49) 44–8; Mommsen, *Staatsrecht* (n 87) vol 3, 645–715.

[112] For a recent discussion see Pierre Sánchez, '*Latini, id est foederati*. Le statut juridique des colonies latines sous la république' (2016) 104 Athenaeum 50–82.

[113] John W Rich, 'Treaties, Allies and the Roman Conquest of Italy' in Philip de Souza and John France (eds), *War and Peace in Ancient and Medieval Italy* (Cambridge University Press 2008) 51–75. Ficulea should be added to the list of possibly attested treaties: *L'Année Epigraphique* 1977, 179 (kindly drawn to my attention by Michael Crawford).

[114] Sigonio, *De antiquo iure Italiae* (n 30) 214, 241, 249, 255.

Sigonio proceeds to discussions of *coloniae*, *municipia*, and *praefecturae*, each of which is accorded four chapters on the same pattern: the first explains the respective community category, the second discusses its *ius* and the third its civic institutions, while the fourth provides a chronological listing of the individual instances. The lion's share of the space is devoted to colonies (twenty-six of the forty-four pages taken up by the book in the 1574 edition). Two further chapters close the book, the first dealing with *ciuitates foederatae*, and the second with *fora* and *conciliabula*, bringing out the naming of the *fora* after their founders as one of the ways by which magistrates perpetuated their glory. As Sigonio recognized, all these categories except for *ciuitates foederatae* continued in post-Social War Italy, and he cites listings of community types from literary sources of that period.[115]

There is a striking mismatch between the subject matter of the first two books of the *De antiquo iure Italiae*. A large part of the second book is devoted to communities of Roman citizens, who were excluded from consideration in the first book. Most of the allied peoples with whom the first book was concerned were, on Sigonio's view, organized as *ciuitates foederatae*, but these are here disposed of in a perfunctory couple of pages.

Sigonio's treatment of colonies will be discussed below. On the remaining community categories, he grapples well with the intractable evidence of Festus and other literary sources, but his drive to systematize again sometimes leads him astray. As we saw above, he insists that even those *municipes* with the vote were not full Roman citizens, and he perversely argues that those without the vote also lacked the private rights of Roman citizenship and participated in citizenship solely by serving in the legions rather than in the *auxilia*, which he takes as honorific.[116] *Praefecturae* gave him particular difficulty, partly because of his misunderstanding of Capua's status, but also because he interpreted the despatch of Roman *praefecti* to these communities as implying that they lacked the autonomy which he regarded as characteristic of all but the lowest,

[115] ibid 215. Similar listings of community types occur in inscribed laws (references at Michael H Crawford, 'How to Create a *municipium*: Rome and Italy after the Social War' in Michel M Austin, Jill Harries, and Christopher Smith (eds), *Modus Operandi: Essays in Honour of Geoffrey Rickman* (Institute of Classical Studies 1998) 42–43; Bispham, *From Asculum to Actium* (n 61) 76–77, but this evidence was not available to Sigonio.

[116] Sigonio, *De antiquo iure Italiae* (n 30) 2.7, 242–45; contrast Panvinio, *Reipublicae Romanae* (n 21) 692–93. Sigonio supports his honorific interpretation with an inaccurate citation of Paul. Fest. 117L (substituting *honoris partem* for *muneris partem*), and does not at this point take account of the case of Anagnia, for whom *ciuitas sine suffragio* was a punishment (Livy 9.43.24, cited later at Sigonio, *De antiquo iure Italiae* (n 30) 248, 252).

provincial grade of *ius*. He recognized that some *praefecturae* had Roman citizenship; in fact they all did.[117]

The third book of the treatise, on the status of Italy in the period from the Social War to the establishment of Augustus' sole rule, shows Sigonio's formidable abilities in marshalling evidence at their best.[118] The first chapter deals with the acquisition of citizenship by the Latins and those he had classed as *Italici*, with careful analysis of the enfranchisement process. On the Italians' desire for citizenship, now so contentious, Sigonio had no doubts: he adduces Livy's reports of migration to Rome as evidence for such aspirations in the early second century and, on Appian's authority, holds that from the time of the Gracchi the Italians were openly seeking the citizenship and would not rest until they achieved it.[119] Accepting an (in fact unfounded) claim by Velleius, Sigonio expresses (for him rare) approval for Tiberius Gracchus: 'although his other proposals were perhaps insufficiently in the public interest, he most aptly for the security of the empire . . . promised citizenship to Italy'.[120]

The next chapter discusses the enfranchisement of Cisalpine Gaul; it was evidently local patriotism that led Sigonio to insist (without evidence) that, although the other Transpadani initially received only Latin rights, the Veneti must have got full citizenship.[121] Next follows a chapter on the post-Social War status of the various categories of community, noting the promotion of the former non-colonial allies to *municipia* and, as we have seen, adducing epigraphic evidence for their allocation to tribes. The remaining chapters continue the listing of colonies for the period from Sulla to the start of Augustus' sole rule (3.4), and discuss the extension of Italy to include Istria and the Alps (3.5–3.6).

[117] ibid 2.10–2.13, 249–52. For a recent discussion of *praefecturae* before the Social War see Bispham, *From Asculum to Actium* (n 61) 95–100.

[118] See the discussion of this book by McCuaig, *Carlo Sigonio* (n 1) 169–70.

[119] Sigonio, *De antiquo iure Italiae* (n 30) 258–62. For recent views on the Italians' aims see Henrik Mouritsen, *Italian Unification: A Study in Ancient and Modern Historiography* (Institute of Classical Studies 1998); Mark P Pobjoy, 'The First *Italia*' in Kathryn Lomas and Edward Herring (eds), *The Emergence of State Identities in Italy in the First Millenium BC* (Accordia Research Institute 2000) 187–211; Seth Kendall, *The Struggle for Roman Citizenship. Romans, Allies and the Wars of 91–77 BCE* (Gorgias Press 2013); Christopher J Dart, *The Social War, 91 to 88 BCE. A History of the Italian Insurgency Against the Roman Republic* (Ashgate 2014); Roselaar, *Italy's Economic Revolution* (n 108) 196–230.

[120] Velleius Paterculus 2.2.3; Sigonio, *De antiquo iure Italiae* (n 30) 260: 'etsi alia parum fortasse e republica promulgauit, illud tamen ad imperium constituendum aptissime . . . ciuitatem Italiae . . . est pollicitus'.

[121] ibid 267.

De antiquo iure prouinciarum

As first published in 1569, Sigonio's third treatise, on the *ius* of the provinces under the Republic, comprised two books. As already noted, the third book added in the 1574 edition dealt with the extraneous topic of Sigonio's controversy with Grouchy. The original two books conformed to the pattern with which we are familiar from the earlier treatises: the first book serves to define the *prouinciae* and expound their *ius*, while the second deals with a different topic also related to that *ius*, in this case provincial administration—as Sigonio puts it, 'by whom and how their *ius* was administered for them'.[122]

The treatise opens with a chapter entitled 'What a province was and how it was established.' Here the parallel with the previous treatise is drawn explicitly:

> If we seek a sure and brief definition of province, just as we called Latium the region endowed with *ius Latii* and Italy the region in receipt of *ius Italicum*, we shall define a province as a region which has obtained *ius provinciale*... *Ius provinciale*, otherwise known as the *formula provinciae*, proceeded, just like *ius Latii* and *ius Italicum*, from the terms of the treaty struck with the Roman people... Since, however, the terms granted to a province had been less favourable than those which had been granted to Latium and Italy, the provinces accordingly received a less favourable *ius* than Latium and Italy. For although Italy was made liable to taxation, it was granted overall liberty. The provinces, however, were penalized not only by taxes, but also by the loss of liberty, since they were deprived of their laws and jurisdiction by their own magistrates. The proof of this is that there was no province which did not have a praetor and quaestor to conduct respectively jurisdiction and tax collection.[123]

Thus once again the gradation of *iura* is at the centre of Sigonio's analysis, and other key concepts deployed as before are residence (or, as here, region)

[122] Sigonio, *De antiquo iure prouinciarum* (n 14) 2.1, 333: 'per quos et quemadmodum ius eis redditum sit'. cf ibid 1.2, 290: 'per quos et quomodo administratae sint.'

[123] ibid 1.1, 286–87: 'Si certam prouinciae breuemque definitionem quaeramus, sane ut Latium regionem iure Latii donatam et Italiam regionem iure Italico affectam dicebamus, sic prouinciam definiemus regionem quae ius prouinciale consecuta sit... Ius autem prouinciale, quod alio nomine formula prouinciae nuncupatur, ut etiam ius Latii atque Italicum, ex legibus percussi cum populo Romano foederis emanauit... Quoniam autem leges quae prouinciae datae sunt iniquiores fuerant quam quae Latio atque Italiae, propterea prouinciae ius etiam deterius quam Latium atque Italia sunt adeptae. Nam Italia uectigalis facta est illa quidem, sed tamen in uniuersum libertate donata; prouinciae vero non solum uectigalibus, sed etiam seruitute mulctatae sunt, quippe quae legibus suis ac magistratibus ius dicentibus spoliatae sint. Id uero argumento est, quod prouincia nulla fuit, quae non Romanum praetorem ac quaestorem habuerit, illum qui ius diceret, hunc qui uectigalia procuraret.'

as a defining criterion, and the treaty (*foedus*) by which a region came under Roman rule as the source of its *ius*.

After a surprisingly short chapter dealing with the establishment of colonies and extension of citizenship in the provinces down to Caesar's dictatorship,[124] Sigonio devotes the rest of the first book to the individual provinces acquired before Augustus' sole rule, assigning a chapter to each province in an order based partly on the chronology of acquisition and partly on location. He defines the subject matter of these chapters as 'when, under which leaders, with which boundaries, and with what *ius* the individual provinces of the Roman people were acquired and established'.[125] They thus perform the same functions for the provinces as had been carried out for pre-Social War Italy by the surveys of individual peoples which formed the bulk of the first book of *De antiquo iure Italiae*. The topics covered here conform closely to those covered in the corresponding Italian chapters. Each chapter seeks to treat successively the region covered by the province in question, the Romans' wars there up to the completion of its conquest, the resulting settlements and the establishment of the province, and its subsequent administration.

Sigonio's treatment of the individual provinces in these chapters is impressively thorough and well informed, and sometimes mitigates through its nuances some of the over-systematic generalizations of the opening chapter. Nonetheless, even here Sigonio tends to envisage Roman provincial administration as a fully developed institution from the outset. This conception has had a very long-lasting influence, and it is only recent research which has fully brought out the extent to which the concepts and institutions of provincial government evolved gradually from the operations of Roman military commanders.[126]

One instance of Sigonian systematizing is his initial insistence, as in the passage cited above, that each province accepted Roman rule by a treaty (*foedus*), just as he had supposed for the Italian peoples, but he makes little attempt to establish this untenable claim in the subsequent treatment of individual

[124] ibid 1.2, 290.

[125] ibid 2.1, 333: 'quo tempore, per quos duces, quibus finibus, quo iure singulae populi Romani confectae ac constitutae prouinciae sint'. cf ibid 1.2, 290: 'quae, et quando, et quibus finibus, et quibus ducibus confectae et quo iure relictae . . . sint'.

[126] For example Andrew W Lintott, 'What was the "Imperium Romanum"?' (1981) 28 Greece & Rome 53–67; Lintott, *Imperium Romanum: Politics and Administration* (Routledge 1993); John S Richardson, *Hispaniae: Spain and the Development of Roman Imperialism 218–82 BC* (Cambridge University Press 1986); John Richardson, *The Language of Empire: Rome and the Idea of Empire from the Third Century BC to the Second Century AD* (Cambridge University Press 2008); Alejandro Días Fernández, Provincia et Imperium. *El mando provincial en la República romana (227–44 a. C.)* (Universidad de Sevilla 2015); Gargola, *The Shape of the Roman Order* (n 66) 55–81.

provinces. Also characteristic is Sigonio's opening treatment of the word *prouincia* itself, acknowledging the range of its usage, but insisting that its primary sense was the one required for his purposes (in fact the last to evolve):

> The term province was used in three ways by the Roman people, which was totally responsible for this matter: the first, for a region which, after having been conquered by arms or brought into their power by whatever means, they had placed under their magistrate for governing; the second, for any region in which a Roman commander waged war; the third, for the responsibility for carrying out any public task. However, in the following treatment of provinces, we shall use the term in the first and proper sense.[127]

One contention of Sigonio's which for long persisted in the handbooks is his claim that the standard procedure for the establishment of the province was for the senate to despatch a commission of ten (or sometimes five) ambassadors (*legati*), under whose guidance the victorious commander brought it *in formam prouinciae*.[128] In fact, although such commissions were often sent out to determine the details of peace settlements, they were (as the individual cases noted in Sigonio's subsequent chapters show) only rarely associated with the establishment of permanent provinces.

Unlike the Latins and the other Italian allies, provincials paid taxes to Rome unless favoured by exemptions, but Sigonio's mistaken belief that the Italians too were taxed prevented him from discerning this important difference in their treatment. For him the inferiority of the provincials' status consisted simply in the loss of liberty: the Italians retained their autonomy, but the provinces 'were deprived of their laws and jurisdiction by their own magistrates'. He acknowledged that exceptions were made for favoured individuals and communities, and, as we have seen, deployed epigraphic evidence in illustration.[129] However, he takes little account of the fact that the remaining provincial communities who lacked such privileged status retained their civic institutions

[127] Sigonio, *De antiquo iure prouinciarum* (n 14) 1.1, 286: 'Prouinciae nomen tribus modis populus Romanus totius huius rationis auctor accepit, uno pro regione, quam aut armis deuictam aut quocunque modo in potestatem adductam, ipse magistratui suo administrandam subiecit; altero, pro quacunque regione in qua bellum Romanus imperator administrarit; tertio, pro quacunque publici muneris procuratione. Nos autem de prouinciis locuturi prouinciam prima et quidem propria significatione sumemus.'

[128] ibid 1.1, 2.5, 288, 358. For such claims in later handbooks see eg Marquardt, *Staatsverwaltung* (n 49) 500; George H Stevenson, *Roman Provincial Administration till the Age of the Antonines* (Blackwell 1949) 68. On commissions of ten *legati* see now Liv M Yarrow, '*Decem legati*: A Flexible Institution, Rigidly Perceived' in Christopher J Smith and Liv M Yarrow (eds), *Imperialism, Cultural Politics, and Polybius* (Oxford University Press 2012) 168–83.

[129] Sigonio, *De antiquo iure prouinciarum* (n 14) 288–89, 317–18.

and, although subject to the Roman governor's authority, in practice enjoyed a good deal of freedom to manage their own affairs.

Sigonio's analysis of provincial government under the Republic in his second book shows to the full his good sense, lucid organization, and superb command of the literary sources. The book treats successively the shifting procedures for appointing governors (2.1), their staff and their quaestors (2.2–2.3), the governors' and quaestors' departure for their provinces (2.4), their functions, civil and military (2.5–2.8), and their return to Rome and its sequels (2.9–2.12). Sigonio throughout maintains the positions he had developed in opposition to Grouchy on the *lex curiata* and the meaning of *imperium*, so making appropriate the fuller restatement given in the third book added in 1574.

Sigonio on Republican Colonization and Agrarian Legislation

We may now at last turn back to take a closer look at Sigonio's treatment of Roman colonization and agrarian legislation under the Republic. As the above analysis has shown, he deals with colonization at three points in the treatises, but the main account comes in the four chapters on colonies in the second book of the *De antiquo iure Italiae* (2.2–2.5), which open its treatment of the various individual categories of community in pre-Social War Italy and take up over half of the book. Although these chapters purport to be restricted to pre-Social War colonies in Italy, some of the discussion ranges more widely, particularly in the long opening chapter entitled simply *De coloniis*.[130] Two further chapters on colonies follow later in the work, but these are mainly concerned with completing the listing of colonies begun at *De antiquo iure Italiae* (2.5), and cover respectively the colonies founded in Italy between the Social War and Augustus' establishment of sole rule (*De antiquo iure Italiae* (3.4)), and those founded in the provinces up to that time (*De antiquo iure prouinciarum* (1.2)).

Sigonio proudly claims that his discussion of colonies has elucidated a previously little understood subject, and his treatment is indeed substantially more thorough than any provided by his predecessors.[131] His account, as we have seen, deploys some epigraphic material, and among the literary sources there is extensive use not just use of writers like Cicero and the historians, but also

[130] Sigonio, *De antiquo iure Italiae* (n 30) 2.2, 215–28.
[131] ibid 216, 228.

of the *agrimensores*, including the *Liber Coloniarum*, which did not appear in print until 1563 and was supplied to Sigonio by Panvinio.[132]

At the start of his opening chapter *De coloniis*, Sigonio defines colonies as 'towns in which the Roman people settled its citizens as inhabitants', and then identifies six reasons why they kept founding colonies: 'first, to control the existing inhabitants; second, to check enemy incursions; third, to increase the stock; fourth, to drain off the urban *plebs*; fifth, to calm sedition; sixth, to provide veteran soldiers with rewards'.[133] He insists that all these reasons are securely attested in the ancient sources, and goes on to cite testimonies. In support of his first two reasons he appeals to Siculus Flaccus, whose wording he has in fact taken over, to various Livian passages, and to Cicero's references to colonies as 'bulwarks of empire'.[134] For his third reason he has again quoted a source's words: Livy, reporting the refusal in 209 BCE by twelve colonies to supply more troops for the war against Hannibal, makes the consuls remind them that they are 'Romans, sprung from there, and sent from there to colonies . . . to increase the stock'.[135] Sigonio regards his final reason as applying only in the late Republic and refers the reader forward to his later treatment. His fourth and fifth reasons are more problematic, since both formulations reflect optimate perspectives, but Sigonio is able to cite supporting evidence across a wide time span: fifth-century BCE instances of colonies reported as founded to distract the plebeians; Livy's statement that the year 300 BCE was not only peaceful externally, but 'at Rome, the unloading of a crowd into colonies made the *plebs* quiet';[136] and references to the need to 'drain off' the urban plebs or the 'dregs of the city' reported at the time of the agrarian laws proposed in 63 and 60 BCE.[137] Thus by careful attention to the diverse testimony of the sources Sigonio here achieved a judicious and well-balanced range of explanation of Republican colonization, taking account both of strategic aims and of socio-economic factors. His analysis was long to remain very influential, and

132 Sigonio's request to Panvinio, May 1560: Sigonio, *Opera omnia* (n 10) vol 6, 1013–14. See also Chapter 2 in this volume by Stenhouse.

133 Sigonio, *De antiquo iure Italiae* (n 30) 2.2, 215–16: 'causas potissimum sex reddi posse reperio, . . . unam ad priores populos coercendos, alteram ad hostium incursiones reprimendas, tertiam stirpis augendae causa, quartam plebis urbanae exhauriendae, quintam seditionis sedandae, sextam ut praemiis milites ueteranos adficerent'.

134 Siculus Flaccus 102 Campbell (*colonos uel ad ipsos priores municipiorum populos coercendos uel ad hostium incursus repellendos*); Cicero, *De lege agraria* 2.73 (*propugnacula imperii*), *Pro Fonteio* 13 (Narbo as *specula populi Romani ac propugnaculum*).

135 Livy 27.9.10–11: 'Romanos, inde oriundos, inde in colonias . . . stirpis augendae causa missos.'

136 Livy 10.6.2: 'Romae quoque plebem quietam exonerata in colonias multitudo praestabat.'

137 Cicero, *De lege agraria* 2.70; *Epistulae ad Atticum* 1.19.4.

was recycled in numerous later accounts down to the nineteenth century.[138] Even today it compares well with the too one-sided explanations favoured by some scholars, such as the overly exclusive emphasis on strategic objectives promoted by Edward Togo Salmon in *Roman Colonization under the Republic* (1969).[139]

Sigonio next informs us that 'for whatever reasons colonies were founded, there was always a need either for a decree of the senate or a law proposed to the popular assembly, each of which I perceive to be comprised under a single name of law, called the agrarian law' (*lex agraria*).[140] In identifying these measures as the 'agrarian law', Sigonio was making a radical departure. Claiming that, in view of its difficulty, this topic required extended treatment, he announces that he will treat what he describes as the 'many headings (*capita*) of the agrarian law', specified as follows: 'it defined which land was to be divided, and prescribed to which and how many persons, by whom, in what way and with what boundaries it was to be divided'.[141] His discussion of these 'headings of the agrarian law' takes up most of the rest of the chapter, with the final pages then devoted to the procedures for founding colonies after their authorization.

Sigonio begins his discussion of the first 'heading of the agrarian law', the definition of the land to be divided, by observing that the settlements could be made either to individuals (viritane allotments) or by founding new communities (*coloniae*), and that the land used for the settlements was 'either captured from enemies and not yet made public, or public land of the Roman people and occupied by them, or public but covertly usurped by powerful private

[138] For a late instance see George Long, 'Colonia' in W Smith (ed) *A Dictionary of Greek and Roman Antiquities* (Taylor and Walton 1842) 256–61. See also Chapter 1 in this volume by Jeremia Pelgrom and Arthur Weststeijn, and Chapter 4 by Mark Somos.

[139] For recent discussions of the ancient and modern historiography of Roman colonization, stressing the need for multi-factorial explanation, see Guy Bradley, 'Colonization and Identity in Republican Italy' in Guy Bradley and John-Paul Wilson (eds), *Greek and Roman Colonization: Origins, Ideologies and Interactions* (The Classical Press of Wales 2006) 161–87; John R Patterson, 'Colonization and Historiography: the Roman Republic' in ibid 189–218; Pelgrom and Stek, 'Roman Colonization under the Republic' (n 2), with assessment of Sigonio's contribution at 16–17. See also Chapter 6 in this volume by Luigi Capogrossi Colognesi.

[140] Sigonio, *De antiquo iure Italiae* (n 30) 2.2, 216: 'quacumque autem de causa deducerentur, omnino aut senatusconsulto opus fuit aut rogatione aliqua populari, quorum utrumque uno legis nomine uideo comprehensum, quae lex agraria appellata est'. The claim that either a senatorial decree or a law was required for founding a colony conforms to the evidence and may be correct: most scholars have followed Mommsen, *Staatsrecht* (n 87) vol 2, 624–39, in supposing that, although Livy often mentions only a senate decree, a law was always necessary as well. Mommsen's view is followed by eg Daniel J Gargola, *Lands, Laws and Gods: Magistrates and Ceremony in the Regulation of Public Lands in Republican Rome* (University of North Carolina Press 1995) 52–58; Amanda J Coles, 'Founding Colonies and Fostering Careers in the Middle Republic' (2017) 112 Classical Journal 283–87. Umberto Laffi, 'Leggi agrarie e coloniarie' in Jean-Louis Ferrary (ed), *Leges publicae. La legge nell'esperienza giuridica romana* (Pavia University Press 2012) 429–61 has made a strong case to the contrary (hereafter Laffi, 'Leggi agrarie').

[141] Sigonio, *De antiquo iure Italiae* (n 30) 216: 'et agrum definiuit, qui esset diuidendus, et quibus, ac quam multis hominibus, et per quos, et quo modo, et quibus limitibus esset diuidendus, praescripsit'.

individuals, or bought with public money for division'.[142] Sigonio then asserts that proposals for agrarian laws which dealt with the other categories of land were carried without contention (an oddly erroneous statement for the late Republic), but those which sought to settle the plebs on public lands occupied by rich individuals always led to the greatest turbulence. With this exordium, he launches into a survey of agrarian laws and other land settlement measures to the end of the Republic.[143]

Thus by redefining measures authorizing colonies as 'the agrarian law' and propounding a wide interpretation of that law, Sigonio has broadened his treatment to cover all land settlement under the Republic, embracing viritane allotments as well as colony foundations, and so enabled himself to include extended coverage of agrarian legislation, one of the most important topics in Republican history. The resulting discussion was important and enjoyed long-lasting influence, but the digressive manoeuvre which led up to it remains of questionable legitimacy. The declared subject of the second book of the *De antiquo iure Italiae* was the *iura* of the various types of communities (*ciuitates*) in pre-Social War Italy, and so viritane allotment could have no direct relevance to that theme. Moreover, Sigonio's very broad conception of the 'agrarian law' was mistaken: until the late Republic, colonies and viritane allotments were always founded by separate measures, and, since uncontentious viritane programmes were normally approved just by decree of the senate,[144] the term *lex agraria* applied only to the contentious viritane settlement programmes proposed as laws to the assembly.

Early modern references to Roman 'agrarian law' are often vague, and Sigonio's own use of the term shows some confusion.[145] Nonetheless, it is hard to avoid the suspicion that he permitted himself some sleight of hand at this point in order to have his say about a topic which had received much recent discussion, on which he thought he could improve. Much the same had happened earlier on the law courts: in his first edition he had devoted a bloated chapter of the *De iure populi Romani* (2.18) to that topic, but there he was eventually able to transfer much of the material to the new treatise *De iudiciis.* In both cases, Sigonio was covering ground which had been dealt with in the

[142] ibid, 217: 'aut de hostibus captum neque dum in publicum redactum, aut publicum populi Romani et a populo Romano possessum, aut publicum quidem, sed furtim a priuatis potentibus usurpatum, aut denique publico aere diuidendi gratia emptum'.

[143] ibid, 217–23.

[144] Laffi, 'Leggi agrarie' (n 140) 433–44.

[145] On early-modern discussions of Roman agrarian law by Machiavelli, Harrington, and others see Alfred Heuss, *Barthold Georg Niebuhrs wissenschaftliche Anfänge* (Vandenbroeck & Ruprecht 1981) 222–46; Eric Nelson, *The Greek Tradition in Republican Thought* (Cambridge University Press 2004) 49–126.

recent collections of Roman laws by Ulrich Zasius (1555), Manuzio (1557), and François Hotman (1558).[146] Sigonio will have known all these works, and on the agrarian laws made close use especially of Hotman, reproducing some of his wording.[147] Nonetheless, his treatment of these laws is more thorough and better documented than those of his predecessors.

Sigonio's survey of agrarian laws (carried or proposed) gives a careful listing from the earliest, said to have been promulgated by Spurius Cassius in 486 BCE, down to Caesar's laws in his consulship in 59 BCE. Sigonio had already included a shorter treatment of the legislation in his discussion of citizens' fiscal obligations in his first treatise, using the levy allegedly payable for the occupation of public land as a peg for a topic which here too was of only marginal relevance, and he had also briefly alluded to the subject in his discussion of the rural plebs.[148]

Like his predecessors, Sigonio does his best to reconcile the evidence of Livy and other sources with the account of developments in respect of the public lands up to and following the legislation of Tiberius Gracchus given by Appian.[149] By contrast with the optimate bias shown elsewhere in his work, Sigonio adopts as his own Appian's hostility to the rich occupiers said to have monopolized the public lands. Like many others, Sigonio takes the Licinian law of 367 BCE, which in fact merely limited landholding, as also providing for land allotments, and he credits it with at last implementing Cassius' proposal. Although his wording is not always clear, he can be seen to have envisaged the Licinian limit as applying just to public land, a view which Niebuhr later established as canonical, but has recently been shown to be mistaken for the Licinian limit itself, although correct for Gracchus' revival.[150] On Tiberius Gracchus' agrarian law Sigonio's stance is ambivalent, at once sympathizing with action

[146] Manuzio's treatise, *Antiquitatum romanarum liber de legibus* (Bernard Turrisan 1557), is arranged thematically and treats the *leges agrariae* at xxvii^{v} to xxviii^{r}. Zasius' work, *Catalogus legum antiquarum* (Guillaume Cavellat 1555) is arranged alphabetically by the authors of the laws, but treats the *leges agrariae* together at 10v–22v. Hotman's work, *De legibus populi romani liber* (Episcopius 1557) is strictly alphabetical, as is Agustín's *De legibus et senatus consultis liber*, to which Sigonio appears not to have had access (it was originally drafted in 1544–45 and revised in 1553–55, but not published until 1583). On all these works see Ferrary, *Recherches* (n 38) 199–228 and Chapter 2 in this volume by Stenhouse.

[147] McCuaig, *Carlo Sigonio* (n 1) 160–61.

[148] Sigonio, *De antiquo iure ciuium* (n 13) 1.16, 2.6, 79–80, 110. On Sigonio's treatment of this legislation see McCuaig, *Carlo Sigonio* (n 1) 153–64.

[149] Appian, *Civil Wars* 1.7–11, 27.

[150] John W Rich, 'Lex Licinia, Lex Sempronia: B.G. Niebuhr and the Limitation of Landholding in the Roman Republic' in Luuk de Ligt and Simon Northwood (eds), *People, Land and Politics. Demographic Developments and the Transformation of Roman Italy, 300 BC–AD 14* (Brill 2008) 519–72; Saskia T Roselaar, *Public Land in the Roman Republic* (Oxford University Press 2010) 95–112; Luigi Capogrossi Colognesi, *Padroni e contadini nell'Italia repubblicana* ('L'Erma' di Bretschneider 2012) 77–83; and see Chapter 5 in this volume by Mattia Balbo.

against the rich occupiers and deploring the disruption of public order, and so juxtaposing a summary of Appian's account with approving quotation of Cicero's statement of the optimates' case against the law.[151]

For his discussion of the three post-Gracchan laws reported by Appian, Sigonio was, as we saw above, able to make use of the inscribed agrarian law of 111 BCE, already in 1560 identifying it as Appian's third law and in his 1574 edition reproducing the fragments which he had been able to inspect.[152] On Caesar's first law, under which land for distribution was acquired by purchase rather than extruding occupiers, Sigonio is strikingly positive, adopting as his own Dio's approval of the measure as transferring the urban mob to agricultural toil, repeopling Italy, and providing veterans and others with livelihoods at no cost to the rich.[153]

After his survey of agrarian laws, Sigonio goes on to deal with his other 'headings of the agrarian law', discussing successively eligibility for settlement and numbers of settlers, the commissions responsible for founding the settlements, the size of allotments, and (drawing on the *agrimensores*) boundary regulations. All these topics are considered in relation to viritane allotments as well as colonies, at some cost in clarity: thus Sigonio fails to make it clear that colony commissions normally had three members, while those making viritane allotments were larger, and he does not discuss the variations in allotment size. Only with the ensuing treatment of foundation procedures does Sigonio resume his original restriction of focus just to colonies.

Sigonio follows this lengthy opening chapter with much briefer discussions of the colonies' *ius* and (drawing on some epigraphic evidence) their civic institutions,[154] and then completes his treatment of pre-Social War colonies in Italy by listing the individual colonies in order of foundation.[155] For this list and for his later list of post-Social War colonies in Italy, Sigonio would have been able to draw on the first such listing, compiled shortly earlier by Panvinio.[156]

[151] Cicero, *Pro Sestio* 103.

[152] On Sigonio's attempt to identify the proposers of these laws see McCuaig, *Carlo Sigonio* (n 1) 163–64, and in general on Appian's account see Daniel J Gargola, 'Appian and the Aftermath of the Gracchan Reform' (1997) 118 AJP 555–81.

[153] Sigonio, *De antiquo iure Italiae* (n 30) 222. Sigonio here closely renders Dio 38.1.3, but in the 1574 edition his words are not italicized, as for other quotations, and so stand as his own view. Sigonio wrongly dates to 60 BCE the law providing for Pompey's and Metellus' veterans attested by Dio 38.5.1, which should in fact be identified with the *Lex Plotia* mentioned at Cicero, *Epistulae ad Atticum* 1.18.6 (overlooked by Sigonio) and dated to 70 BCE, following Pompey's return from Spain.

[154] Sigonio, *De antiquo iure Italiae* (n 30) 2.3–2.4, 228–33.

[155] ibid, 2.5, 233–41.

[156] Panvinio, *Reipublicae Romanae* (n 21) 702–53. Sigonio appears to have drawn on Panvinio's list (705) for the Signia inscription he cites at *De antiquo iure Italiae* (n 30) 232. The later list of post-Social War colonies is at ibid, 3.4, 272–79.

However, Sigonio's list is his own independent work, and on the difficult topic of the first-century colonies is much superior to Panvinio's treatment.[157]

Sigonio begins his discussion of colonies' *ius* by correctly observing that, contrary to the opinion of certain unnamed writers, Livy's evidence shows that the distinction between the two categories of colonies, Roman citizen and Latin, was based not on their location or their settlers' origin, but on their *ius*, and he then goes on to expound the *ius* enjoyed by each group. Latin colonies, Sigonio maintains, held the *ius Latii* as he had previously defined it, namely a limited right to vote at Rome and the right to the Roman citizenship itself for their magistrates, but none of the private rights of Roman citizens. He also reiterates his view that they were required not only to supply troops but also to pay tax to Rome, a doctrine which, as we saw above, was mistaken, but was to play a prominent part in later debates on the obligations of colonies, particularly at the time of the American Revolution.[158]

As for the Roman citizen colonies, Sigonio insists that, while they enjoyed the private rights of Roman citizens, which he believed to have been designated by the term *ius Quiritium*, they did not have the public rights, namely voting in the assembly and eligibility for office.[159] Their distance from Rome may well have prevented the colonists from making much use of these rights, but Sigonio provides no adequate arguments for supposing that they formally lacked the rights. Nonetheless, such was his authority that this doctrine continued to be generally held until it was refuted in a youthful work by the great Danish scholar Johan Nicolai Madvig (1804–86), which was of fundamental importance in setting the future direction of studies of Republican colonization.[160]

Sigonio's discussion of colonies is bedevilled by uncertainty about which of the foundations down to the Second Punic War were Roman citizen colonies, and which were Latin. This question was finally resolved in the same study by Madvig, which proved that it was only in the early second century that larger citizen colonies came to be founded: until then all the larger colonial

[157] Panvinio's list is numbered and contrives to make Placentia the fifty-third colony, as claimed by Asconius 3C. On Asconius' puzzling claim, with which Sigonio attempted to grapple, see now Simon J Northwood, 'Asconius' Fifty-Three Colonies: A Regal Solution' (2008) 58 Classical Quarterly 353–62 (whose solution, like Panvinio's, involves counting the regal colonies).

[158] See Chapter 4 in this volume by Somos.

[159] It should be noted that the reading *ut Quiritium aliae* in modern texts of Asconius (3C), referring to citizen colonies, is merely an emendation of the manuscript reading *itaque*, first proposed in Johann G Baiter's 1833 edition, and in fact very dubious.

[160] Johan N Madvig, 'De iure et condicione coloniarum populi Romani quaestio historica' in *Opuscula Academica* (Gyldendal 1834) 228–55 (hereafter Madvig, 'De iure'). As he makes clear at the outset, Madvig's study was written in direct response to Niebuhr's discussion of colonies and Latin Right in *Römische Geschichte* (n 111) vol 2, 48–93, but he acknowledges Sigonio's pre-eminence in this field before Niebuhr.

foundations had Latin status, and the citizen colonies were all smaller coastal settlements.[161]

Earlier writers including Sigonio can be forgiven for their confusion on colony classification before the second century BCE in view of the extreme lack of clarity on the matter in Livy and Velleius, our two main sources for colony foundation in the early and middle Republic. Velleius in his list of Roman colony foundations from the Gallic sack to the end of the second century BCE never distinguishes between citizen and Latin colonies.[162] Livy often distinguishes carefully between citizen and Latin colonies in his reports on the early second-century foundations (calling the former *coloniae ciuium Romanorum*). Before that, he only twice speaks of colonies as Latin, and elsewhere speaks of colonies which were in fact Latin as 'Roman colonies' or 'colonies of the Roman people'.[163] Livy's focus here is not on the colonists' formal status but on their origin and allegiance, envisaging all the early colonies as founded by Rome and their settlers as Romans.[164]

These obscurities help to account for inadequacies in Sigonio's treatment of Latin colonies and their *ius*. In his colony list, he explicitly characterizes colonies as Latin only for the early second-century foundations, and does not attempt to resolve the apparent conflict of evidence on the earlier colonies.[165] Failing to recognize that Ariminum was a Latin colony, Sigonio misinterprets Cicero's reference to rights of *nexa* and *hereditates* with Roman citizens enjoyed by twelve colonies, of which Ariminum was one, as relating to citizen colonies and supporting his view that they held only the private rights of Roman citizenship, whereas in fact it shows that (contrary to his doctrine) at least

[161] Madvig, 'De iure' (n 160) 264–69, 285–87. Madvig showed that Livy's language at 27.9.2 and 29.15.2 must entail that all the thirty listed colonies (both the twelve who refused to supply troops in 209 and the eighteen who complied) were Latin. For Livy's list of these colonies see 27.9.7, 10.7–10.8; 29.15.5. Confirmation for Spoletium and Placentia is supplied by Cicero, *Pro Balbo* 48, and Asconius 3C.

[162] Velleius 1.14–1.15.

[163] *Coloniae Latinae*: Livy 2.16.8; 29.15.2. *Coloniae Romanae*: Livy 7.42.8, 8.3.9, 10.36.16, 31.10.7. *Coloniae populi Romani*: Livy 27.19.7.

[164] cf Livy 27.9.10, where he makes the consuls of 209 remind the defaulting Latin colonies that they were 'Romans, sprung from there' (*Romanos, inde oriundos*). Only at 34.42.5 does Livy use *colonia Romana* as a designation for a colony with citizen status, which he elsewhere terms *colonia ciuium Romanorum*. Michael H Crawford, 'La storia della colonizzazione romana secondo i Romani' in Alfredina Storchi Marino (ed), *L'incidenza dell'antico. Studi in memoria di Ettore Lepore* 1 (Luciano 1995) 187–92, and Edward Bispham, 'Coloniam deducere: How Roman was Roman Colonization During the Middle Republic?' in Guy J Bradley and John-Paul Wilson (eds), *Greek and Roman Colonization. Origins, Ideologies and Interactions* (Classical Press of Wales 2006) 81–85, take Livy's and Velleius' usage as showing that early colony categories were less normative and more labile than has traditionally been supposed, but it is better interpreted as reflecting the Romanocentric perspective of their own age.

[165] Sigonio, *De antiquo iure Italiae* (n 30) 238, noting the different terminology used by Livy at 27.9.7 and 29.15.2. Unlike Sigonio, Panvinio in his listing classes each of the twelve colonies refusing troops in 209 as Latin on the basis of Livy 29.15.2 (and other evidence where available).

some Latin citizens enjoyed some of those rights.[166] Sigonio's confusion over the Latin colonies may also shed light on his handling of *ius Latii* in the first book of the *De antiquo iure Italiae*, where, as we saw above, he erroneously interpreted it as held primarily by the residents of the extended Latium from the Tiber to the Liris, and took little note of the Latin colonies who were in fact its principal holders before the Social War. Later, in his discussion of colonies' *iura*, he recognizes that the defining characteristic of Latin colonies was not their region of residence but their enjoyment of the Latin Right, but fails to explore the contradiction between this finding and his earlier interpretation of that *ius* in terms of residence in the extended Latium.

Conclusion

Sigonio's focus on *ius* and its gradations enabled him to endow the three treatises which he eventually brought together as the *De antiquo iure populi Romani* with a clearly articulated structure giving scope for a comprehensive analysis of the institutions of the Roman Republic and its empire. In the first treatise the Aristotelian definition of citizenship provided the model for a treatment in which the first book defined the Roman citizen and analysed his *ius*, that is, his rights and obligations, and the second book dealt with the related topic of the divisions in the Roman citizen body which affected *iura*. In the second and third treatises Sigonio adapted this procedure for his three further, progressively inferior categories of *ius* and their holders. In each of these treatises, the first book defined the grouping or groupings in question, surveyed the steps by which its members came under Roman rule, and analysed its *ius*, while the second (and, where required, third) book discussed related topics bearing on *iura*.

This lucidity of structure, allied with his control of (principally, but not exclusively literary) evidence and thoroughness of treatment, gave Sigonio's treatises a quality unmatched by the productions of his peers and ensured that on many topics they were not surpassed until the nineteenth century. The first and third treatises are particularly successful. The *De antiquo iure populi Romani* includes admirable treatment of numerous topics relating to the Roman citizen body, ranging from the citizens' claims to *libertas* to the composition of the urban plebs, and notable insights such as the highlighting of the plebeians'

[166] Sigonio, *De antiquo iure Italiae* (n 30) 229; Cicero, *Pro Caecina* 102. On the vexed question of Cicero's 'right of Ariminum' see Coşkun, *Bürgerrechtsentzug oder Fremdenausweisung?* (n 110) 63–70; and Roselaar, 'The Concept of *commercium*' (n 110) 406 (with earlier bibliography).

achievement of participation in office and the resulting emergence of the patricio-plebeian nobility and its association with *imagines*. The *De antiquo iure prouinciarum* provides what was long to remain the best treatment of provincial administration under the Republic.

The treatises are far from flawless. The huge accumulation of evidence and improvement of texts since Sigonio's day has exposed many errors for which he can hardly be blamed. Other failings arise from tendencies which he shared with his contemporaries, for example his (by our standards) often uncritical acceptance of the ancient sources' claims and perspectives. However, the urge to systematize which is one of Sigonio's great strengths can also sometimes be a weakness, especially in relation to the classification of *iura*, and this particularly affects the *De antiquo iure Italiae*. Examples of this aspect of the treatise include the misunderstanding of the ancient usage of *ius Italicum*, the misconception of *ius Latii* as primarily regional in application, and the doctrines that all the Latins lacked the private rights of Roman citizens and the inhabitants of citizen colonies lacked their public rights.

Some of these weaknesses affected Sigonio's treatment of colonies. The obscurity of the sources impaired his understanding of Latin colonies, and it was only by a rather slippery manoeuvre that he was able to extend the treatment to viritane allotment and agrarian laws. However, this section also displays his characteristic virtues, and it is particularly notable for its balanced treatment of agrarian legislation and recognition of the importance of socio-economic as well as strategic factors in Republican settlement programmes.

The huge advances made by Mommsen and his contemporaries meant that, after retaining their predominance for so long, Sigonio's treatises were at last comprehensively superseded, and as a result they have long suffered almost complete neglect. Nonetheless, the treatises' long pre-eminence meant that they had wide impact outside specialist studies, and the use made of them in early modern discussions about politics and empire richly deserves investigation, as the next chapter by Mark Somos shows. For modern students of Roman institutions Mommsen has long served as the starting point when inquiring into the unfolding of research controversies, but scholars have rightly now begun to recognize that it is often fruitful to look back beyond Mommsen's generation to earlier stages of debate, and in such investigations Sigonio should loom large. On occasion, as with the doctrine that all Rome's Italian allies had treaties, they may even show that we have all remained unwittingly in Sigonio's thrall.

4

Sigonio in Anglo-American Projects to Reform the Imperial Constitution, 1751–1777

Mark Somos[*]

Sigonio's Reception and Influence

The waning of Carlo Sigonio's name recognition deserves a separate study. Intellectual historians are used to the rediscovery of forgotten figures and the contested reassessments of thinkers we still remember. Is Niccolò Machiavelli none too relevant due to his purported blindness to economics? Was James Harrington typical of English republicanism? When did people outside England start to read Thomas Hobbes's *Leviathan*, not only *De cive*? Is there a profound change of heart and mind between Adam Smith's *Theory of Moral Sentiments* and *The Wealth of Nations*? Alongside such revolutions in reception history, we also discover texts, from a large portion of Cicero's *De re publica* in 1822 (*pace* Sigonio, the *Consolatio* remains lost) to Hugo Grotius' *Meletius* in 1984, with a frequency that invites regular disciplinary self-reflection.

Yet there are reasons why Sigonio poses unusual problems in this regard, making his impact particularly hard to measure. First, writers often fail to acknowledge him as their source. This was not an unusual practice in early modern texts, especially when a source was understood to be widely known, and was consequently treated as a handbook of commonly assumed authority.[1] This is the case not only with Sigonio's own writings but also with his editions.

[*] For opportunities to work on Sigonio I am grateful to the Jack Miller Center for fellowships at the Huntington Library and the Center for the Study of Representative Institutions at Yale University, the Edmond J Safra Center for Ethics, the John Carter Brown Library, the British School at Rome, and the Alexander von Humboldt Foundation for a fellowship at the Max Planck Institute for Comparative Public Law and International Law in Heidelberg. With many thanks to Daniel Margócsy for his comments.

[1] Christopher Smith notes this effect as late as Niebuhr and Mommsen in the nineteenth century: Christopher J Smith, *The Roman Clan: The* Gens *from Ancient Ideology to Modern Anthropology* (Cambridge University Press 2006) 70.

Mark Somos, *Sigonio in Anglo-American Projects to Reform the Imperial Constitution, 1751–1777* In: *The Renaissance of Roman Colonization.* Edited by: Jeremia Pelgrom and Arthur Weststeijn, Oxford University Press (2020). © the Several Contributors. DOI: 10.1093/oso/9780198850960.003.0004

For instance, Sten Bodvar Liljegren argues that when James Harrington referred to Livy in his 1656 *The Commonwealth of Oceana*, instead of Livy he drew on Sigonio's *De antiquo iure ciuium Romanorum* to understand the Roman Republic's constitution.[2] Another case is James Abercromby's 1766–75 *De jure et gubernatione coloniarum*, a key text discussed in this chapter. His direct references to Sigonio are discussed below; but Abercromby also drew his interpretation of Cicero's agrarian orations from Sigonio. In addition to affording him fewer explicit acknowledgments than more contentious authors would receive, the reception of Sigonio as both an editor and a secondary source on ancient Rome and feudal Italy further conceals the originality and impact of his arguments.

A second reason is that Sigonio was often copied and abstracted in intermediary sources, including popular histories. Thomas Godwyn's *Romanae historiae anthologia*, a long-influential school textbook first published in 1614, drew heavily on Sigonio. A case of its direct impact in the period examined here is the copy owned by Ezra Stiles (1727–95), President of Yale College. Stiles inherited it from his father in 1760 and covered it with annotations, especially Godwyn's treatment of the relationship between colonies and the mother country, based almost entirely on the works of Sigonio.[3] This copy represents an extraordinary continuity of interest in modern applications of ancient colonialism. Stiles' great-grandfather, who emigrated to New England, was born around 1633 in Milbrook, fifty miles from Abingdon School, where Godwyn taught and wrote the *Anthologia*. Through his grandfather, Abiel Holmes, a historian of the American colonies who married Stiles' daughter, the copy passed to Oliver Wendell Holmes, Jr (1841–1935), a prodigious Supreme Court justice and one of the most cited American legal historians. In short, this copy of Sigonian passages was in colonial use for over two centuries. The compression of authoritative sources required in such school textbooks could, in itself, further obscure Sigonio's importance. We catch a glimpse of this in Alexander Adam's 1791 *Roman Antiquities*. In this very popular textbook that went through numerous editions, Adam handsomely acknowledges his debt to Sigonio as a chief source on 'assemblies of the people, the rights of the citizens,

[2] Sten Bodvar Liljegren (ed), *James Harrington's Oceana* (Winter 1924) 292. One may add that this includes the voting assemblies, all-important to Harrington, and sometimes confused by Livy. See William McCuaig, *Carlo Sigonio: The Changing World of the Late Renaissance* (Princeton University Press 1989) 190 (hereafter McCuaig, *Carlo Sigonio*).

[3] Thomas Godwyn, *Romanae historiae anthologia* (John Lichfield 1631), Houghton Library, STC 11962.

the laws and judicial proceedings' in the Preface; but hardly ever references him in the text.

Third, some of Sigonio's works, including his discussions of colonialism, were updated and reissued by writers who reproduced substantial passages from Sigonio. The reception of the 1585 *Antiquitatum romanarum corpus absolutissimum* by Johannes Rosinus (*c* 1550–1626), for instance, and of its emended editions by Thomas Dempster, Paolo Manuzio, Andreas Schottus and others, should often be considered as a proxy for Sigonio's influence.[4] The same holds for Basil Kennett's (1674–1715) *Romae antiquae notitia*, first published in 1696 and reissued in numerous revised editions until 1822, as well as for the works of Archbishop John Potter (*c* 1674–1747). Sir William Jones (1746–94), in his edition of the speeches of Isaeus, recommends that readers consult

> the elegant treatise of CAROLUS SIGONIUS, *On the Athenian Republick*: that most judicious antiquary has, indeed, so completely exhausted the subject, that POTTER has done little more than translate his work with some additional authorities and a multitude of quotations, which are so far from improving his book, that they render it intolerably dry and tedious.[5]

Sometimes these effects combine to disguise or almost hide Sigonio's influence. This is the case with aggregated commentaries on Livy. One of the great editions, the 1644–45 Leiden Elzevier version (reissued in 1653–54) by Jan Frederik Gronovius (1611–71), professor of rhetoric and history first at Deventer, then at Leiden, relied extensively on Sigonio's edition and annotations.[6] While trying respectfully to supersede him, Gronovius drew on Sigonio to such a degree that Gronovius' son, Jacob (1645–1716), re-issued his father's comments together with Sigonio's, whose name he then added to his father's as

[4] For instance, Abercromby's modern editors think that sometimes Abercromby was using Rosinus instead of Sigonio, but credited Sigonio, because he knew that Rosinus lifted passages from Sigonio *verbatim*: James Abercromby, *Magna Charta for America: James Abercromby's "An examination of the acts of Parliament relative to the trade and the government of our American colonies" (1752) and "De jure et gubernatione coloniarum, or An inquiry into the nature, and the rights of colonies, ancient, and modern" (1774)* (Jack Philip Greene, Charles F Mullett, and Edward C Papenfuse eds, American Philosophical Society 1986) 289 n 76 (hereafter Abercromby, *Magna Charta*). Another conduit for Sigonio, with an impact on American colonial writings, was a set of antipapal Anglican arguments published under Elizabeth I. See inter alia. John Rainolds, *The summe of the conference betwene Iohn Rainoldes and Iohn Hart* (John Wolfe 1584) and John Bridges, *A defence of the gouernment established in the Church of Englande for ecclesiasticall matters* (John Windet 1587).

[5] William Jones (ed), *The Speeches of Isæus in Causes Concerning the Law of Succession to Property at Athens* (J Nichols 1779) Prefatory discourse, 27.

[6] *Titi Livii Historiarum libri, ex recensione I.F. Grouovii* (Elzevier 1644–45, 2nd edn, 1654). For other background see McCuaig, *Carlo Sigonio* (n 2) 24–26.

an editor of Livy.[7] A similar story can be told about several editions of Cicero, including the three key speeches on the agrarian law.

Another difficulty in detecting and understanding Sigonio's influence concerns interpretation. It is often complicated and sometimes impossible to distinguish historical from political works in eighteenth-century comparative constitutionalism, a field where Sigonio was recognized as a towering authority. It was rare for a historian to write a book without contemporary political debates in mind. When they did, someone would, more likely than not, find a political use for it. Editions of Aeschines and Demosthenes on the Crown that cite Sigonio's 1564 *De republica Atheniensium*, including a 1732 annotated translation by Thomas Dawson, chaplain to Richard, third Viscount Molesworth, are a case in point. Sigonio's Demosthenes served periodically at least until the 1770s as a philological pretext to criticize reigning British monarchs.

Frequent lack of acknowledgment; hard-to-detect dissemination via popular histories; extensive use by proxy writers, copycats, or in cases of collective authorship; and complexities of interpretation recoverable only through close contextualization, are the four methodological problems this chapter draws attention to, and leaves unresolved. There are other authors whose reception is complicated by the same issues. In Sigonio's case, they make it unusually problematic to fully and properly chart his influence. Fortunately, we can learn a great deal even in the limited cases when his impact is easy to identify. Sigonio was an important source of Renaissance and early modern thinking on numerous issues, including social progress, prudent international relations for small states, effective colonial governance, and comparative constitutionalism. Moreover, Sigonio's reconstruction of the history of ancient Rome and feudal history and, if one may borrow a term from political science, the path dependences that these histories created, shaped subsequent discussions of themes both relevant to colonialism and wide-ranging enough to include social mobility, stratification, and the *homines novi*, or the distinction between *imperium* at the centre, and *potestas* in the provinces. [8] This chapter explores

[7] *Titi Livii Historiarum quod extat, cum perpetuis Car. Sigonii et J. F. Gronovii Notis. Jac. Gronovius probavit, suasque et aliorum Notas adjecit* (Elzevier 1679).

[8] Sigonio's impact on these issues is charted in Mark Somos, 'Irenic Secularization and the Hebrew Republic in Harrington's *Oceana*' in Gaby Mahlberg and Dirk Wiemann (eds), *European Contexts for English Republicanism* (Ashgate 2013) 81–103, esp 92–93; Mark Somos, '*Mare clausum*, *Leviathan*, and *Oceana*: Bible Criticism, Secularisation and Imperialism in Seventeenth-Century English Political and Legal Thought' in Carly Crouch and Jonathan Stökl (eds), *In the Name of God: The Bible in the Colonial Discourses of Empire* (Brill 2013) 85–133, at 116–17; Mark Somos, *Varieties of Secularisation in English and Dutch Public and International Law* (PhD dissertation Leiden University 2014) 73–91; Mark Somos, 'Harrington's Project: The Balance of Money, A Republican Constitution for Europe, and England's Patronage of the World' in Béla Kapossy, Isaac Nakhimovsky, and Richard Whatmore (eds), *Commerce and Peace in the Enlightenment* (Cambridge University Press 2017) 20–43, at 23–26, 31.

another aspect of Sigonio's still uncharted influence by zooming in on a short, twenty-six-year period when Sigonio was invoked as authority during Anglo-American controversies concerning the British imperial constitution.

Sigonio in America: Greek and Roman Models in the Anglo-American Controversy

Broadly speaking, one way to classify positions on the relationship between ancient and modern colonialism in debates surrounding American independence is to divide writers into three groups: those who thought that the British Empire followed the Greek pattern; those who thought it followed Rome; and those who thought that modern colonialism was radically different from the ancient. The Greek–British parallel usually entailed the argument that Greek colonies, driven by natural population growth, were more or less independent. The mother states had little or no influence, let alone the right to tax them. If the colonies acted in harmony with them, they did so out of uncompelled loyalty and as some kind of federation. The camp that held the Roman and British empires analogous usually argued that Roman colonies were ordered and supported by Rome, which retained the right to tax its colonies and command their military allegiance; therefore so did Britain toward the American colonies. Finally, a few writers developed their arguments in opposition to the assumption that the lessons of ancient colonialism applied to the modern management of colonies.

James Otis, Jr (1725–83) was one of the most influential early revolutionaries. In February 1761, he represented sixty-three Boston merchants in *Paxton's Case*, challenging the legality of writs of assistance.[9] His concluding speech was described by John Adams as the beginning of the American Revolution.[10] From this speech, Otis built *The Rights of the British Colonies Asserted and Proved* (1764), which many historians cite as the document that galvanized colonial public opinion. *The Rights* created a template for several arguments for imperial constitutional reform, and later for independence,

[9] Maurice Henry Smith, *The Writs of Assistance Case* (California University Press 1978); William J Cuddihy, 'Paxton's Case and the Writs of Assistance Controversy in Massachusetts, 1755-1762' ch 17' in *The Fourth Amendment: Origins and Original Meaning, 602–1791* (Oxford University Press 2009). For a brief overview of the history and kinds of writs of assistance, see Horace Gray in *Quincy's Reports*, Appendix I, section A, 395–400.

[10] On the auspicious day of 3 July 1776, Adams described the case to his wife as the starting point of the British–American controversy. In a letter, one in a series he sent to William Tudor on Otis's speech in 1816–19, Adams again declared: 'Then and there, the child Independence was born. In fifteen years, i.e. in 1776, he grew up to manhood and declared himself free.'

that were often repeated or adapted in hundreds, if not thousands, of pamphlets.[11] One such colonial criticism of the metropolitan analogy with the Roman empire, drawing on Thucydides, Grotius, and Pufendorf, was that the Greek model, in which colonies were independent and owed only a sort of reverence to the mother country, applied to the American case, and that Rome's approach to colonies was one reason for its downfall.[12]

Otis' treatise prompted a wave of response and debate. Two years after its publication, the Virginian representative Richard Bland (1710–76) published *An Inquiry into the Rights of the British Colonies*, offering substantive discussions of what distinguishes modern from ancient colonialism. Recognized as an unusually astute argument ever since it first appeared in 1766, Bland contended that the actual relationship between the mother country and the colonies cannot be found in the laws, nor in historical examples, since previous imperial systems dealt with conquered provinces—but the American Colonies are free. Without relevant English laws and ancient history, the only source for this relationship is the law of nature.[13]

In this debate on the significance of ancient models for modern colonial governance, Sigonio was seen as a respected authority. His impact is made manifest particularly in James Abercromby's *De jure et gubernatione coloniarum, or An Inquiry into the Nature, and the Rights of Colonies, Ancient, and Modern*, which explicitly intended to refute both Otis and Bland. Abercromby (1707–75) personified a whole class of well-trained and experienced Anglo-American colonial administrators who can be difficult to understand in retrospect, in light of the American Revolution. In terms of sociological and intellectual historiography, their work, thoughts, and ambitions are best seen as akin to Loyalists such as Joseph Galloway, Daniel Leonard, or William Franklin, Benjamin Franklin's son—creole elites with a deep attachment to the colonies who worked not to overthrow but to reform the British imperial constitution, but who eventually left America when the revolutionary party and impetus proved too radical for them.[14] Similarly, people like Abercromby came into their own as administrators of a transatlantic empire with a relatively common constitutional identity and set of military and economic interests. In retrospect, the differences that led to American independence can be easy to overestimate,

[11] See Mark Somos, *American States of Nature: The Origins of Independence, 1761–1775* (Oxford University Press 2019) (hereafter Somos, *American States of Nature*).

[12] James Otis, Jr, *The Rights of British Colonies Asserted and Proved* (Edes and Gill 1764) 26–27, 39–42.

[13] Richard Bland, *An Inquiry into the Rights of the British Colonies* (Alexander Purdie 1766) 14.

[14] On this group see Daniel Hulsebosch, *Constituting Empire: New York and the Transformation of Constitutionalism in the Atlantic World, 1664–1830* (University of North Carolina Press 2005).

leading us to lose sight of the relative coherence of an imperial identity that is vital for interpreting the reform proposals that invoked Sigonio. Abercromby felt equally at ease as elected assemblyman in South Carolina, later colonial agent for North Carolina and Virginia in London, and eventually Member of Parliament in 1761–68.

Abercromby was educated at Westminster School, Leiden University, and Lincoln's Inn. Appointed at twenty-three, he served as attorney general and advocate general of the court of the vice-admiralty in South Carolina from 1730 until 1744. He was one of two commissioners tasked with drawing the boundary between North and South Carolina in 1735, and he sat for two terms in the South Carolina Assembly in 1739–42 and 1744. In this capacity he drafted legislation on stimulating immigration, regulating settlement, on the province's judicial system, paper money, and other matters. In October 1748 he became North Carolina's first colonial agent in London, and continued to represent its interests until December 1758. From 1752 until 1775, Virginia also employed him as its colonial agent. Always interested in colonial defence, Abercromby acted as attorney for his cousin, General James Abercromby, and managed pay and provisions for the General and his Royal American Regiment. By all accounts, he was remarkably effective and conscientious in all his duties, which made him familiar with colonial affairs to a degree that was rare among those who wrote about imperial reform.

According to Abercromby, reforming the imperial constitution became an 'object [of serious concern] under the Government during the late 1740s'.[15] He himself wrote one of the most learned and innovative reform plans, *An Examination of the Acts of Parliament Relative to the Trade and the Government of our American Colonies*. Originally intended for publication, he decided that it should be circulated only among high-ranking members of government, partly because colonists would react to its publication with avoidable hostility, and partly because Abercromby hoped to advance his career through confidential dissemination. Between 1751 and 1756, he duly sent copies to Prime Minister Henry Pelham; John Carteret, 2nd Earl Granville, Lord President of the Council; John Campbell, 4th Earl of Loudoun, and others. There is evidence of substantial emendations between surviving copies. At the end of the *Examination*, Abercromby noted his desire to find time to broaden his analysis by comparing the British with ancient colonial administrations. That extension

[15] Abercromby, *Magna Charta* (n 4) 4. For the persistence of this effort see Craig Yirush, *Settlers, Liberty, and Empire: The Roots of Early American Political Theory, 1675–1775* (Cambridge University Press 2011).

turned into the treatise, *De jure et gubernatione coloniarum*, which is also a revision of the original proposal that no longer seemed practicable. Abercromby recorded that he finished parts of *De jure* during the Stamp Act crisis of 1765–66. The 1986 editors of the treatise argue that internal evidence shows that he was revising the text until 1775.[16]

Abercromby begins *De jure* by raising the same problem that, according to Liljegren, Harrington adapted from Sigonio's editorial apparatus on Livy: can an empire survive having distant colonies? Abercromby admits that it is difficult, but adds that he came to realize the great potential inherent in a written transatlantic constitution from studying 'the Lex Julia of the Romans conveyed to their Italian Colonys' and 'the Imperial Constitution by the Emperor Antonius Caracalla . . . granted universally to all the Roman Colonys and afterwards extended to all People within the Roman Dominions'.[17] His research led him to distinguish between Greek and Roman methods of colonialism. When Greek cities became naturally overpopulated, a group of inhabitants set off to colonize, with the agreement of the whole city-state. When successful, they became independent states, acknowledging the 'Seniority, not the Superiority . . . of the Mother City' and acting as allies or confederates. By contrast, Roman colonists were sent out by the state, for one of six reasons: to subdue the natives; 'to restrain the incursion of Enemies'; to encourage population growth; to remove idle and superfluous population from Rome; to stifle tumults and seditions; and to reward veterans.[18] According to Abercromby, Sigonio's classification of these six Roman reasons applies equally to the British Empire.[19]

[16] Abercromby, *Magna Charta* (n 4) 5–6. A word about the text is in order. As with the *Examination*, Abercromby circulated *De jure* confidentially. Two drafts survive, an early version at the John Carter Brown Library (JCB) in Providence, Rhode Island (Codex-Eng. 50), and a later draft at the Huntington Library in San Marino, California (HM 513). The JCB manuscript, dated roughly to 1766, and the Huntington's 1774 version of *De jure*, both contain a wealth of references to Sigonio. The modern edition from 1986 is generally of high quality, but the editors fail to note that the JCB manuscript was cropped close after composition, and probably misses marginal amendments. They also acknowledge that they could not read some words, and could not identify some of Abercromby's references. Moreover, in some cases Abercromby's allusions to sources remain unnoticed; and the editors often omit significant deletions in Abercromby's manuscripts that are still possible to read—eg a long section on 156–58 of the mss at the Huntington, HM 513. I draw my arguments from the JCB and Huntington manuscripts, and give page references to the 1986 edition whenever possible.

[17] Abercromby, *Magna Charta* (n 4) 6. Abercromby is referring to the 90 BCE Lex Iulia de Civitate Latinis et Socii Danda.

[18] William Barron, *History of the Colonization of the Free States of Antiquity Applied to the Present Contest between Great Britain and Her American Colonies* (Cadell 1777) 83 (hereafter Barron, *History of the Colonization*), probably draws on Sigonio for the same list of motives. In contrast with Abercromby, Barron argues that the Julian Law destroyed the Republic, and a similar scheme for accommodating the claims of American colonists would destroy the British Empire: ibid 50, 108–10, 137, 150, *passim*.

[19] Abercromby, *Magna Charta* (n 4) 198.

With this argument, Abercromby departed from the claim he had made earlier in the *Examination*, in which he posited that most modern powers followed the Roman model, but Britain followed the Greek.[20] This was the Patriot and revolutionary position. Now, in *De jure*, Abercromby explains that further study of sources like Sigonio and Rosinus convinced him that all modern states followed Rome. Consequently, American colonies were neither founded nor encouraged to be independent. The ultimate source and authority was and remains King-in-Parliament, even though for expediency, and to respect colonists' rights to representation, jury, and other English liberties, they are allowed to have provincial laws and institutions.[21] The colonists' problem is that they mistakenly believe that the British Empire follows the Greek model.[22] Though clearly well versed in American pamphlets and treatises, Abercromby selects only two texts to represent the arguments he intends to refute: Otis's *Rights*, and Richard Bland's 1766 *Inquiry*. As we saw, Otis built a case on the analogy between Greek and British colonialism, thus he was a fit subject for Abercromby's criticism, but Bland held that ancient and modern colonialism are far from analogous, and therefore he was a more puzzling target for Abercromby.

Unlike most British writers, Abercromby did not consider the colonists' ingratitude as a chief cause of conflict. Their efforts to contravene the Navigation Acts and other British measures that limited their trade was natural and understandable. The fault lay with Westminster, which neglected colonial affairs. Even when it paid attention, it unwisely prioritized commerce over politics.[23] A revived common political identity was needed, with a comprehensive, coherent, and written imperial constitution at its heart. This would benefit both Britain and the colonists by securing the rule of law, including legal equality and the protection of colonial rights similar to those of ancient Greek colonists, as well as remedy for colonial administrators' abuse and corruption—a British version of the Julian *lex repetundarum*.

According to Abercromby, ancient writers such as Cicero and Velleius Paterculus often argued that holding distant colonies is hard or impossible, and history has shown them to be right. American colonies are far from Britain. In

[20] That said, in one passage of the *c* 1752 *Examination* Abercromby already suggests that the Roman Empire was closer to the British in some respects, and cites Rosinus and Sigonio in support: ibid 68.

[21] ibid 25–27.

[22] ibid 222. In a fascinating, undated and unpublished draft entitled 'Dominion of the Colonies', written sometime after he attended the Stamp Act Congress in 1765, William Samuel Johnson argued that the American colonies were patterned not on the Roman but on the Greek model, and cited Grotius as his source for the distinction (Connecticut Historical Society, MS 22977, Box 4, Folder 5).

[23] Abercromby, *Magna Charta* (n 4) 13–14. Here Abercromby may be echoing Montesquieu, *Spirit of the Laws* 20.6, Book 2, 7 in Thomas Nugent's second edition of 1752, which was widely read in the colonies.

order to both respect colonists' rights and enable effective provincial government, they need more extensive autonomy than cities, corporations, and counties palatine in Britain (Durham, Lancaster, and Chester), or even Scotland and Ireland ever had.[24] At the same time, another principle that ancient and modern colonialism have in common is that colonial affairs are subservient to the mother country's interest. Britain has every right to reconstitute the relationship with its colonies, notwithstanding provincial custom, charters, and other pretended sources of right.[25] Abercromby's immediate recommendations include enforcing and extending the Navigation Acts, strategically limiting the colonies' trade and economic development, and using vice-admiralty courts to do so.[26]

Sigonio is Abercromby's main source for the argument that the colonies owe taxes in exchange for liberties and protection, because Roman colonies did the same. In one passage to this effect, Abercromby cites Sigonio's chapter on colonization in *De antiquo iure Italiae* 2.3, sometimes referred to by its section heading, 'De iure coloniarum', as if it were a free-standing text. His illustrative case is the refusal of twelve Roman colonies in Italy to pay their assessments during the Second Punic War.[27] The Senate chastised them, the colonies relented, paid the higher dues demanded in punishment and, as a sign of good will, the Senate formally thanked their agents. Throughout the discussion, Abercromby spells out similarities and differences between the Roman and British colonies' agents, relations with the metropolis, possible mechanisms for negotiating between the mother country and the colonies concerning the assessment of taxes, and the like.[28] Abercromby also relies on Sigonio to show

[24] On the contentious analogy between counties palatinate and the American colonies see John Phillip Reid, *Constitutional History of the American Revolution: The Authority to Tax* (University of Wisconsin Press 1987) 19–20, 150–53.

[25] Abercromby, *Magna Charta* (n 4) 16–18, 22–23.

[26] ibid 20–21.

[27] Livy 27.9, 42.29. Abercromby, *Magna Charta* (n 4) 223–24. Abercromby gives further instances and again cites Sigonio on 282–83.

[28] On assessing taxes in the Roman and British empires: ibid 283, citing Sigonio, *De antiquo iure Italiae* 2.4. Abercromby's editors speculate that much of his *De jure* was written in the late 1760s. John Pettingal, *An Enquiry into the Use and Practice of Juries among the Greeks and Romans* (Cadell 1769) vol 2, 76–78, uses the same story and the same Sigonio and Livy references to argue that the Gothic or feudal constitution preserves not only the Greek, but also the Roman principle that military and financial obligations are incurred in return for protection, both at home, and between the colonies and the mother country. The book contains numerous important references to Sigonio, and its relevance to the relationship between Britain and America was well understood. To the passage where Pettingal argued from Livy that Britain has the right to tax its American colonies (ibid 78–79), Thomas Hollis added a respectful but firm note wishing that Pettingal had not drawn this false analogy. Hollis then sent his annotated copy to Harvard (Houghton f*EC75.H7267.Zz769p).

that Roman colonies 'were bound to the Quartering of Troops', another bone of contention in America at the time.[29]

Unlike Harrington, Abercromby finds some of Rome's conquests as enlightened as Britain's. Praising the degree of autonomy and toleration that Britain granted to Canada with the 1774 *Quebec Act* (14 Geo. III c.83), Abercromby berates the American colonies' opposition to the Act, asserting that colonists are trying to deny Canadians the same fruits of beneficent imperialism that they themselves enjoyed. Abercromby starts to discuss British rule over both the long-established American colonies, and the new dominion over Canada, in the same breath.

> It is the first Instance, where the Humanity and Faith of Conquerors, engaged and pledged to the conquered, have been impeached, and for the honour of the Nation, I wish the last; England, has done, by the American conquest, what the Romans did, more particularly by theirs of Greece, and the Kingdom of Macedonia, declaring to the conquered, that they the Romans conquered, not to enslave, which did not become the dignity, and Magnanimity of the Romans, but to share, with the conquered people, the Happiness of Roman Subjects, under Roman Government and Laws, and thereupon new Modelled, for their New Subjects, their System of Government, allowing to such their new Subjects, the enjoyment, and exercise of particular Laws and Customs, which they had theretofore enjoyed, <Populi Romano> adding thereto, such New Laws, as suited the Roman Sovereignty, and accordingly amongst the Roman Laws, we find, the *Jus Coloniarum*, the *Jus Municipiorum*, and the *Jus Provinciarum*, all distinctly treated of, by Sigonius, Rosinus, Lazius, and others, but more particularly so, by Sigonius, who takes Notice, that though these Laws, do in many instances differ, yet all, have relation, to the Laws of Rome.[30]

Abercromby singles out Sigonio as the most authoritative source for the constitutional arrangement between the colonies and the mother country in ancient Rome. Given Abercromby's thesis on the similarity between Rome and Britain, the demonstrative and prescriptive authority of Sigonio is considerable in his scheme. The parallels that Abercromby continues to draw show how seriously he took the analogy. A Roman colony, Abercromby

[29] Abercromby, *Magna Charta* (n 4) 225. This is one of Abercromby's references to Sigonio that the editors could not identify: 294 n 159. Another relevant one is 291 n 114.

[30] ibid 265.

cites Sigonio, was governed by the laws of the mother country, and by its own provincial laws. The forms of government may vary among the colonies. Some have a Governor and a Senate. Others, like Rhode Island and Connecticut, have popular governments. Citing Sigonio's chapter, 'De republica coloniarum' (*De antiquo iure Italiae* 2.4), Abercromby stresses that the important thing is that

> every Colony is *sui juris*, with regard to each other, but not *sui arbitrii* as to this Kingdom, or other Colonys, and with us, as with the Romans—whose Colonys had peculiar Laws, distinct from those of Rome [and of Great Britain] and so with our Colonys—All of them nevertheless, deriving their Authority in the first Instance theirs, from Rome, ours, from Great Britain.[31]

Colonists often argued that they were not represented in Parliament, and therefore could not be taxed. Otis famously made this case in the 1764 *Rights of the British Colonists*. A stock British rejoinder was that corporations, and large industrial towns in Britain that experienced rapid population growth, were also unrepresented in the same sense. In other words, the conclusion that Britain was the most just society in the world despite flaws in representation, including rotten boroughs, was used to try and support the premise that British justice depended on virtual representation, whereby every member of Parliament represented the interests of the whole state, and the whole empire, not only their voters. Thomas Whately, MP in 1763–65 and Lord of Trade in 1771–72, described virtual representation in his refutation of Otis.[32] Bland in turn formulated an enduring colonial rejoinder in his *Inquiry into the Rights of the British Colonies*, where he denied that virtual representation made any sense at all.[33] As noted above, Otis' and Bland's treatises are the only two colonial texts that Abercromby explicitly cites in *De jure*. However, instead of endorsing Whately's virtual representation model in opposition to these colonial texts, Abercromby mobilizes the typology and gradation of citizenship that Sigonio described for the Roman empire.[34] Sigonio gave Abercromby a new way to square the circle of justifying colonial taxes without either instituting actual representation for

[31] ibid 201–02.

[32] Thomas Whately, *The Regulations Lately Made Concerning the Colonies* (J Wilkie 1765).

[33] Somos, *American States of Nature* (n 11) ch 4.

[34] William Smith, *A Dictionary of Greek and Roman Antiquities* (Taylor and Walton 1842), s.v. 'Colonia,' regarded Sigonio as the origin of the mistaken view that colonists lost some of their rights. In any case, this was close to the British polemical uses of Sigonio in the 1770s, even though they usually held that it was the American colonists' decision to suspend or renounce their rights.

colonists, or explicitly denying their rights as Englishmen. His argument is the following.

Colonists as individuals have all the English rights of citizenship, but no collective sovereignty distinct from the empire. By becoming colonists, they chose to suspend their right to vote, 'of which they have no Right to complain, because their Absence is their own free choice, by going to America, for better accommodation'. They are legally distinct from residents of Britain partly due to the suspension of this right, and partly because they have rights provided by their own provincial laws, which derive their authority from Britain but obviously do not apply in Britain. The two legal identities are, according to Abercromby, the same as Sigonio's description of the Roman colonists' two countries, one by natural birth and one by politics. The latter allegiance is the greater, and natural identity is subsumed under the political. In giving examples and elaborating how this system works, with particular focus on colonial suffrage, Abercromby extensively cites Sigonio's *De antiquo iure Italiae* 1.1, 1.8, 2.3, and other passages.[35] Another possible resolution that Abercromby explores, citing Sigonio, is sending *decuriones colonici*, comparable to leading burgesses in American colonies (and presumably to colonial agents like himself) to give the colonies a vote in the mother country.[36] The authority of Sigonio, in short, frames Abercromby's various arguments in favour of British imperial policy.

Sigonio Cited and Manipulated

Abercromby was not the only participant in the Anglo-American controversy to rely so heavily on Sigonio. Another example is the scurrilous and pugnacious Philadelphia lawyer Isaac Hunt (*c* 1742–1809). Whilst Abercromby's confidential, long treatise was intended for ministers and high-ranking civil servants, Hunt's thirty-page pamphlet, *The Political Family: or a discourse, pointing out the reciprocal advantages, which flow from an uninterrupted Union between Great-Britain and her American Colonies* (1775), was addressed to 'the worthy merchants, farmers, and mechanics of the Province of Pennsylvania'. It argues that the British Empire must be a 'union of laws and government' in order to be sustainable and effective as a body politic that provides protection and happiness.[37] There are two kinds of legitimate colonies, Hunt states: those that were

35 Abercromby, *Magna Charta* (n 4) 212, 214–15.

36 ibid 246, citing Sigonio, *De antiquo iure Italiae* 2.4.

37 Isaac Hunt, *The Political Family: or a discourse, pointing out the reciprocal advantages, which flow from an uninterrupted Union between Great-Britain and her American Colonies* (James Humphreys 1775) 6.

established by settlers on land bought from the natives, and colonies based on conquest in just war. In both, colonists are bound by acts of Parliament.[38]

The constitutions of colonies consist of laws in force in England at the time of settlement: 'Acts of parliament made since, in which they are expressly named', and laws the colonists passed in accordance with their royal charters for limited self-government, and subsequently approved in England.

> This also is similar to the constitution of the *Roman colonies*. They received their laws from the people of *Rome*, or they enacted them by their inferior senates, or by the consent of the people of the *colonies*. Though every particular colony had laws distinct from the general laws of *Rome*, yet they were either dictated to them, or confirmed by the Triumviri. They are of that sort of colonies which Baron Puffendorff mentions as united to the mother country by a kind of unequal confederacy.[39]

In support of this point, Hunt cites four sources: Sigonio, Livy, Flaccus, and finally Pufendorf.[40] Hunt's citation of Sigonio runs:

> Omnis *coloniarum* respublica in legibus et legum curatoribus fuit posita. Leges vel a populo Romano acceperunt, vel ipse sibi per senatum aut populum condiderunt. Leges autem suas quaeque *colonia* habuit praecipuas, a Romanis quidem legibus separatas; sed tamen a Romanis Triumviris datas. —In *coloniis* concilium erat et Senatus. (*Sigonius de antiq. jure civ. Rom. L. 2*, 185)

The page number suggests that the reference is to the 1593 Frankfurt edition of Sigonio's collected works. Apart from a few omissions, Hunt's citation is by and large accurate. However, there is nothing like the last sentence in Sigonio. A comparison with an Abercromby passage may point to Hunt's source, or at least show an interesting common feature of their use of Sigonio citations.

The introduction in one of the four surviving copies of Abercromby's *Examination*, known as the Harrisburg 1 version, differs substantially from the other manuscripts. Here Abercromby compares the British imperial constitution to that of Rome in general, but especially the Republic.[41] In

[38] ibid 8.
[39] ibid 9–10.
[40] The last citation may be from Pufendorf's 1738 *An Introduction to the History of the Principal Kingdoms and States of Europe*, which was available in Philadelphia already in 1741: *A Catalogue of Books Belonging to the Library Company of Philadelphia* (Benjamin Franklin 1741).
[41] Abercromby, *Magna Charta* (n 4) 311.

support he cites a passage from Rosinus 10.24, 'De republica Coloniarum, Municipiorum, Praefecturarum, & Provinciarum'.[42] This chapter begins with Rosinus' praise of Sigonio, and expands on Sigonio's discussion of colonial assemblies and magistrates. It corresponds to the part of Sigonio's *De antiquo iure ciuium Romanorum* that Hunt cites. The specific textual echoes between Abercromby's and Hunt's citations of Sigonio may be due to Hunt having gained access to Abercromby's draft; or they are strikingly coincidental, parallel adaptations of Sigonio to the American colonies. Neither scenario explains where Hunt drew the last sentence from, which omits the citizens of colonies as a source of laws entirely.

In *De jure*, Abercromby cites Rosinus 10.24 again, to make precisely the same point as Hunt, namely that the colonies derive all their legal authority from Britain. Abercromby first cites Sigonio, then Rosinus:

> *Fuisse, praeter haec, alias leges, ab ipsis Coloniis, a Coloniae concilio, hoc est, Senatu populo que suo latas, Argumento, illud est, quod in Coloniis, Concilium erat et Senatus, et Populi; Senatores in Coloniis, Decuriones Vocabantur.*[43]

According to Abercromby, the senate and the people together make up the colonial *concilium*, and in this, as in many other features, the Roman empire during the Republic resembles the British Empire. However, this passage in this form is absent from Rosinus. While Sigonio was a frequently cited authority in the British-American controversy, writers could be cavalier with the original text. Abercromby made up a passage to support his views on the correct composition of colonial assemblies. While Sigonio, Rosinus, and Abercromby all include the people as a source of colonial law, Hunt omits them from the odd final sentence, which he probably added himself, in the passage he presented as a direct Sigonio quotation.

Sigonio himself was accused of similar distortion. In a remarkable passage, Adam Ferguson argued that colonists of the Roman Republic were not disenfranchised but stopped exercising their deliberative rights when they left Rome. Instead of introducing a legal gradation of citizenship, any Roman references

[42] Johannes Rosinus, *Antiquitatum romanarum corpus absolutissimum* (Chouët 1558) 469–70. In the 1620 edition of Rosinus, with Dempster's and Schotte's additions, chapter 10.24 is on 1608–11, the passage that corresponds to Sigonio's *De antiquo iure ciuium Romanorum* is also on 1608–11, and the passage Hunt cites is on 1609. Provenance records show that this Sigonio passage, transmitted in Rosinus, was at Harvard already in the 1760s. The College of New Jersey (now Princeton) held a copy by 1760, together with Sigonio's *De Republica Hebraeorum*. See *A Catalogue of Books in the Library of The College of New-Jersey, January 29, 1760* (Parker 1760) 28, 30.

[43] Abercromby, *Magna Charta* (n 4) 202.

to different tiers of rights simply reflected this fact. Ferguson blamed Sigonio for 'a wonderful perversion' of Livy's text to prove legal gradation.[44] Ferguson's interpretation of Sigonio mirrors exactly a standard and widespread British response to the American colonists, namely that the colonists were not deprived of representation, but chose to render themselves incapable of participation when they moved to America.

Sigonio and Colonial Taxation

It shows the diversity of Sigonio's impact that not only the various treatises of *De antiquo iure populi Romani* but also his treatise on Athens and Sparta, *De Atheniensium et Lacedaemoniorum temporibus* (1565) were used to score political points even in the limited context of the Anglo-American controversy concerning legitimate colonialism during the brief period of 1751–77 examined in this chapter.

As John Pocock has argued, the American crisis was seen less as a case of the decline and fall of the British Empire and more a recurrence of the Social War between the Roman Republic and Italian allies (*socii*).[45] In his 1777 *History of the Colonization of the Free States of Antiquity Applied to the Present Contest between Great Britain and Her American Colonies*, the Scottish William Barron, later professor of logic, rhetoric and metaphysics at St Andrews, set out to analyse Carthaginian, Greek, and Roman colonialism explicitly in order to settle the debate between Britain and its American colonies, and to prepare the public, and the politicians, for the settlement that must follow 'the submission of the colonies'.[46] Among other things, Barron criticized Adam Smith's proposal for colonial representation, and took up a point of Montesquieu's concerning the lex Julia of 90 BCE. Montesquieu proposed that extending the rights of citizenship to Rome's colonies and allies was one of two causes of Rome's ruin. Barron thought that it alone would have sufficed.[47]

Placed in the context of other accounts of the nature of the British Empire and the consequent degree of the American colonies' autonomy, we can appreciate

[44] Adam Ferguson, *The History of the Progress and Termination of the Roman Republic* (Strahan 1783) 1.3, 71–72.

[45] John GA Pocock, 'Political Thought in the English-speaking Atlantic, 1760–1790. Part I: The Imperial Crisis' in John GA Pocock and others (eds) *The Varieties of British Political Thought* (Cambridge University Press 1993) 246–82.

[46] William Barron, *History of the Colonization* (n 18) 4.

[47] ibid 50, 108–10, 137, 150, *passim*. See Iain McDaniel, *Adam Ferguson in the Scottish Enlightenment* (Harvard University Press 2013) 186.

that one of the cardinal points Barron makes is that it was only at first, in the primitive stage of Greek colonialism that Greek colonies had full autonomy, and mother states had no power to tax them, as they could offer no protection in return. As Sparta and Athens rose to prominence, both the remaining Greek city-states and their colonies had to ally with one or the other. Even if allegiances shifted, the imperative to choose sides meant that Sparta and Athens could effectively claim and institutionalize the right to tax for defence.[48]

However, this was a gradual process. Barron surveys disputes between Corinth and Corcyra at length to show that at that time 'the respective rights and privileges, both of the metropolis and the colony among the Greeks, were still extremely undetermined'.[49] Even for events as late as 414 BCE, the middle of the Peloponnesian War, Barron could argue that Richard Price in his 1776 *Observations on the Nature of Civil Liberty* misled his readers when he claimed that the failure of the Athenian siege of Syracuse held a lesson for the British who wished to reduce the American colonies by force. On the contrary, Barron argued, Greek colonialism was still in its early stage, therefore Syracuse was not a subordinate colony but an independent state, and therefore Price's analogy was invalid. At this stage, none of the Greek states had the power to tax colonies, and raised funds for defence from them only by specific, *ad hoc* arrangements.[50]

Barron introduces the new stage of Greek colonialism in chapter 2, section 4 of his treatise. The turning point came after the second Persian invasion ended in 479 BCE with Greek victories at Plataea and Mycale. The Greek colonies in Asia, Aeolis and Ionia, formerly under Persian rule, were wary of a renewed Persian attack. As a cautionary measure, the Lacedaemonians and Peloponnesians suggested transplanting the Asian colonies to Greece. Athens resisted, and offered the Asian colonies its protection instead. The Greeks agreed, and Aristides promptly proposed a general tax 'for the purposes of common defence against the future attacks of Persia'.[51] According to Barron, this was the tax that made Athens, and the whole of ancient Greece, flourish.[52] The federal state that colonial taxes had built gave rise to philosophy, the arts, natural science, political liberty, and so on. Throughout this section, Sigonio is the only modern authority Barron cites.

[48] William Barron, *History of the Colonization* (n 18) 32–33.
[49] ibid 62–67; quotation from 64.
[50] ibid 44–47.
[51] ibid 51. Also see 74, 133–34.
[52] ibid 52.

Only Athens and Sparta acquired the right to tax colonies, Barron continues; therefore modern politicians are wrong to believe that the balance of power is a new *arcanum imperii*. That said, there are better and worse ways to tax an empire. Due to its flawed constitution that prohibited taxation, Sparta still taxed its colonies, but in a dangerously, destructively haphazard manner.[53] Here is the same desire for a clear, written imperial constitution that we saw in Abercromby—a constitution based on the best of ancient imperialist prudence as formulated by Sigonio, who was not only one of several sources, but the most eminent authority on many of the issues discussed here.

Barron takes the mainstream British position that the British Empire most strongly resembles the Roman empire at its best. Like Abercromby, Barron argues that due to their membership in a beneficent empire, Americans have the right to establish their own, albeit inferior government, and that they chose to suspend their political rights to representation in the parent state when they moved to the colonies.[54] Barron's conclusion, namely that Britain has every right to tax the American colonies, does not come as a surprise. What is more interesting is that despite coming down on the Roman side of the puzzle of which ancient empire is analogous to the British, Barron appreciates the complexity of positions sufficiently to try to further ground this conclusion in what he asserts was the Carthaginian, Greek, and Roman practice of taxing colonies. When it comes to taxes, all ancient imperial prudence points the same way, even though in other features, such as rights given to colonies, the British Empire most closely resembles the Roman. Importantly, Barron uses Sigonio to break the 'Greek or Roman' dichotomy, harmonize ancient practices to support the British claim, and argue that the American colonies were in a similar constitutional relationship with Britain as Greek colonists in Asia were vis-à-vis Athens after the second Persian invasion.[55] Barron cited and criticized Sigonio when he did not fit his scheme, for instance when Sigonio mistakenly argued (according to Barron) that Rome did not allow Latium to adopt Roman laws, and restricted the Latins to retaining their own laws, subject to Roman approval.[56]

Barron's work found great success even by eighteenth-century standards. It was translated into German and French immediately, the latter by Antoine Marie Cerisier, a clearinghouse of information and a publicist of the Anglo-American controversy. Several works were published in response, and the

[53] ibid 75–76.
[54] ibid 91–94.
[55] ibid 133–34.
[56] ibid 91–92.

resulting controversy naturally involved Sigonio, Barron's main source for distinguishing the non-taxing and the taxing stages of Greek colonialism.[57]

Conclusion: Sigonio's Expansive Relevance

In Anglo-American debates between 1751 and 1777 concerning the desirable reform of the British imperial constitution, a context seldom connected to Sigonio's Renaissance scholarship, we find Sigonio directly and formidably present, with several of his works cited and manipulated to support rival interpretations of ancient colonial prudence, enduring international law, and advisable colonial policy. In the short span of twenty-six years, Patriot lawyers in northern and southern colonies (Hunt and Bland), a Scottish professor of rhetoric (Barron), and a transatlantic colonial agent and MP (Abercromby) all turned to centuries-old works by Sigonio for pragmatic inspiration and authoritative evidence for their proposals to reform the failing imperial constitution. Further research may find many more cases of the lasting, expansive but so far unappreciated influence of Sigonio in the same period in other contexts, for example his relevance for Rousseau's account of Roman institutions in the 1762 *Social Contract*.[58] Indeed, as Mattia Balbo shows in the next chapter, Sigonio's shadow continued to loom large over scholarly interpretations of Roman agrarian law and colonization in the eighteenth and early nineteenth centuries.

[57] See Giovanna Ceserani, *Italy's Lost Greece. Magna Graecia and the Making of Modern Archaeology* (Oxford University Press 2012) 107–10.

[58] Edmond Dreyfus-Brisac pointed out that Rousseau borrowed from Sigonio some of the key insights in book 4, chs 4–7: Jean-Jacques Rousseau, *Du contrat social* (Dreyfus ed, Alcan 1896) xix. It is a long-held and quite frequently repeated opinion that these chapters are inferior and irrelevant to the rest of the work. See eg Charles E Vaughan, *The Political Writings of Jean-Jacques Rousseau* (Cambridge University Press 1915) vol 5, 2 n 109: 'It must be confessed that these four chapters are barely relevant to the subject and quite unworthy of the setting in which they stand. The beggarly elements of the Servian Constitution are a fitter theme for Sigonius than for Rousseau.' Roger D Masters, *The Political Philosophy of Rousseau* (Princeton University Press 1968) 305–06 n 21 notes that this was cited with approval in the edition of *Du contrat social* by Robert Derathé in *Oeuvres complètes* (Gallimard 1964) vol 3, 1495. While Masters is right to criticize these views, his solution, namely to emphasize Rousseau's distinction between the ideal government and the prudential lessons derivable from Rome, is wanting. It is enough to consider one American aspect of Rousseau's extensive adaptation of Sigonio to see how relevant and significant these chapters are. This aspect is the role that Rousseau's Sigonian version of the tribunate played in the American formulation of the doctrine of judicial review: Samuel Freeman, 'Constitutional Democracy and the Legitimacy of Judicial Review' (1990–91) 9 Law and Philosophy 327–70; Rousseau further noted the importance of Machiavelli and Sigonio in a letter from 26 March 1767: Jean-Jacques Rousseau, *Oeuvres* (Déterville et Lefèvre 1817) vol 8, 394.

5

Roman Colonization and Land Division between Enlightenment and Romanticism

Beaufort and Niebuhr

Mattia Balbo[*]

In the eighteenth and early nineteenth centuries, several studies on Roman colonization and on the relations between Romans and Italians stressed the importance of land management and of the rules by which Rome granted, to its own citizens and to its allies, access to this fundamental resource. These studies were strongly influenced by political and ideological discourses of the Enlightenment, as well as of the American and French Revolutions and, as a consequence, the questions they posed to ancient texts (and sometimes even their answers) echo the social and political concerns of that era. Arguably, the most innovative theories in this period concerned the study of the ancient land laws, which were often taken as examples for proposing a reform of the social structure of the Ancien Régime. Of particular importance are the studies of two influential scholars: Louis de Beaufort, a representative of the Francophone Enlightenment of the mid-eighteenth century who was affected strongly by Montesquieu's theories on the separation of powers; and Barthold Georg Niebuhr, who wrote in the post-revolutionary context, when, after the Restoration, liberalism and a reformist attitude began to spread through the German states. This chapter explores the innovative aspects of the works of Beaufort and Niebuhr against the background of Sigonio's Renaissance scholarship and assesses their impact on the ensuing historiography. It focuses on Beaufort and Niebuhr because they offer two crucial case studies for understanding the cultural developments in the period 1750–1830 and because their writings have greatly influenced the historiographical debate, forming a turning point in the study of several aspects of Roman Republican history.

[*] I should like to thank Professor John Rich for his careful reading of this chapter and for his very useful comments.

Mattia Balbo, *Roman Colonization and Land Division between Enlightenment and Romanticism* In: *The Renaissance of Roman Colonization.* Edited by: Jeremia Pelgrom and Arthur Weststeijn, Oxford University Press (2020). © the Several Contributors. DOI: 10.1093/oso/9780198850960.003.0005

Indeed, Beaufort is considered the forerunner of the modern sceptical approach to the history of archaic Rome, an approach that conditioned his attitude towards the most ancient phases of Roman colonization and land distribution. He also proposed a strongly positive, almost unprecedented, reappraisal of the tribunate of the plebs, which played a fundamental role in his analysis of agrarian and colonial policies (an analysis clearly indebted to Sigonio, and also to Montesquieu) as the plebeian tribunes were the main sponsors of legal reforms in this matter. Niebuhr, on the other hand, was one of the protagonists of the early-nineteenth-century paradigm shift in history that transformed the study of Roman history and law radically. His attention to agrarian and colonial history chiefly centred around the legal definition of landholding and of the personal status of farmers—a theme with direct topical relevance in the political context of his time. As this chapter shows, Niebuhr softened many revolutionary aspects that previous scholars ascribed to Roman popular institutions, and he introduced a reformist, liberal conception of Roman politics which was further developed by the first scholar who truly overshadowed Sigonio: Theodor Mommsen.

Beaufort: Politicizing Roman Colonization and Land Division

Little is known about the life and the education of Louis de Beaufort (1703–95). As a member of a French Huguenot family that moved to the Dutch Republic after the revocation of the Edict of Nantes in the late seventeenth century, Beaufort spent his whole life in the Dutch milieu. For some years he was tutor to the young Frederick IV, the future landgrave of Hesse-Homburg, whom he accompanied to the University of Leiden and to whom he dedicated a historical treatise on Germanicus (*Histoire de César Germanicus*, 1741). In 1746, Beaufort was elected fellow of the Royal Society of London. He later moved to Maastricht, where he apparently resided until his death.[1] His *Dissertation sur l'incertitude des cinq premiers siècles de l'histoire romaine*, first published in 1738 and then reissued in 1750 in order to reply to many criticisms, was widely

[1] An exhaustive biography of Beaufort can be found both in Ronald T Ridley, *Gibbon's Complement: Louis de Beaufort* (Istituto Veneto di Scienze, Lettere ed Arti 1986) 13–41 and in Mouza Raskolnikoff, *Histoire romaine et critique historique dans l'Europe des lumières. La naissance de l'hypercritique dans l'historiographie de la Rome antique* (École Française de Rome 1992) 389–408 (hereafter Raskolnikoff, *Histoire romaine*).

circulated throughout Europe and also in Britain, thanks to an anonymous English translation printed in 1740.

Beaufort's chief thesis, which guides his general view on Roman history, stresses the absolute unreliability of the traditional accounts about the history of archaic Rome. The *Dissertation* entails a long and detailed argumentation on the lack of historical sources before the third-century BCE, and of the fictional character of the accounts of Rome's origins that were written after the Punic Wars. In Beaufort's opinion, these accounts mostly served the interests of late Republican and early imperial aristocratic families. He posited that Roman historiography was born only around 200 BCE, with Fabius Pictor, whereas the most ancient documentary sources (if they existed) perished in the Gallic sack of 390 BCE. His strict criticism of ancient sources—notably Polybius, Livy, Dionysius of Halicarnassus, Cicero, Pliny the Elder, Tacitus, Suetonius, and Plutarch—informed his extremely sceptical approach to Rome's archaic history.[2] In the intellectual milieu of the eighteenth century, Beaufort's radical scepticism represented a minority (but not altogether unprecedented) tendency, but it gained momentum in the nineteenth century. Niebuhr, for example, praised Beaufort in the second edition of his *Roman History* and in his Bonn Lectures, although he diverged from him in his attempt at rewriting archaic history.[3] As Ronald Ridley has observed, Beaufort's 'real successor in the nineteenth century' was the mid-Victorian statesman and scholar, Sir George Cornewall Lewis (1806–63).[4] His *Inquiry into the Credibility of the Early Roman History* (1855) aimed to refute Niebuhr's imaginative rewriting of Rome's early history, in favour of the sceptical view that it could not be reconstructed, the perspective championed by Beaufort, whom Lewis held in high esteem.[5]

[2] Hendrik J Erasmus, *The Origins of Rome in Historiography from Petrarch to Perizonius* (Van Gorcum 1962) 130; Arnaldo Momigliano, 'H. J. Erasmus, The Origins of Rome in Historiography from Petrarch to Perizonius, 1962' in Arnaldo Momigliano (ed), *Terzo contributo alla storia degli studi classici* (Edizioni di Storia e Letteratura 1966) vol 2, 769–74; Raskolnikoff, *Histoire romaine* (n 1) 288–89; 409–19. Important forerunners of Beaufort's scepticism were Philipp Cluver (1580–1622), Henry Dodwell (1641–1711), Louis-Jean Lévesque de Pouilly (1691–1750), and partly also Perizonius (Jakob Voorbroek, 1651–1715).

[3] Barthold G Niebuhr, *The History of Rome* (Julius C Hare and Connop Thirlwall ed, Taylor, Walton, Maberly 1851) vii (hereafter Niebuhr, *The History of Rome*); Barthold G Niebuhr, *Lectures on Roman History* (Havilland M Chepmell and Franz Demmler tr, Chatto & Windus 1875) 3 (hereafter Niebuhr, *Lectures*). In the preface to the first edition, Niebuhr declares that he read the *Dissertation* when his first part was already in print: Barthold G Niebuhr, *The Roman History* (Francis A Walter tr, Rivington 1827) xiii (hereafter Niebuhr, *The Roman History*). cf Raskolnikoff, *Histoire romaine* (n 1) 737–48.

[4] Ridley, *Gibbon's Complement* (n 1) 111–16.

[5] George Cornewall Lewis, *An Inquiry into the Credibility of the Early Roman History* (JW Parker 1855) 4–12 (comparison between Beaufort and Niebuhr). cf Arnaldo Momigliano, 'George Grote and the Study of Greek History' in Arnaldo Momigliano, *Contributo alla storia degli studi classici* (Edizioni di Storia e Letteratura 1955); Arnaldo Momigliano, 'G. C. Lewis, Niebuhr e la critica delle fonti' in Arnaldo Momigliano, *Contributo alla storia degli studi classici* (Edizioni di Storia e Letteratura 1955) 249–62.

Eventually, in the twentieth century, the so-called hypercritical historiography followed and independently developed many themes proposed by Beaufort,[6] although many of these 'hypercritics' intended to rewrite the story rather than just insisting on the impossibility of recovering it (and such an approach is perhaps rather in the tradition of Niebuhr than of Beaufort and Lewis).

The publication of the *Dissertation* caused much controversy in which Beaufort was accused of historical pyrrhonism. Among his critics were Nathaniel Hooke, who nevertheless accepted some fundamental aspects of Beaufort's argumentation, and notably Christoph Gottlob Sachs (Christophorus Saxius).[7] In reply to his critics, Beaufort sought to give further substantiation to his claims. While the *Dissertation* contains a very strong *pars destruens*, the work lacks a comparable and adequate *pars construens* that explores the alternative solutions to an approach that otherwise might seem mere 'nihilism'. To offer such an alternative, in 1766 Beaufort published an impressive treatise on the Roman Republic (*La république romaine, ou plan général de l'ancien gouvernement de Rome*), printed in The Hague in two quarto tomes and then in Paris in six octavo volumes (1767).[8] This work does not aim either to refute the reliability of ancient literary sources or to affirm the impossibility of studying Roman archaic history, but rather to provide the *pars construens* that was missing in Beaufort's previous treatise. Although reasserting in principle the thesis of the *Dissertation*, Beaufort does not question the traditional chronology of the events but pragmatically accepts it, as explained in the *Discours préliminaire* in the first volume: Beaufort maintains that he accepts several elements of the traditional story and that in so far as the details are unreliable, they are not important for his purpose. In this sense, the *Republic* is more conventional than the *Dissertation*, since it operates in a much less sceptical fashion.

[6] For instance Ettore Pais, *Ancient Legends of Roman History* (Mario E Cosenza tr, Dodd, Mead, and Company 1905) 2 considers Beaufort as the real founder of modern criticism (on this judgement see Raskolnikoff, *Histoire romaine* (n 1) 781–82). On the hypercritical approach: Moses I Finley, *Ancient History. Evidence and Models* (Chatto & Windus 1985) 9–10; Timothy P Wiseman, *Unwritten Rome* (University of Exeter Press 2008); Cristiano Viglietti, *Il limite del bisogno. Antropologia economica di Roma arcaica* (Il Mulino 2011) 59–62.

[7] Nathaniel Hooke, *Roman History. From the Building of Rome to the Ruin of the Commonwealth* (reprint Thomas Davison 1830) 399–436. Saxius attacked Beaufort in a series of articles published in Latin in the Nova Acta Eruditorum (June 1741, June 1742, April 1743, September 1744), in the Ephemerides Lipsienses (1744), and especially in Christophorus Saxius, 'Ἐπίκρισις φιλολογική, sive stricturae in nuperum Franci cuiusdam libellum de incerto historiae Romanorum antiquissimae' (1742) 1 Miscellanea Lipsiensia nova ad incrementum scientiarum 40–79; (1743) 2 Miscellanea Lipsiensia 409–95, 620–712; (1744) 3 Miscellanea Lipsiensia 235–329, 743–49.

[8] I follow the quarto version: Louis de Beaufort, *La république romaine, ou plan général de l'ancien gouvernement de Rome* (Nicolas van Daalen 1766). The English translation of Beaufort's passages is mine.

As it is suggested by its subtitle, the *Republic* investigates the power relationships between the Roman governmental institutions and analyses the functioning of each institution, public office, and law in the light of the clash of powers. Beaufort explicitly states that he intends to use Montesquieu's political theory to fill up the gap that his sceptical approach had created, in particular the *Considerations on the Causes of the Greatness of the Romans and their Decline* (1734) and the *Spirit of the Laws*, first published in 1748, which Beaufort had in his own library.

> We will find [many new ideas] in the small volume, by the eminent *Président* de Montesquieu, on the *Causes of the Greatness of the Romans and their Decline*, and in his masterpiece on *The Spirit of the Laws*. We cannot enough admire the sagacity and the depth that permeate these books, as well as his wisdom in seizing the essentials and rejecting all that mess which entangles the works of the half-scholars. The theories of such a wise man have often acted as guides in my researches, and have helped me to outline the links that existed between each part of the Roman government.[9]

Beaufort's debt towards Montesquieu is evident in the 'trias politica' principle that he applies to the Roman constitution—anachronistically, for in antiquity such a separation did not concern power per se, but its holders.[10] This approach reveals how modern analytical categories helped Beaufort to show how Roman institutions worked. For example, he distinguishes the legislative, executive, and judicial inside the prerogatives of the assemblies, magistracies, and senate. In the same manner, he dwells upon the balance of these powers by reconsidering Polybius' notion of a mixed constitution, paving the way for the

[9] Beaufort, *La république* (n 8) Discours préliminaire, vol 1, ii. On Beaufort's personal library see Raskolnikoff, *Histoire romaine* (n 1) 527–33; on the circulation of Montesquieu's works in the eighteenth-century Dutch Republic, see Wyger RE Velema, *Republicans. Essays on Eighteenth-Century Dutch Political Thought* (Brill 2007) 94–98. Some scholars suppose that Beaufort was also inspired by Machiavelli's *Discorsi*, even if there is no evidence that he possessed this book. He could have read it elsewhere, or he may have had an indirect knowledge of it through the large use made by Montesquieu himself. See Ridley, *Gibbon's Complement* (n 1) 138–39 and cf the more cautious assessment in Thibaud Lanfranchi, *Les tribuns de la plèbe et la formation de la République romaine, 494–287 avant J.-C. Rome* (École Française de Rome 2015) 14–15 (hereafter Lanfranchi, *Les tribuns de la plèbe*). We might also recognize some influence from Rousseau, especially from the *Discourse on Inequality* (1755) and, of course, from the *Social Contract* (1762). However, neither of these are recorded among Beaufort's personal books and there is no evidence that Beaufort took direct inspiration from Rousseau's works. Their thinking indeed contains some elements that are apparently similar, for instance the positive reappraisal of the tribunate of the plebs (as we will see below); but this could be an independent development, even though it is uncommon in early-eighteenth-century historiography.

[10] Beaufort, *La république* (n 8) vol 2, 400–06: 'Considérations sur les différends du Sénat et du Peuple', article 3 (hereafter 'Considérations').

later eighteenth century when the Founding Fathers of the United States (and partly also the French Constituents) sought to reproduce the Roman constitution by adopting the idea of checks and balances that Polybius had outlined in the sixth book of his *Histories*.[11]

The way Beaufort deals with colonies and landholdings is also influenced by this approach. His reflection on colonies is part of a larger discussion about the legal relations between Romans and other peoples, in which he surveys the colonies and the characteristic qualities that distinguish this kind of town from the other urban settlements in Italy (*municipia*, *praefecturae*, *ciuitates foederatae* etc). Beaufort's chief purpose does not consist either of providing a reconstruction of the agrarian landscape of ancient Italy, or of reassessing the history of Roman colonization. On the contrary, he aims to outline the juridical features that regulate colonies and land division in the late Republic. His discussion partly continues in the section about provinces, which follows almost the same structure.[12] He considers the various forms of citizenship (*droit de bourgeoisie*), the relations with local peoples, and the juridical differences among the cities in the territories conquered by Rome. He briefly deals with the legal measures that authorize the creation of colonial settlements. In this respect, Beaufort mentions the beneficial function that colonies had for the Roman social structure as ways of relieving population pressure and meeting the social claims of the plebeians, thanks to land allotments which are linked to colonization:

> During the frequent wars against the nearby peoples, Romulus had a very soft attitude towards the vanquished: their punishment was to move to Rome and become fellow citizens. Since for this reason, the city of Rome could quickly become overpopulated, he arranged to relieve it of a useless youth and of a needy plebs, by distributing among them the conquered lands and by transferring them in the towns which he had emptied . . . It is uncertain whether Romulus had suggested this policy to the Roman Senate, but it is certain that the latter has always applied it: instead of destroying the conquered towns, he was content to confiscate their lands, that were to be divided among the poor citizens who were transferred in these towns.[13]

[11] Andrew Lintott, *The Constitution of the Roman Republic* (Oxford University Press 1999) 251–55 (hereafter Lintott, *Constitution*); see also Eric Nelson, *The Greek Tradition in Republican Thought* (Cambridge University Press 2004) 195–233 (hereafter Nelson, *The Greek Tradition*); Sergio Roda, *Il modello della repubblica imperiale romana fra mondo antico e mondo modern* 'Fecisti patriam diversis gentibus unam' (Monduzzi 2011) 155–68.

[12] Beaufort, *La rḗpublique* (n 8) 7.2–7.6 (On provincial government).

[13] ibid 7.4, vol 2, 236.

Beaufort's discussion of colonies clearly follows that of Sigonio, who is frequently mentioned in the *Republic* and to whom he attributes an unrivalled authority.[14] Yet Beaufort also differs from Sigonio's analysis, in particular by making a sharper distinction between viritane distributions and colonial allotments.[15] Sigonio also separated viritane distributions from colonial allotments, stating that both kinds of provisions are agrarian measures but that their objectives and outcomes are different. However, he considered the whole agrarian matter as a sort of 'subcategory' of the colonial policy resulting from Roman expansion. Beaufort applies a different hierarchy. Of course, he is aware that colonial settlements and agrarian laws can be considered as parts of the same problem, namely land management, but he prefers to treat the two aspects separately, in two different chapters which are quite far apart in the general structure of his treatise. Beaufort must have felt that Sigonio's choice to put the agrarian laws under the heading of colonies is a questionable decision, since it forces the interpretation of an issue that does not derive only from colonization. Although there are no great differences in the contents of their discussions on colonies, in this respect Beaufort makes a crucial departure from Sigonio. Because of the theoretical distinction between colonies and viritane distributions, Beaufort does not give to colonization the same weight that he gives to the agrarian reforms as a solution for political and social issues. He is primarily interested in the legal relations between institutions, as well as in the political struggle that can arise from these relations. From this perspective, agrarian reforms are crucial, as they entailed a change in the existing property situation that, according to the ancient sources on the middle and late Republic, provoked the harshest political struggles among Rome's citizen body. Compared to these agrarian reforms, colonial policy left less traces of internal struggles in the ancient source material.[16] Moreover, viritane distributions can be stopped or limited,[17] whereas the foundation of a colony cannot exclude land allotments for the settlers. In this case the political struggle chiefly involves the *creation* of the colony, rather than the subsequent land distribution.

[14] ibid vol 2, 256, on the colonies established by Sulla, Caesar, and the triumvirs: 'This subject is so confused that I only refer to Sigonius, who has collected all the best that could be said about it.' However, Beaufort occasionally disagrees with Sigonio on some related topics: eg ibid vol 2, 199, 201, 223.

[15] Carlo Sigonio, *De antiquo iure Italiae* (Giordano Ziletti 1560) 2.2, 60 (hereafter Sigonio, *De antiquo iure Italiae*). On Sigonio's approach see Chapter 3 in this volume by John Rich.

[16] For example the dismantling of the colonies at Carthage (121 BCE) and Capua (83 BCE), just after their creation.

[17] See, for instance, Appian, *Civil Wars* 1.19.78–82, about Scipio's attempt to stop the Gracchan distributions in 129 BCE.

Beaufort's discussion of the *leges agrariae* in the context of colonization again follows Sigonio, with some differences.[18] First of all, Beaufort uses the ancient sources analysed by Sigonio, reproduces his line of argument, and accepts his conclusions. Sigonio, after having introduced the main reasons that led Rome to create colonies, showed the ways of managing the *ager publicus* and distinguished colonial allotments from viritane distributions (a distinction Beaufort endorses). Then, he listed every agrarian law attested in the ancient tradition, from the Roman Kingdom to the Triumvirate, and offered a short description of their contents.[19] Here Sigonio gave much importance to the first book of Appian's *Civil Wars* that describes the social consequences of Roman expansion in Italy, and so does Beaufort. Both seem to prefer Appian to other sources.[20] Sigonio knew Appian's text well, and probably used Carolus Stephanus' *editio princeps* (1551).[21] Unlike Machiavelli and many others, he considered Appian a very reliable source for the reconstruction of the agrarian and economic history of Roman Italy. Beaufort follows this appraisal of Appian, which became predominant again in the nineteenth and twentieth centuries.[22]

Beaufort however diverges from Sigonio about chronology, as may be expected. Sigonio completely followed the traditional dates of Roman history. He provided a synthetic but exhaustive abridgement of the agrarian laws under the Republic. If his critical reading of the texts was very careful and rigorous, his reconstruction of the historical context may seem a bit sketchy: Sigonio does not appear greatly concerned to define the proper background of each law, but only reconstructs as far as possible their contents by comparing every single attestation. His study of the agrarian laws is subordinate to the purpose of exposing the ways in which the Romans managed their lands after the colonization of Italy. Beaufort changes that historical approach. He is not interested in any single agrarian statute (and of course he is sceptical as to the reliability of

[18] Beaufort, *La république* (n 8) 3.6, vol 1, 240–44; 'Considérations' (n 10) art 6, vol 2, 415–17; cf Sigonio, *De antiquo iure ciuium Romanorum libri II* (Giordano Ziletti 1560) 2.16 (hereafter Sigonio, *De antiquo iure ciuium*); *De antiquo iure Italiae* (n 15) 2.2.

[19] See Chapter 3 in this volume by Rich.

[20] Appian, *Civil Wars* 1.7.26–1.8.33. Compare Sigonio, *De antiquo iure Italiae* (n 15) 2.2, 67 with Beaufort, 'Considérations' (n 10) art 6, vol 2, 417.

[21] William McCuaig, *Carlo Sigonio. The Changing World of the Late Renaissance* (Princeton University Press 1989) 9. Machiavelli and earlier generations of humanists were mostly dependent on the Latin version by Pier Candido Decembrio (1452–54): see Edmund B Fryde, *Humanism and Renaissance Historiography* (Hambledon Press 1983) 104–05; Massimo Zaggia, 'La traduzione latina da Appiano di Pier Candido Decembrio: per la storia della tradizione' (1993) 34 Studi Medievali 193–243; Lintott, *Constitution* (n 11) 239.

[22] See Gianfranco Tibiletti, 'Il possesso dell'ager publicus e le norme de modo agrorum sino ai Gracchi' (1948–49) 26 Athenaeum 173–236; 27 Athenaeum 3–42. In the nineteenth century, Appian was much appreciated by, for instance, Karl Marx (*Letters*, 27.02.1861), whose classical formation was based on Niebuhr's *Roman History*.

the most ancient attestations) but in the notion of *lex agraria* as such and in the political struggles that followed the proposal of a land reform. Beaufort treats the agrarian law twice, in two extended passages that constitute a chronologically ordered discussion in which he argues that the grievances of the people against the 'grandees' were well founded and pursued with moderation by the tribunes.[23] He stresses the link between the *lex Licinia de modo agrorum* (traditionally dated to 367 BCE) and the *lex agraria* of the Gracchi much more than Sigonio does.[24] Here, Beaufort's work is more a political treatise than a study in ancient history: being interested in the consequences of the struggle around the proposal of land laws, and notably in the conflicts between the parts of the republican constitution (senate, magistrates, assemblies), Beaufort essentially builds a political history of agrarian legislation.

In this context, Beaufort may have been influenced by Montesquieu's notion of equality. In his *Considerations on the Causes of the Greatness of the Romans and their Decline*, Montesquieu affirms that the greatness of the ancient republics consisted in granting to their citizens a fair access to the resources. Rome, during its Republican history, was able to maintain a high and steady level of military participation thanks to this equality: the equal partition of lands, encouraged by the agrarian laws, gave rise to an efficient army, because soldiers were strongly motivated to protect their own possessions as well as those of the state. This harmony of interests permitted the city-state Rome to prevail against bigger and more populous states that were ruled by despotic governments where the king and a restricted aristocracy monopolized wealth (for Montesquieu, the comparison between the Hellenistic kingdoms and eighteenth-century absolutism is manifest).[25] In the *Spirit of the Laws*, he further illustrates this concept with more examples taken from the history of

[23] Beaufort, *La république* (n 8) 3.6 ('considérations sur les comices'); and then in the 'Considérations' (n 10) art 6: 'de la loi agraire ou du partage des terres'.

[24] Several ancient authors state that the *lex Sempronia* of 133 BCE reformed a previous, obsolete law that most of them identified with the plebiscite of C. Licinius Stolo passed in the fourth century BCE (except for Cato the Elder and Appian, who do not specify its promoter). The *lex Licinia* has been sometimes interpreted in the light of the terms and purposes of the *lex Sempronia*. To the pre-Gracchan rule are ascribed some clauses very similar to the Sempronian law (for instance the supposed seizure of lands), and of course the specific aim of recovering *ager publicus* (to be subsequently divided among poor people). No such provisions are attested for the Licinian law, whose original background is completely lost (apart from the traditional and ambiguous reference to the Conflict of the Orders). We only know that the archaic law set a limit on landholding and, perhaps, on cattle breeding, and envisaged a fine for offenders. This indefiniteness, as well as the statement that the Gracchi wanted to restore and reform a prior rule, has much helped the overlapping of the two laws. For further documentation see Mattia Balbo, 'La *lex Licinia de modo agrorum*: riconsiderazione di un modello storiografico' (2010) 138 Rivista di Filologia e di Istruzione Classica 265–311 (hereafter Balbo, 'La *lex Licinia*').

[25] Charles-Louis de Secondat, Baron de La Brède et de Montesquieu, *Considérations sur les causes de la grandeur des Romains et de leur decadence* (Jacques Desbordes 1734) 21–24.

the Greek *poleis*.[26] Montesquieu considers the *leges Licinia* and *Sempronia* as fair measures, and supposes that they were adopted in order to limit the monopolization of landholding and to grant a reasonably balanced access to the resources, with the aim to increase military recruitment (the source is again Appian). Montesquieu is not suggesting a communist view *ante litteram*, nor does he propose to replace private properties with collective tenures; he simply remarks that a fair property status would increase the power of the state, drawing on the ancient ideal of the citizen-soldier.

Montesquieu's remarks on land laws are very short and lack detail, but his general view of the plebeian movement certainly influenced Beaufort's attitude towards the political claims of the plebs. Beaufort further stresses the intrinsic benefit of the agrarian reforms for the people. His argument can be summarized as follows: the land distribution envisaged by the Gracchi only hurt a small part of the aristocrats and benefitted the multitude of poor citizens. Therefore, when viewed from a costs and benefits point of view, the land reform was beneficial to the whole community.[27] It should be noted that Beaufort, to illustrate the reasonableness of Tiberius Gracchus' proposal, does not identify the recipients of the *lex Sempronia agraria* as the needy plebs of Rome, often considered as an easy prey to riots and as sensitive to the blandishments of demagogues (if anything, Gaius Gracchus' *lex frumentaria* was addressed to these plebs); rather, he specifically singles out the class of citizen–soldiers who had become impoverished after the richest aristocrats had encroached on the lands with the consent of the senate.[28]

These so-called *assidui* of the fifth class are therefore interpreted as a sort of 'middle class', distinct, even politically, from the *proletarii*. Such a specification helps Beaufort to better defend Montesquieu's sympathy for the plebs and to solve some problems posed by several alternative theories, notably that of Machiavelli, who was much more critical towards the policy of the tribunes. Machiavelli pragmatically recognized the usefulness of some agrarian norms, namely the practical importance of a limit on landholding (*lex Licinia*), that he

[26] Charles-Louis de Secondat, Baron de La Brède et de Montesquieu, *De l'esprit des lois* (2nd edn, 1768) 5.5, 7.2, 16.15, discussed by John Rich, 'Lex Licinia, Lex Sempronia: B.G. Niebuhr and the limitation of landholding in the Roman Republic' in Luuk de Ligt and Simon Northwood (eds), *People, Land and Politics. Demographic Developments and the Transformation of Roman Italy, 300 BC–AD 14* (Brill 2008) 528–29 (hereafter Rich, 'Lex Licinia, Lex Sempronia').

[27] Beaufort, *La république* (n 8) 3.6, vol 1, 241–42. On Beaufort's sympathy for the plebeians cf Ridley, *Gibbon's Complement* (n 1) 138–39.

[28] Beaufort, *La république* (n 8) 3.6, vol 1, 237–38. Although Beaufort sometimes seems to contradict himself, as when he affirms that the poorest urban plebeians were concerned by agrarian distributions ('Considérations' (n 10) art 6, vol 2, 416), it is clear enough that in his mind, the Gracchan programme was mainly directed to the *assidui*.

considered a manner to prevent the excessive enrichment of individuals at the detriment of the state.[29] However, Machiavelli ascribed to the agrarian laws of the Gracchi the fault of having excited, with the promise of land distribution, an immoderate desire among the poor people to become rich, stirring up the plebs against the senate. In contrast, Beaufort follows the ancient sources (notably Appian and Plutarch) that report Tiberius Gracchus' worries about manpower and the traditional military recruitment and so affirms that the agrarian reform intended to protect smallholdings.[30] By clarifying this point, he can refute the claim of demagogy and sedition often assigned to the Gracchi.[31]

Beaufort continues to give a positive interpretation of the legislative activity of the plebeian tribunes. First of all, he justifies the 'seditious' behaviour of the Gracchi by asserting that it was an inevitable reaction both to the pressing social-economic issues of Roman Italy and to the deafness of the senators towards demands for reform. In order to prevent riots, the senate permitted some minor viritane distributions or promoted colonial foundations, but harshly opposed any comprehensive programme of a fairer reorganization of the agrarian landscape of Italy.[32] The agrarian measures of the senate were one-time provisions, rather than large-scale reforms. Beaufort considers the tribunate as the real promoter of social change and, subsequently, as the institution that, more than others, cared for the general interest of the state. In other words, as regards agrarian policy, the senate protected the interests of its members, whilst the tribunate helped Rome to sustain the needs of its citizen–soldiers.[33]

Such a reappraisal is absent in Montesquieu, who seems to prefer Machiavelli's judgement on the political conduct of the plebeian tribunes. Rousseau, by contrast, assigns a fundamental role to the tribunate in his *Social Contract*, since he considers it as a fundamental mediator between different powers that prevents the breaking of the institutional balance.[34] There is no

[29] Compare Niccolò Machiavelli, *Discorsi* 1.37 with Beaufort, *La république* (n 8) 3.6, vol 1, 237, both stressing the strategy of keeping individual citizens poor.

[30] Appian, *Civil Wars* 1.9.35; 11.45; Plutarch, *Tiberius Gracchus* 9.4. cf Daniel J Gargola, 'The Gracchan Reform and Appian's Representation of an Agrarian Crisis' in Luuk de Ligt and Simon Northwood (eds), *People, Land and Politics. Demographic Developments and the Transformation of Roman Italy, 300 BC–AD 14* (Brill 2008) 487.

[31] Most early modern antiquarian writers followed Cicero's (and Machiavelli's) famous opinion on the Gracchi in Cicero, *De legibus* 3.19: '[the tribunician power] seems to me truly pestilent, as you might expect from something born in sedition and for sedition'. On Cicero's opinion on the Gracchi, see Jean Béranger, 'Les jugements de Cicéron sur les Gracques' (1972) 1 ANRW 732–63. On early modern attitudes to the tribunate see Nelson, *The Greek Tradition* (n 11) 49–86; a good summary of the modern positions can be found in Lanfranchi, *Les tribuns de la plèbe* (n 9) 1–30.

[32] Beaufort, *La république* (n 8) 3.6, vol 1, 236; 'Considérations' (n 10) art 6, vol 2, 417.

[33] Beaufort, *La république* (n 8) 4.7, vol 1, 361–62.

[34] Jean-Jacques Rousseau, *The Social Contract* (Christopher Betts tr, Oxford University Press 1999) 151–53. cf Mouza Raskolnikoff, *Des Anciens et des Modernes* (Publications de la Sorbonne 1990) 97–99, 156; Lanfranchi, *Les tribuns de la plèbe* (n 9) 14.

conclusive evidence if Beaufort's positive reappraisal of the tribunate is based on Rousseau, but he clearly shares Rousseau's positive view of the tribunes, as in his judgement on the Gracchi: 'Their aims could have been right and praiseworthy; and if we find in their conduct many blameable things, we can impute them to the ardour by which they strove to accomplish their task, that was every day obstructed by new obstacles.'[35] However, Beaufort does not explicitly ascribe a contemporary relevance to the Roman model: in the *Republic*, he does not take the *lex Sempronia agraria* as a pretext to claim a land reform in modern Europe. Yet it may be argued that Beaufort's scholarly analysis paved the way for more topical readings of the example of Rome in the Age of Revolutions.

Indeed, some years after the publication of the *Republic*, the Scottish historian Adam Ferguson published his renowned *History of the Progress and Termination of the Roman Republic* (1783), in which he affirms that both the Licinian and Sempronian laws envisaged a limitation of private property, according to a 'Montesquieu-fashioned' principle of equality.[36] Ferguson recognizes that the equal partition of land is perfectly suitable, and very desirable, for small states, but he admits that it is difficult and dangerous to impose such a reform in a bigger empire, where the social gap has become too large (there is a bit of Machiavelli's realism in this specification). The hypothesis that the agrarian law affected private properties in order to reallocate the wealth had been proposed in the previous centuries, and was now further popularized by Ferguson. This intellectual development reached a climax during the French Revolution with the proposal by François-Noël Babeuf (1760–97) to abolish landed property. Babeuf had a solid training in fiscal matters thanks to his experience as *commissaire à terrier* (a sort of land surveyor) in Picardy, where he experienced the large social inequalities of the Ancien Régime. Inspired by Rousseau's *Discourse on Inequality* (that moreover considers private property as the first inequality in the history of the world, the origin of all social differences), [37] Babeuf sponsored a radical reform during the Revolution that envisaged the replacement of private property with collective tenures. His interest in

[35] Beaufort, *La république* (n 8) vol 1, 242.

[36] Adam Ferguson, *The History of the Progress and Termination of the Roman Republic* (Strahan 1783) 2.2, 283–85.

[37] Jean-Jacques Rousseau, *The Discourses and Other Early Political Writings* (Victor Gourevitch tr, Cambridge University Press 1997) 161: 'The first man who, having enclosed a piece of ground, to whom it occurred to say *this is mine*, and found people sufficiently simple to believe him, was the true founder of civil society. How many crimes, wars, murders, how many miseries and horrors Mankind would have been spared by him who, pulling up the stakes or filling in the ditch, had cried out to his kind: Beware of listening to this impostor; You are lost if you forget that the fruits are everyone's and the Earth no one's.' On Rousseau's account of property, see Peter Garnsey, *Thinking about Property. From Antiquity to the Age of Revolution* (Cambridge University Press 2007) 159–65.

classical models, notably the Roman Republic, is well known: he adopted the surname Gracchus, called his third-born son Gaius (as a tribute to the most 'revolutionary' of the Gracchi brothers), and founded a newspaper named *Le tribun du peuple*, which acted as a megaphone for the programme of the *Society of the Equals* that blamed both Robespierre and the Directory that succeeded him for not having adopted a veritable reform of landholding after the formal abolition of feudalism. Baubeuf thought the *lex Sempronia* limited private property (he might have taken this idea from Machiavelli, or also partly from Montesquieu) and intended to impose in France an updated model of this restriction.[38]

Among the first and most resolute opponents of Babeuf's ideals was the German academic Christian Gottlob Heyne (1729–1812). In 1793 he published a virulent pamphlet in which he reaffirmed that the Roman state would never have limited private property but rather the individual occupation of lands that legally belonged to it, namely public lands.[39] Thus, Heyne intended to remove the most powerful argument of those who were proposing the return to a supposed ancient communism, notably the idea that the fundamental character of the Roman Republic consisted in the limitation of private landholdings. Heyne's work in turn contributed to the development of the new vision on Roman agrarian history propagated by Niebuhr.

Niebuhr: A New Juridical Approach

The life of Barthold Georg Niebuhr (1776–1831) is well known, as is the genesis of his famous *Roman History*. This masterpiece contains two full treatises on the agrarian laws. In the first edition from 1812, there is a long discussion on agrarian legislation (*Das agrarische Recht*) as part of the analysis of the Licinian-Sextian laws.[40] In the second edition from 1830, this discussion is shortened and highlighted, with the meaningful title *Vom gemeinen Feld und dessen Nutzung* (*On Public Land and its Occupation*), in the context of the agrarian proposal made by Spurius Cassius in 486 BCE.[41] The same choice

[38] On Babeuf's inspiration cf Andrea Giardina and André Vauchez, *Il mito di Roma. Da Carlo Magno a Mussolini* (Laterza 2000) 131; Lanfranchi, *Les tribuns de la plèbe* (n 9) 1n1, 8n20.

[39] It was entitled *Leges agrariae pestiferae et execrabiles*, and then reprinted several times before it appeared as Christian G Heyne, *Opuscula academica collecta et animadversionibus locupletata* (Dieterich 1796) vol 4, 350–73.

[40] Barthold G Niebuhr, *Römische Geschichte* (Realschulbuchhandlung 1811–12) vol 2, 349–94 (= Niebuhr, *The Roman History* (n 3) vol 2, 353–95).

[41] Barthold G Niebuhr, *Römische Geschichte* (2nd edn, Reimer 1828–32) vol 2, 146–76 (= Niebuhr, *The History of Rome* (n 3) vol 2, 130–55; plus Appendix I at 620–33).

occurs in Niebuhr's *Bonn Lectures* (posthumously published), and stems from his wish to outline a common thread to all occurrences of any agrarian issue in the history of the Roman Republic.[42]

Niebuhr was born in Denmark, in a German family, and after his early studies he became private secretary of the Danish Finance Minister, Count Schimmelmann, a reformist politician.[43] During the Napoleonic era, he continued his education in Great Britain (in London and Edinburgh) and then returned to Copenhagen, where he held several financial offices, until he entered in 1806 into the service of the Prussian government, always with duties relating to public finances. In 1810 a sharp disagreement with chancellor Hardenberg led to his resignation from the Prussian ministry. During the following two years he gave lectures at the University of Berlin, which were published as the *Roman History*. Then, he returned to public life, serving as Prussian Ambassador in Rome (1816–23). In 1825 he finally retired to Bonn, resuming an academic life (although not holding a regular university post) and producing the radically revised new edition of the *Roman History*.

Although Niebuhr retired from public engagement, he nevertheless remained concerned with the political matters of his time, not only in Germany. He supported the first timid attempts at a liberal government in France (led by Martignac) and feared that the July Revolution of 1830 could brusquely stop any reformist progress and plunge Europe back into war.[44] The political context of the early nineteenth century also influenced his strong interest in agrarian issues. First of all, Niebuhr felt the influence of the historiographical debate of the later Enlightenment on ancient property: as he publicly admitted, he was influenced by Heyne's arguments against radical thinkers such as Babeuf.[45] Yet the background against which he composed his *Roman*

[42] Barthold G Niebuhr, *Vorträge über römische Geschichte, an der Universität zu Bonn gehalten* (Meyer Isler ed, Reimer 1846–48) vol 1, 251–59 (= Niebuhr, *Lectures* (n 3) vol 1, 250–58).

[43] On Niebuhr's biography see Seppo Rytkönen, *Barthold Georg Niebuhr als Politiker und Historiker. Zeitgeschehen und Zeitgeist in der geschichtlichen Beurteilungen von B.G. Niebuhr* (Suomalainen Tiedeakatemia 1968); Alfred Heuss, *Barthold Georg Niebuhrs wissenschaftliche Anfänge. Untersuchungen und Mitteilungen über die Kopenhagener Manuscripte und zur europäischen Tradition der lex agraria (loi agraire)* (Vandenhoeck & Ruprecht 1981) (hereafter Heuss, *Barthold Georg Niebuhrs wissenschaftliche Anfänge*); James Q Whitman, *The Legacy of Roman Law in the German Romantic Era* (Princeton University Press 1990); Gerrit Walther, *Niebuhrs Forschung* (Steiner Verlag 1993); Arnaldo Momigliano, 'New Paths of Classicism in the Nineteenth Century' in Glen W Bowersock and Tim J Cornell (eds), *Studies on Modern Scholarship* (University of California Press 1994) 223–85; Rich, 'Lex Licinia, Lex Sempronia' (n 26).

[44] For an interesting political biography of Niebuhr, see the appendix to the Italian version of his *Roman History*: *Storia romana* (Bizzoni 1832–33) vol 2, 371–419: 'Vita e studi di Niebuhr.' On his reaction to the July Revolution see also John E Sandys, *A History of Classical Scholarship* (Cambridge University Press 1908) vol 3, 78.

[45] Niebuhr, *The History of Rome* (n 3) vol 2, 133. See also Rich, 'Lex Licinia, Lex Sempronia' (n 26) 534.

History was particularly related to the reformist demands that circulated in the German states at the beginning of the nineteenth century as a consequence of the Napoleonic experience. Niebuhr was especially interested in the movement for serf emancipation against feudal privileges. Such a reform took place in Denmark in 1788, in 1796 serf emancipation was also proposed in Holstein (Niebuhr's home region, which was under Danish rule at the time), but it was only adopted in 1804, after a harsh struggle between reformers and conservatives; eventually, Prussia, where Niebuhr made a political career, also abolished serfdom in 1807. As a public officer with financial duties, Niebuhr's political engagement with the reformist agenda pushed his scholarly interest towards the study of ancient land laws. While the claim for the abolition of landed property almost ceased with the end of Babeuf's movement in 1797, the reform of the legal relationships between landlords and farmers remained an important concern at the beginning of the nineteenth century. This ongoing relevance of the agrarian issue made Niebuhr pay specific attention to agrarian regulations in his *Roman History*.

It is commonly accepted that Niebuhr's major contribution to this topic consists in a reconsideration of the main categories employed to define Roman legislation. He was fascinated by the important innovations that affected juridical thought at the beginning of the nineteenth century, especially thanks to the contribution of his friend (and mentor) Friedrich von Savigny, whose importance Niebuhr mentions explicitly.[46] Initially, Niebuhr intended to compose a specific treatise on agrarian regulations, modelled on Montesquieu's *Spirit of the Laws*. Its title was to be *Geist der Gesetze des Landeigentums* (*Spirit of the Laws of Landed Property*), and it would provide, among other things, a methodical analysis of the history of the Roman *ager publicus* and its rules, with appropriate comparisons with modern Europe. The two *excursus* on the agrarian laws in his *Roman History* are what remains of this original project.[47]

Niebuhr's starting question concerns the proper field of application of Roman agrarian regulations, as well as the different legal forms of landholding. His central thesis is that every agrarian law introduced by the Roman state concerned only the *ager publicus*, and he provides an exhaustive reconstruction of the legal features of this kind of land. He clearly defines the different forms of

[46] Niebuhr, *The Roman History* (n 3) vol 2, 372 n88; Niebuhr, *The History of Rome* (n 3) vol 2, 149 n316, 152. Savigny in turn acknowledges Niebuhr's theses in the third edition of his treatise on the law of *possessio* (1818): Friedrich C von Savigny, *Das Recht des Besitzes. Eine civilistische Abhandlung* (6th edn, Heyer 1837) 215–24.

[47] There are also two manuscripts, written between 1803 and 1806, that contain some materials of this project and are partially published in Heuss, *Barthold Georg Niebuhrs wissenschaftliche Anfänge* (n 43) 501–05, 530–31. cf Rich, 'Lex Licinia, Lex Sempronia' (n 26) 524.

landholding, starting from the notion of *possessio* attested in Festus (following Savigny) and from the descriptions provided by the Latin *agrimensores*.[48] Therefore, he gives a legal definition of what a *lex agraria* is, stating that it can only affect the properties of the state (*ager publicus populi Romani*). According to Niebuhr and Savigny, Roman law (*ius*) did not consider any limitation of the *dominium ex iure Quiritium*, which was instead left to the private initiative of individuals.

The 1830 *excursus* starts with a clear statement in which Niebuhr aims to refute what he regarded as the great misconception of his era that the agrarian rules affected private lands, mobilizing the scholarly tradition since Sigonio:

> It is not exactly true that the agrarian law of Cassius was the earliest so called. Every law by which the commonwealth disposed of its public land, bore that name; as for instance that by which the domain of the kings was parcelled out among the commonalty, and those by which colonies were planted. Even in the narrower sense, of a law whereby the state exercised its ownership in removing the old possessors from a part of its domain, and making over its right of property therein, such a law existed among those of Servius Tullius. In the room of these significations, very general currency has been given to the term, *an agrarian law*, in the sense of an enactment relating to the landed property of all the citizens, setting a limit to it, and assigning all beyond that limit to the destitute. The regulation of Cleomenes, the equal partition of land demanded by the frantic levellers in the French Revolution, are termed agrarian laws . . . This misconception is as old as the revival of philology. Neither Sigonius nor Manutius doubted that the tribunes had limited landed property to 500 jugers, and had assigned the excess to the poorer citizens: nor had Beaufort any other notion, nor Hooke; though they all had the statement before their eyes, that the measure referred to the conquered lands, which the Greek historians insist on as so essential a point. They only mention this by way of explaining how such vast estates could have arisen. That there was a kind of landed property to which no limit had been set, they had no conception. Yet every one of them must have been aware that there was a riddle to be solved here: but they tacitly gave it up. Ferguson on the other hand never perceived that there was one: nor did Machiavel, or Montesquieu; the value of whose reflections on Roman history is no way affected by their mistakes as to the historical facts.[49]

[48] Festus 260–262 L; Hyg. Grom. *cond. agr.* 74–80 Th.; Sic. Flac. *cond. agr.* 100–02 Th.; *quaest. agr.* 116–17 Th.; *divis. et ass.* 118–20 Th.

[49] Niebuhr, *The History of Rome* (n 3) vol 2, 130–31.

These words are quite renowned and have been widely debated, and they show how the specific application of the Roman agrarian laws had become an important topic in the revolutionary context and the rising demands for a radical reform of land tenure.[50] Were the limits of the agrarian laws applied to public lands only, or also to private property? Among the authors cited by Niebuhr, only Ferguson clearly stated that both the Licinian restriction and the Sempronian reform affected private property.[51] Sigonio and Beaufort considered the public land as the main field of application of the agrarian measures. As regards colonization and viritane distributions, Sigonio spoke about the conquered lands that belong to the republic,[52] and Beaufort explicitly stated, at least once, that land laws affected the public domain. Yet Beaufort did not discuss this problem further, making it seem as if he had forgotten it, or rather that he did not judge it as important.[53] In any case, his statements are too brief to ascertain that he held that limits were only applied to *ager publicus*, the position taken by Niebuhr.

The notion that the *ius ciuile* could not conceive a limitation of private enterprise fits with Niebuhr's liberal conception of history, and his theory on the *ager publicus* gave rise to a long debate. Following Niebuhr, German scholarship in the first half of the nineteenth century started to explore more deeply

[50] See for instance Momigliano, 'New Paths' (n 43) 231–32; Ronald T Ridley, '*Leges agrariae*: Myths Ancient and Modern' (2000) 95 Classical Philology 459–67 (hereafter Ridley, '*Leges agrariae*'); Rich, 'Lex Licinia, Lex Sempronia' (n 26) 526–43; Balbo, 'La *lex Licinia*' (n 24) 265–311; Luigi Capogrossi Colognesi, *Padroni e contadini nell'Italia repubblicana* ("L'Erma" di Bretschneider 2012) 77–84.

[51] See the excellent discussion in Rich, 'Lex Licinia, Lex Sempronia' (n 26) 527–43.

[52] Sigonio, *De antiquo iure Italiae* (n 15) 2.2, 64–66: 'I found there was plenty of land of both kinds, either obviously taken from enemies and not yet given back to the public, or public land of the Roman people and thus possessed by the Roman people itself, or land that was in fact public but seized clandestinely by mighty citizens, or, finally, land bought with public money for the sake of dividing it. . . For if any division of land took place in the meantime [after the Licinian-Sextian Laws], it was not a division of private property, but of land taken from enemies or declared property of the Roman people' (Isabelle Buhre tr). See also Sigonio, *De antiquo iure ciuium* (n 18) 1.16, 71: 'Since the [Licinian] Law was not observed, causing great damage to the Roman plebs, the tribune Tiberius Gracchus decided to re-enact it with a new provision: in the 620th year of Rome, under the consulate of Scaevola and Piso, he ordered that nobody could hold more than 500 *iugera* of *ager publicus*, as it was already stated by the Licinian law' (the English translation is mine). That Sigonio envisaged the Licinian restriction as relating to public land is also confirmed by his assertions that this law implemented the Cassian law on public possessions: *De antiquo iure Italiae* (n 15) 2.2, 217, 219.

[53] Beaufort, *La république* (n 8) 3.6, vol 1, 240: 'In order to understand the reasons why the Senate was so intolerant towards any proposal of land distribution, we have to know what land was concerned. When the Romans had conquered a territory, they added to the domain belonging to the Commonwealth the lands that previously belonged to the conquered people, who lost part of their estates as well.' On this passage see Ridley, '*Leges agrariae*' (n 50) 464. However, in his main discussion of the agrarian laws Beaufort just speaks about 'land partition', without defining which kind of land he intends. Whereas he is clear that the Cassian law sought to reclaim *ager publicus* held by rich *possessores* and holds that the failure to implement it led to the Licinian law, he only speaks of the Licinian law as 'limiting the possessions of the rich' (3.6) and says nothing to suggest that its application was restricted to *ager publicus*. cf Rich, 'Lex Licinia, Lex Sempronia' (n 26) 531 n38.

the genesis of the *ager publicus* and its relationship with agrarian rules. Some of the most important scholars were very critical of Niebuhr's model, including Georg Huschke (1801–86), Adolf Rudorff (1803–73), and Rudolf Jhering (1818–92), who all thought that the Licinian norms could have set various kinds of restrictions on any form of landholding.[54] On the other hand, the 'pandectist' Georg F Puchta (1798–1846) continued to assert that the agrarian reforms intended to limit only private property.[55] The question about the forms of land tenure became increasingly dominant in the historiography, with Niebuhr's model being part of a wider reconsideration of Roman law. Theodor Mommsen particularly contributed to the affirmation of Niebuhr's thesis on land laws, followed by Benedikt Niese (1849–1910), who reproduced the idea that land laws only regarded *ager publicus*.[56] This interpretation became almost universal. For example, in the twentieth century a famous study by Gianfranco Tibiletti further developed the hypothesis on the ways of managing public lands in ancient Rome. Starting from the idea that every restriction was related to the *ager publicus*, he judged that an archaic Licinian law could not contain a 500-*iugera* individual limit, because such an amount only matched the extent of the *ager Romanus* in the second century BCE; and, therefore, the ancient sources might have anticipated a late Republican clause (the 'sceptical' Beaufort would have appreciated such an argument).[57] This example illustrates how Niebuhr's approach has effectively changed our perception of Roman history. Recently, the consensus around Niebuhr's model has been challenged, and several scholars are now starting to reconsider the application of some archaic measures beyond the theoretical dualism between *dominium* and *ager publicus* (which seems more fitting to the middle and late Republic). If we reconsider

[54] Philipp Ed Huschke, *Ueber die Stelle des Varro von den Liciniern (de re rust. I, 2. §. 9), nebst einer Zugabe über Fest. v. Possessiones und Possessio. Zwei Abhandlungen aus dem Gebiete der Alterthumswissenschaft und Rechtsgeschichte* (JCB Mohr 1835); Adolf AF Rudorff, *Römische Rechtsgeschichte* (Bernhard Tauchnitz 1857) vol 1, 38–39; Rudolf von Jhering, *Geist des römischen Rechts auf den verschiedenen Stufen seiner Entwicklung* (Breitkopf und Härtel 1854) 2.1, 247–48.

[55] Georg F Puchta, *Cursus der Institutionen* I (Breitkopf und Härtel 1841) 202–04, 272–73; Georg F Puchta, 'Remarks on Professor Long's Paper on the Licinian Law *de modo agri*' (1846) 3 Classical Museum 67–77.

[56] Theodor Mommsen, *Römische Geschichte* (3rd edn, Weidmann 1861) vol 1, 294, 301; Benedictus Niese, 'Das sogenannte Licinisch-Sextische Ackergesetz' (1888) Hermes 410.

[57] Tibiletti, 'Il possesso' (n 22) 5–14. His argument is essentially the following: the cattle clause (Cato, *Pro Rhodiensibus* frg. 167 Malc.; Appian, *Civil Wars* 1.8.33) allows 1,800 *iugera* more (estimated at the mean consumption of grazing land), that should be added to the previous 500 (which are reserved to agriculture). Thus, the individual limit should reach the amount of 2,300 *iugera* (575 ha), which seems too large for the *ager Romanus* in the fourth century BCE. Such an extent could only apply to the beginning of the second century BCE, after the Hannibalic War. On Tibiletti's sources see Dario Mantovani 'L'occupazione dell'ager publicus e le sue regole prima del 367 a.C.' (1997) 85 Athenaeum 575–98; on the twentieth-century historiography see esp. Capogrossi Colognesi, *Padroni e contadini* (n 50) 1–60, and his contribution in Chapter 6 of this volume.

the ancient sources, we may assume that the original Licinian limit applied to all landholdings, public and private, and that the second-century practice (as the Gracchan reform) only considered the *ager publicus*.[58]

If Niebuhr's contribution is crucial to the modern understanding of Roman land reforms, his analysis of colonization had less impact. He included extensive sections on Latins, colonies, and *municipia* only in the second edition of his *Roman History*, replacing the brief account of the Latin League in the first edition,[59] and clearly planned a more detailed treatment which he never completed, except for the sketch on the political rights of the allies included in the third volume.[60] Perhaps Niebuhr came to feel that his discussion of this topic in his first edition was inadequate. However, he gives no overt hints as to how he reached this conclusion. The only modern writer he cites in these sections is Machiavelli, who was already known to him when he composed the first edition.[61] Savigny's influence could have played a part in this decision, as it did for the juridical treatment of the agrarian laws. Savigny delivered an important lecture on Latinity in 1812, and another on *ius Italicum* in 1814, challenging aspects of Sigonio's account; it is likely that Niebuhr knew these works and that he may have been inspired by them.[62]

In the second book of the *Roman History*, Niebuhr devotes a short chapter to the properly called Roman colonies, outlining some important features of Roman colonial practice.[63] Due to his interest in the whole of ancient history, he establishes an interesting comparison between Greek and Roman colonizations. Greek colonies, he argues, originated from a secession within the citizen body of the mother city and, as a result, the new *polis* was almost

[58] I have followed this hypothesis in Balbo, 'La *lex Licinia*' (n 24) and Mattia Balbo, '*Lex tam acerba*: la sanzione per i trasgressori del modus agrorum nella Roma repubblicana' (2014) 142 Rivista di Filologia e di Istruzione Classica 75–90. For the application of the Licinian restriction to all landholding see Wolfgang Kunkel, *Staatsordnung und Staatspraxis der römischen Republik, II: Der Magistratur* (Beck 1995) 493–97; Rich, 'Lex Licinia, Lex Sempronia' (n 26) 546–52; Saskia Roselaar, *Public Land in the Roman Republic. A Social and Economic History of Ager Publicus in Italy, 396–89 BC* (Oxford University Press 2010) 95–112. cf also Luigi Capogrossi Colognesi 'Le radici storiche della lex Licinia de modo agrorum' in Cosimo Cascione and Carla Masi Doria (eds), *Fides humanitas ius: Studii in onore di Luigi Labruna* (Editoriale scientifica 2007) vol 2, 677–94 and Capogrossi Colognesi, *Padroni e contadini* (n 50) 77–83, who cautiously admits such an alternative to Niebuhr's theory. On the contrary, Dominic W Rathbone 'The Control and Exploitation of *ager publicus* in Italy under the Roman Republic' in Jean-Jacques Aubert (ed), *Tâches publiques et entreprise privée dans le monde romain, Actes du Diplôme d'Études Avancées* (Université de Neuchâtel 2003) 135–78, esp. 143–49, 159–62 prefers to suppose, like Puchta, that it applied only to private land and that it was introduced only at the beginning of the third century BCE.

[59] Niebuhr, *The Roman History* (n 3) vol 1, 384–89.

[60] ibid vol 3, 523–47 (unfinished).

[61] ibid vol 2, 47.

[62] They were first published in 1816 and 1818 in the Transactions of the Berlin Academy, and then reprinted in Friedrich C von Savigny, *Vermischte Schriften* (Veit und Comp 1850) vol 1, 14–80.

[63] Niebuhr, *The History of Rome* (n 3) vol 2, 43–49.

independent; the Roman ones, instead, were planned and directly sponsored by Rome in order to extend and maintain its domination. Therefore, if the Greek cities must be considered as separate states (with their own history), Rome and its colonies were a sole entity. Niebuhr also specifies that Roman colonization should not be considered as a unique case, but rather that it may be part of a wider Italic model (on which he does not expand because of a lack of sources). Significantly, Niebuhr does not address the problem of land allotment in this chapter, nor does he address it later on in the discussion of other kinds of allied towns (Latin colonies and *municipia*). He briefly repeats that colonization contributed to the amount of *ager publicus* and that any colonial settlement included an equal distribution of land to the settlers.[64] Like Beaufort, he notices that these allotments generally did not pose a great political problem for Rome and did not give rise to struggles dangerous for the Republic.

While Niebuhr does not discuss colonization in detail, he pays great attention to other forms of citizenship: Latin Rights and privileges accorded to the Italians. The chapter on colonies is followed by two long sections about the different kinds of relationships established between the Romans and the Italians.[65] Given Niebuhr's strong juridical interest, he extensively discusses the features of the different rights in the Italian communities. He compares Greek and Roman models here as well (see, for instance, the long discussion of *isopoliteia* alongside with *municipium*).[66] Moreover, when dealing with the different kinds of citizenship, Niebuhr does not consider the role of towns and cities, but that of their inhabitants. Thus, the *municipium* is not approached as a single institution, but as the whole of the rights accorded to its members (*municipes*); it is not a Latin colony that enjoys the *ius Latii*, but its citizens, and so on. In other words, Niebuhr considers ancient citizenship as the personal right of the inhabitants of a city, and not as the right of the city itself. This is a subtle, but interesting, distinction. As we have seen, Sigonio and Beaufort approached this problem in the opposite manner, namely by considering citizenship as the right of a precise urban settlement (colony, *municipium*, allied town etc.). They both offered a well-constructed catalogue of the towns that existed in Italy, and their rights. Niebuhr, by contrast, focuses on the peoples.

[64] ibid vol 2, 45; cf vol 3, 531.

[65] ibid vol 2, 50–76 (On the rights of isopolity and municipium); 77–81 (On the franchise of the Latins). The discussion continues in vol 3, 523–47 (Entire subjugation of Italy, and the political rights of the Italian allies).

[66] Central to Niebuhr's thesis here was his use of Dionysius to argue for a parallel between the rights accorded by the Romans and Greek *isopoliteia*; for an attack on this influential view, see Michel Humbert, *Municipium et civitas sine suffragio. L'organization de la conquête jusqu'à la guerre sociale* (École française de Rome 1978) 93–97.

Since Niebuhr's treatment of this subject is incomplete, we can only formulate conjectures in order to explain his approach. First, there might be an obvious philological intent. The ancient sources, when dealing with treatises and privileges, often affirm that these are granted to some peoples (ie the citizens of a community, which may or not be a proper urban settlement). This is more evident in Greek texts (since Niebuhr continues comparing different models) and is, of course, more valid in a study on the Early Republic (as Niebuhr's *Roman History*), when the peoples of Italy were organized within structures very different from each other. The history of the Italian peoples before Rome (and at the beginning of Roman dominion) occupies a great part of the first volume of Niebuhr's *Roman History*, and so the sections on the Italic rights matches with such a historiographical intent.

Second, in order to understand Niebuhr's strong interest in the Italian peoples, we might also consider the political and cultural setting in which he composed his treatise. In the third, unfinished, volume of Niebuhr's *Roman History*, the contemporary political context of the 1820s comes explicitly to the surface in the comparison between the unwisdom of Rome's refusal to extend franchise to the Italians and similar inequalities existing in modern states. In a passage written in 1824, so before Catholic emancipation was enacted in the United Kingdom, Niebuhr makes a specific parallel with the condition of Irish Catholics.[67] Moreover, in the chapter devoted to the integration of Roman Italy, he stresses the importance for the survival of a powerful and stable state of granting political rights at the proper moment. He compares the background that led to the Social War with the contemporary situation in Europe, as he fears that the refusal to gradually reform social inequalities (again he cites the problem of serf emancipation) will lead to a new revolution.[68]

Particularly significant in this context is the development of Romantic nationalism and, especially, the Italian *Risorgimento*. If the Napoleonic era stressed the unifying role of the Roman Empire, upcoming national movements instead focused on the Middle Ages and, as concerns Roman history, the peoples that were included in the empire. In the *Risorgimento*, the ancient notion of Italy (composed of several different peoples) and the Social War were used to define the origins of the modern identity of the

[67] Niebuhr, *The History of Rome* (n 3) vol 3, 537–38 and n969 (the *Roman Catholic Relief Act* was passed in 1829). A similar statement recurs in the first edition, in the chapter about the secession of the plebs, where Irish Catholics are compared to the position of the plebeians in the early Republic: ibid vol 1, 394.

[68] Niebuhr, *The History of Rome* (n 3) vol 3, 537–38.

Italians. As Roman dominion included many cultures, all with their own institutions (reflected in the variety of cities and rights of citizenship accorded by Rome), so modern Italy could rise from the unification of several 'Italian' states. A similar and contemporary process occurred in Germany, even though Niebuhr probably did not have the 'German question' in mind when he was dealing with ancient Italy. Yet in this case as well, Niebuhr can be seen as a forerunner of Mommsen, who was deeply involved in German unification as a member of the Prussian parliament and effectively made the liberal-nationalist approach dominant in Roman historiography.[69]

Conclusion

The close attention to agrarian issues, in particular the agrarian legislation inspired by the popular tribunes, is an important connection between Beaufort and Niebuhr. However, both scholars approached the issue from a different perspective, reflecting the crucial changes of the Revolutionary Era. Beaufort was among the first historians to offer a positive judgement on the Roman plebs and their champions, denying the seditious character of the tribunes' policy and justifying the historical need for their reforms, thus mitigating the revolutionary character of the tribunate in a time when 'revolution' was usually reputed a synonym of 'sedition'. The French Revolution overturned the notion of revolution itself and, subsequently, the Gracchan policy recovered its revolutionary character, but in this case with a new positive meaning. Niebuhr, by contrast, refuted that interpretation of the agrarian laws as totally misleading. Instead, he proposed a reformist view of Roman law: the agrarian measures did not act against the status quo but were simply rules by which the state disposed of its own goods. In other words, Niebuhr normalized a kind of provision that previously was considered as destabilizing. His judgement of the Roman plebs was also positive, but in a different way from more radical thinkers as he perceived the plebeians to be the guardians of the rule of the law. This argument eventually led to Mommsen's notion that the *populus* was the real keeper of sovereignty and the source of law.

[69] Ian Wood, *The Modern Origins of the Early Middle Ages* (Oxford University Press 2013) 175–77; Silvia Giorcelli Bersani, *Torino capitale degli studi seri. Carteggio Theodor Mommsen – Carlo Promis* (Celid 2014) 23–25, 150; Henrik Mouritsen, *Italian Unification. A Study in Ancient and Modern Historiography* (University of London, Institute of Classical Studies 1998) 23–37.

On the other hand, neither Beaufort nor Niebuhr provided a thorough reconsideration of Roman colonization that could be compared to their discussions of agrarian policy. There is still a question to be posed in this regard. If Beaufort and Niebuhr approached the land laws with a political intent, why do they not seem to have considered colonization (namely land distribution that follows colonial foundations) as a solution for the needy? The answer is neither simple nor univocal. As we have seen, Beaufort briefly touches on this aspect (taking it from Sigonio), but he soon moves on, and does not repeat it when dealing with the Gracchan 'revolution'. Niebuhr, instead, applies to the colonial ambit the same interpreting model that he had drafted for the agrarian regulations, but he prefers to focus on the general problem of the rights (including property rights) granted to the peoples in a multi-ethnic state. Both scholars focus on the political meaning of land division, which appears more evident in the struggles around the agrarian reforms than in colonization. Indeed, most of the revolutionary and reformist claims at the end of eighteenth and the beginning of the nineteenth century addressed changes of property situation and power relations inside European countries, requesting a more equal repartition of the existing resources. Colonization, in this context, was of increasingly less relevance, as colonies were perceived as a remedy for overpopulation and not for social inequalities.

Beaufort's and Niebuhr's relative silence on Roman colonization may therefore be seen as a reflection of the demise of the farmer–settler model in European overseas colonialism. European practices of colonization in the eighteenth and nineteenth century proved in fact more suitable to a comparison with Roman Republican provinces than with Roman colonies in Italy. For example, the first Roman provinces were created after commercial penetration and the establishment of various forms of indirect hegemony, which often led to eventual military conquest and territorial annexation. They also entailed the appointment of governors (delegates of the centralized power), and the settlement of few Roman citizens with a very privileged status vis-à-vis the natives. Most provinces of the second century BCE corresponded to territories far from the political centre of the empire and at first they were economically exploited without sharing the benefits of the empire. While Roman colonies were founded in the *ager Romanus*, and so Rome and its colonies could be considered together as a single state or even as a single social and economic setting (as Niebuhr does), modern European colonies turned out to be very different from this model, being located far away from the mother country and more similar to economic protectorates meant for commercial exploitation. Scholars interested in domestic agrarian and social reform around the turn of the nineteenth century would therefore find more inspiration in a reformist programme that set out to change the existing situation within Roman society (which is how the Gracchan attempt can be interpreted) than in the colonial settlements that were central to the Renaissance scholarship of Sigonio.

6

Roman Colonization in Twentieth-Century Historiography

*Luigi Capogrossi Colognesi**

This panoramic survey of the history of twentieth-century studies of Roman Republican colonization focuses on the development of modern ideas on the role and function of Roman colonies, as they were proposed in the twentieth century, thus excluding the more recent contribution made in the last decades.[1] In this study I leave aside the complex problems of colonization in the imperial age, in particular the role played by colonies as a crucial tool for governing the provincial territories. Also, it is important to note that it has not always been easy to draw a clear distinction between historiographical works on Roman colonization and research dedicated instead to the municipal order. The interrelationships between these two histories are so obvious and persistent that there is no need to press the point. The difficulty of tracing clear boundaries has thus forced me to make incursions into neighbouring fields and has led me to reconstruct the paths taken by individual scholars at varying length. In consequence, the potential for omissions, distortions, and misunderstandings has been multiplied by judgments as questionable as they are subjective (frankly, sometimes impressionistic). I am well aware of this, but I can do no more than apologize for my inadequacy: I have taken the risk in the attempt; it is not for me to determine its success.

* This text was translated into English by John Dillon and Jeremia Pelgrom, to whom my deep gratitude and appreciation goes.

[1] I have benefited from the excellent reference point provided by the important essay of Jeremia Pelgrom and Tesse D Stek, 'Roman Colonization under the Republic: Historiographical Contextualization of a Paradigm' in Tesse D Stek and Jeremia Pelgrom (eds), *Roman Republican Colonization. New Perspectives from Archaeology and Ancient History* (Palombi 2014) 10–44 (hereafter Pelgrom and Stek, 'Roman Colonization') which in many ways has set the coordinates within which this chapter has been conceived and around which it revolves. The focus of this chapter will be on the first half of the twentieth century, which spares me from delving into a history that extends into my own generation with the risk of creating a questionable autobiographical narrative. Of course, it has not always been easy to respect this decision: see for example the discussion of Laffi's and Grelle's early work below.

Luigi Capogrossi Colognesi, *Roman Colonization in Twentieth-Century Historiography* In: *The Renaissance of Roman Colonization.* Edited by: Jeremia Pelgrom and Arthur Weststeijn, Oxford University Press (2020). © the Several Contributors.
DOI: 10.1093/oso/9780198850960.003.0006

In reviewing the history of these studies, I had to give much space to institutional problems because of their objective importance as well as their influence on modern studies on these topics. It is also true, however—and the reader deserves to know this—that this may also be partly a distortion caused by my own interests. In fact, I believe it is of paramount importance that we seek to understand how the invention and systematic exploitation of the peculiar institutional and political instrument that was the Roman colony affected the original constitution of the city and the Roman conception of it as the exclusive embodiment of their political and juridical community.

A Promising Start

At the start of the twentieth century, the discourse on Roman colonial structures was very much alive as is demonstrated by the works of two important scholars who both wrote crucial contributions in the form of lexicon entries: Ettore De Ruggiero's article on *colonizzazione* for the *Dizionario Epigrafico*, which appeared between 1896 and 1900,[2] and Ernst Kornemann's entry on *coloniae* for Pauly-Wissowa's *Realencyclopädie* in 1901.[3] With his article on *coloniae*, Kornemann, indisputably one of the foremost post-Mommsen scholars of Roman-Italic political and territorial structures, offered the scholarly world a vast and exhaustive framework for understanding the rich and complex history of the Roman colonial system, comprising a multitude of different types of colonies, established by the Romans in different historical periods and in varying territorial contexts. As a result of its erudite character, this article would remain for a long time an important reference point in Roman colonial studies. Nevertheless, it did not explicitly open up new historiographical perspectives, nor did it encourage independent interpretive hypotheses about the morphology and function of Roman colonization.

Far more important and ground-breaking was the work of the complex scholarly personality of Ettore De Ruggiero, a student of Mommsen from Naples. In an earlier article I took the opportunity to emphasize that despite his heavy reliance on Mommsen, De Ruggiero possessed an original intuition for new problems, which bore fruit only much later.[4] This multifaceted scholarly attitude

[2] Ettore De Ruggiero, 'colonia', *Dizionario Epigrafico II* (1900) (hereafter De Ruggiero, 'colonia'). The article had been published independently under the title *Le colonie dei Romani* (Tipografia dell'Umbria 1896) (hereafter De Ruggiero, *Le colonie*).

[3] Ernst Kornemann, 'coloniae' (1901) *Realencyclopädie IV* (1901) 511–88.

[4] Luigi Capogrossi Colognesi, *De Ruggiero e l'Italia romana* (Arbor Sapientiae 2004), now in Luigi Capogrossi, *Scritti scelti* vol 2 (Jovene 2010) 1199–220. In this article I have already discussed his

is evident in his discussion of Roman colonies in the *Dizionario epigrafico*. Although this lemma clearly shows his deep understanding of the studies of his German teacher, it does not slavishly summarize these teachings. His reliance on Mommsen can be seen in the first part of his paper, where he differentiates three types of Roman colonies—*civium Romanorum*, *Latinorum*, and *peregrinorum*—which reflects Mommsen's general classification of the different juridical forms of settlement know in the Roman world.[5] However, De Ruggiero continues his analysis using an original and multifaceted analytical structure that centres on the difficult-to-translate concept of *comune*: an Italian world which has a technical meaning, referring to a minor municipality inside the modern state, which had a certain autonomous legal status. He differentiates colonies associated with the foundation of a *comune* from those that were not.[6] He further drew attention to cases in which colony status was conferred on an existing community and to cases in which land was reallocated to an existing community that had been weakened demographically and economically. Such reallocations were carried out in forms typical of colonization, facilitating also the integration of a new population in a pre-existing community, but with distinct outcomes each time.

In this respect, De Ruggiero—breaking with the approach of his famous teacher from Berlin—irreparably distanced himself from the rigid view of the jurists, which operated according to logical classifications by *genera et species*. Of course, also for De Ruggiero the two legal entities of Roman colonization, *civitas Romana* and especially *Latinitas*, were fundamental, but this distinction is considered in a less systematic way than in Mommsen's *Staatsrecht*.[7] Although he too had to reduce the complex reality into an artificial framework, a practice already present in the ancient evidence,[8] he was far less rigid in his approach than his predecessors had been.

scholarly ordeal with the *Dizionario epigrafico*, and his anything but secondary, albeit relatively isolated, part in the revival of classical studies in Italy.

[5] See esp De Ruggiero, 'colonia' (n 2) 417.

[6] The first one is subdivided in those that were created as new realities and those that were added to already existing and acknowledged communities. The latter category can be further subdivided in two typologies: those consisting of relocated peoples to whom Rome assigned new territories, like what happened to the *Ligures Baebiani*, and those formed by the more conventional viritane distribution of territory.

[7] Theodor Mommsen, *Römisches Staatsrecht* (Hirsel 1887) (hereafter Mommsen, *Staatsrecht*). This seems all the more significant when we consider the justified remark of Pelgrom and Stek, 'Roman Colonization' (n 1) 15, that the distinction between Roman and Latin colonies is more prominent among 'modern scholars' than it was among the ancients.

[8] As we can see in the texts of Roman land surveyors in which heterogeneous settlement forms and various territorial structures are forced to fit relatively incongruous models based essentially on juristic reasoning.

That is not to say that De Ruggiero refused to address specialized legal problems and concepts in his analysis. Hence we find in his article on *coloniae* an extensive discussion on a topic that reappears in his subsequent scholarly work: the legal foundations of the formal, 'semi-sovereign' independence of Rome's Latin colonies.[9] Nonetheless, also in that case in which he aligned himself with an approach so typical of nineteenth-century historiography, he seems to have been less interested than his master Mommsen in interpreting the Roman political architecture in terms of contemporary constitutional paradigms. His more eclectic approach gave him the advantage of an uncommon insight into the peculiarities of Roman territorial power. Even today, we might endorse what he wrote concerning colonies that, like Italic states, whether allied with Rome or not,

> and in certain respects even more so than them, [Latin colonies had] so much political autonomy that they might be considered sovereign at least in legal terms; for example, the use of their own laws and their own institutions, the right to coin money, internal administration free from all Roman interference, the right of exile, private property exempt from all Roman tribute, political territory exempted from the tribes and administrative districts of Rome, a right of citizenship distinct from Roman citizenship; and along with that, they enjoyed private law reciprocity with the Romans and could acquire Roman citizenship with greater ease than other allies. Rome reserved itself supremacy only in military and international affairs.[10]

The exclusion of the territory of the Latin colonies from the sphere of Roman *ius civile* was a natural consequence of this arrangement. The land was in fact allocated to the colonists as private property, but as property that stood outside the system of *dominium ex iure Quiritium*.[11] All these facts were known to earlier authors, but De Ruggiero was the first to put them in a more explicit, coherent form.

[9] For De Ruggiero, 'colonia' (n 2) 418, such Latin colonies were 'cities allied with the Romans, which, although they had been founded by Rome for the most part and had an internal order that increasingly resembled that of Roman colonies over time, never ceased to have such extensive political autonomy as to make them, at least in legal terms, virtually sovereign states vis-à-vis Rome itself'. This may be a simple model, but in some ways it is more accurate than the reconstruction in Mommsen's *Staatsrecht*. De Ruggiero derived this independence thesis, probably correctly, from their status prior to 338 BCE (besides the status of the cities of the Latin League at the time, on which the new colonies were presumably modelled in various ways).

[10] De Ruggiero, 'colonia' (n 2) 419. cf De Ruggiero, *Le colonie* (n 2) 19, with a few modifications, where we find the following conclusion: 'Hence the Latin colonies were the equals of Rome's other allies and in some respects enjoyed a more favorable position.'

[11] De Ruggiero, 'colonia' (n 2) 441.

The question of relations between the 'sovereign' city of Rome and other cities dependent on it, such as colonies or *municipia*, became a key theme of a series of publications by De Ruggiero. These studies focused on the way in which the city-state model developed over time, and, above all, on the tensions caused by the extraordinary expansion of Rome's territory and its sphere of sovereignty.[12] In a long series of articles on Roman *municipia* and 'semi-citizens' (*cives sine suffragio*), and on individual Roman and Latin colonies, De Ruggiero progressively focused on the heterogenesis of the civic foundation of the Roman political order. He outlines convincingly the crisis of the 'city-state'[13] in the rapidly expanding Roman Empire. His analysis of the development of this archetypical political institution of classical antiquity tends in two directions. On the one hand, he highlights the increasing difficulty to interpret through this model the Roman political-institutional character after 338 BCE. Even though Rome remained a city-state, and a supremely powerful one, it had also become the political centre of myriad other 'city-states'. The complex hierarchic system of rights and duties Rome developed for its dealings with subordinate communities increasingly eroded their original status as sovereign states. On the other hand, De Ruggiero shows that, despite their loss of autonomy, they retained a strong civic identity and even a capacity for self-organization and government. The change in the status of subject cities after 338 BCE he thus interpreted as the loss of their original 'statehood' while retaining their 'communitarian' physiognomy. The legal consequences in particular of this process became one of the key questions at the heart of De Ruggiero's thought, culminating in the volume *La Patria nel diritto pubblico romano*, which appeared in 1921.[14]

It should be noted that De Ruggiero avoids the expression 'city-state' in his writings far too systematically to be a coincidence.[15] This choice, however, did not help him in clarifying the actual technical-legal dimension of the processes he was describing, for which he clearly lacked appropriate terminology.[16] The

[12] cf the seminars in Berlin in Santo Mazzarino, 'Storia e diritto nello studio delle società classiche' in *La storia del diritto nel quadro delle scienze storiche* (Olschki 1966) 42ff.

[13] De Ruggiero does not actually uses the term city-state. On this see the discussion below.

[14] Ettore De Ruggiero, *La Patria nel diritto pubblico romano* (Maglione 1921) (hereafter De Ruggiero, *La Patria nel diritto*). The opening pages of the book had been published as an autonomous minor work titled *Stato e comune, cittadinanza e patria presso i Romani* (without date or place), but see also Ettore De Ruggiero, 'Lo Stato e la città capitale nel mondo romano' (1918) 2 Nuova Rivista Storica 3ff (hereafter De Ruggiero, 'Lo Stato').

[15] The meaning of the term, as I have recently had the opportunity to point out, seems more immediately intuitive the more uncertain its hermeneutical force is. On this point, see my reservations in Luigi Capogrossi Colognesi, *Storia di Roma tra diritto e potere* (2nd edn, Il Mulino 2014) 11–16 (hereafter Colognesi, *Storia di Roma*).

[16] This is a problem that plagued him throughout his long academic career, if one considers the obvious definitional difficulties that we find already in his work from the 1870s. cf his well-known work *La 'gens' in Roma avanti la formazione del commune* (Tipografia del Genio Artistico 1872), which was

truth is that it is no easier, even today, to find the technical terms to represent phenomena of such peculiar physiognomy as the political developments of ancient Italy, which ultimately resulted in the breakdown and disintegration, on various levels of autonomy, of the unitary concept of sovereignty.

Although they seem quite inadequate today, De Ruggiero used the terms 'state' (*stato*) and 'community' (*comune*)[17] to highlight the progressive separation of these two entities in the Roman experience, culminating in the formation 'of the grand Italic state' with Rome, not as its 'capital' in the modern sense but rather as the first and fundamental 'community' of the empire, constituted by the metropolis.[18] He seems to imagine a development of Roman political power, from an original federal arrangement, first Latin, later Italic, that dissolved after 338 BCE into a hegemonic political system in which Rome assumed the role as the 'capital of a federal national state'. The organizational process was concluded with the extension of Roman citizenship to the Italic peoples, with the *lex Rubria* of 49 BCE, when a federal state composed of 'non-sovereign petty republics', as De Ruggiero colourfully named it, was created.[19] He calls them 'petty republics' (*repubblichette*) because, although deprived of real sovereignty, they did preserve a strong political identity: namely, as 'communities' of citizens. Under this new arrangement each of these 'petty republics'—the 'communities' that made up the federal state—was recognized as having 'citizenship rights of its own'. In this reconstruction these rights were not so much the product of a 'direct concession by the state, but rather a survival from the days of their political independence as allied states that Rome had permitted to remain'.[20]

intended as part of a more extensive work on *Diritto di cittadinanza romano*, which obviously was a central reference point for him over the course of his long scholarly career.

[17] Whether derived from the administrative law of his day or whether the German word *Gemeinde* lurks behind it is unclear.

[18] More explicitly, cf De Ruggiero, 'Lo Stato' (n 14) 7. He also states, however, that Rome is the collective subject of the sovereignty of the 'state' exercised over all its 'communities'. The same interpretation based on the antithesis of 'state' and 'community/*Gemeinde*' indeed reflected tension derived from a lack of clearly defined terms. The roots of this deficit ultimately lay in the extensive use of the category of the 'state' in virtually all nineteenth-century historiography, with Mommsen as its greatest proponent.

[19] De Ruggiero, *La Patria nel diritto* (n 14) 17: 'repubblichette non sovrane'.

[20] ibid 18. In substance, a twofold and contradictory element is in play here: on the one hand, the subaltern nature of the Latin city, insofar as it is subject to the sovereignty of Rome; on the other, the persistence of its original sovereign physiognomy, insofar as it has not been modified by being placed under and absorbed by Roman power.

The Development of the Discourse on Roman Colonization after De Ruggiero

Despite the promising start, the discourse on Roman colonization and expansion in Italy was only marginally advanced in the decades following De Ruggiero's seminal contribution. It seems that any interest in the great gains that had been made by the masters of the nineteenth century with respect to the history of Italic and provincial territory had vanished. Certainly, some studies appeared, but they did not change the overall trend of decline of interest in the discourse. For example, the few pages Gaetano De Sanctis dedicated to the subject in the second volume of his *Storia dei Romani*,[21] or Arthur Rosenberg's 1913 monograph on the *Staat der alten Italiker* can hardly be considered important turning points in this discussion.[22] The latter work focused on the collision of the institutions of various Italic peoples and those of the Romans, but largely neglected the subject of Roman colonization (and of *Latium vetus*).[23] The topic was likewise overlooked in the subsequent work by Hans Rudolph, *Staat und Stadt im römischen Italien*, published in 1935, with its heavy, dogmatic language.[24] It is even more difficult to find anything important in Anglophone scholarship at the time.[25] The only important exception is represented by the great scholarly achievements of Karl Julius Beloch, whose academic approach reflected his personal biography, divided between his German roots and his Italian life. In particular, his grand *Geschichte* warrants special attention, since it offered an unparalleled comprehensive and analytical framework—based on an extremely rich collection of evidence—for Roman territorial control in Italy, providing the reader with exhaustive evidence for each colony and *municipium*.[26] In some respects, despite the fact that

[21] Gaetano De Sanctis, *Storia dei Romani* (2nd edn, La Nuova Italia 1960) 425–39 (hereafter De Sanctis, *Storia*).

[22] Arthur Rosenberg, *Der Staat der alten Italiker* (Weidmann 1913).

[23] Felice Senatore, '"Der Staat der alten Italiker" nella storia degli studi sull'Italia antica' in Arthur Rosenberg, *Lo stato degli antichi Italici* (Scienze e Lettere 2011) 235–95.

[24] Hans Rudolph, *Staat und Stadt im römischen Italien. Untersuchungen über die Entwicklung des Munizipalwesens in der republikanischen Zeit* (Dieterich 1935) (hereafter Rudolph, *Staat und Stadt*). As for the reception of this work, it is interesting to note the rather cold review by Ludwich Schnorr v Carolsfeld (1936) 56 Zeitschrift der Savigny-Stiftung für Rechtsgeschichte: Romanistische Abteilung 302–04. The book was also subjected to very harsh remarks by Pietro De Francisci, which he wrote in the margins of the copy in my possession that came from his library. De Francisci criticizes Rudolph's tendency to rule out autonomous local jurisdiction even for the period before Caesar (224ff) on the basis of highly preconceived notions.

[25] This is the case with Frank F Abbott and Allan C Johnson, *Municipal Administration in the Roman Empire* (Princeton University Press 1926), where it is hard to find anything besides old data from the nineteenth century, from Mommsen and Marquardt to entries in the major encyclopaedias.

[26] Karl Julius Beloch, *Römische Geschichte bis zum Beginn des Punischen Kriege* (Walter de Gruyter 1926). But we must remember also the peculiar relevance of Karl Julius Beloch's *Italische Bund unter*

it was published virtually at the end of Beloch's scholarly life in 1926, it seems to me to be an extension of the heights reached by German historiography of the late nineteenth century. Hence its eccentric nature: isolated in an Italian context, where the author settled despite so many vicissitudes, but also far from the culture and orientation dominant north of the Alps. It thus remained the solitary product of in ingenious but unlucky scholar, which only time could confer the stature it deserved.[27]

Other important contributions that appeared in Germany during these years include the two articles that appeared in 1918 on *ius Italicum* and *ius Latii* respectively by Anton v Premerstein and Arthur Steinwenter,[28] and an article by Matthias Gelzer on *Latium* of 1924.[29] Steinwenter's contribution and, still further, that of Gelzer brought to the fore a series of problems that are essential for better understanding the complex bundle of statutes and legal statuses associated with *Latinitas*: from the *Prisci Latini* to the impact of the *Foedus Cassianum*, as well as the different legal condition of Latin colonists and colonies, from the early colonization of the Latin League, to the twelve colonies under the *ius Ariminense*. This new wave of historiographical reflection, characterized by exhaustive inventory of existing knowledge and data, was taken even further by an extensive article on *municipia* by Ernst Kornemann of 1933, which, in hindsight, marked a turning point in historiographical interest in the territorial structure of Roman power in Italy.[30]

In the same years, in Italian academia few important contributions to our argument can be mentioned. A notable exception that deserves our attention is Ettore Pais (I will discuss the other, even greater exception of Plinio Fraccaro below). He was a singular and in some ways anomalous Italian student of the great Mommsen, who like a lonely outcrop in an otherwise flat and monotonous landscape continued the tradition of Roman colonial studies in Italy.[31]

römische Hegemonie (Teubner 1880). We have also to consider that another important contribution to our knowledge of Italian political geography and its changes can be found in De Sanctis, *Storia* (n 21).

[27] Paradoxically, Beloch's *Geschichte* was destined to remain at the margins of subsequent developments in historiography on antiquity in the latter half of the twentieth century: its very structure virtually condemned it to serve as a vast mine for later research.

[28] Anton von Premerstein, 'ius Italicum', *Realencyclopädie X* (1918) 1238–53; Arthur Steinwenter, 'ius Latii', ibid 1267–70.

[29] Matthias Gelzer, 'Latium' *Realencyclopädie XII* (1924) 940–63.

[30] Ernst Kornemann, 'municipium', *Realencyclopädie XVI* (1933) 570–638 (hereafter Kornemann, 'municipium'). On his work see also below.

[31] Recently, Jeremia Pelgrom and Tesse Stek have rightly drawn attention to his work on colonization: it is in my view quite telling that they do not clarify the actual impact of Pais's contribution to the historiographical debate on Roman colonization (Pelgrom and Stek, 'Roman Colonization' (n 1) 14ff). It seems to me that, in their eyes, his impact lies in the updated list of various colony types—no big deal, given his well-known reliance on earlier work by Beloch and Kornemann. Ettore Pais, 'Serie cronologica delle colonie romane e latine dall'età regia fino all'impero' (1924–25) 17 (s 5) Mem. Acc. Lincei 311–55

In his, in some ways, so singular study on the *Storia della colonizzazione romana*, published in 1923,[32] he reconsiders *ab imis fundamentis* a major problem that had received extensive treatment by Mommsen, yet which had been left in a state of suspense: namely, the value of the unique evidence of the *Corpus Agrimensorum*, edited by Karl Lachmann as the *Liber coloniarum* I and II, for understanding Italic colonial systems.[33] Mommsen dedicated a study to this work,[34] but never developed his thoughts further in subsequent research.[35] In contrast to the caution shown by his great German teacher with respect to the overall value of the manuscript tradition used to reconstruct the *Liber coloniarum*, Pais was more optimistic. His reassessment, however, was asserted rather than based on the necessary re-examination of the manuscripts, their origin, composition, and internal stratigraphy.[36] His attempt to integrate other indirect information[37] was not enough to fill the void left by the interruption of the new edition of the *Gromatici veteres* by Carl Olof Thulin.[38] At best, this additional material augmented the commentary on an already well-known text, but certainly did not provide a new critical edition of these texts or lay the groundwork for independent and more comprehensive research on Roman colonization. This shortcoming explains, at least in part, why this work did not inspire a serious revival of interest in the subject.

In this rather barren landscape, Kornemann's article on *municipium* of 1933 constituted an important turning point and the beginning of a new chapter of Roman colonial and institutional studies. His historiographical approach,

and 1 (s 6) Mem. Acc. Lincei 345–412. If my interpretation is correct, then I must concur wholeheartedly with Pelgrom and Stek, since I also consider the most interesting aspect of Pais's work on Roman colonization to be the attempt to expand the traditional sources on which earlier historiographical work had been based.

[32] Ettore Pais, *Storia della colonizzazione di Roma antica* vol 1 (Nardecchia 1923) (hereafter Pais, *Storia*).

[33] cf Friedrich Blume, Karl Lachmann, and Adolf Rudorff, *Die Schriften der römischen Feldmesser* vol 1 (Georg Reimer 1848) 209–62.

[34] As is well known, the ancient manuscripts associate this collection of texts with the name of Balbus, possibly an agrimensor from the early imperial age, and also make reference to a liber Augusti Caesaris et Neronis in the book edited with commentary by Lachmann (cf Mommsen's contribution to that work).

[35] Theodor Mommsen, '*Die* libri coloniarum' in Friederich Blume, Karl Lachmann, and Adolf Rudorff (eds), *Die Schriften der römischen Feldmesser* vol 2 (Georg Reimer 1852) 157ff and 176ff and his later paper 'Die Interpolationen des gromatischen Corpus' (1895), now in Theodor Mommsen, *Gesammelte Schriften* vol 7 (Weidmann 1909) 464–82.

[36] cf Pais, *Storia* (n 32) xxiv–xxxiv.

[37] ibid 145–360.

[38] Carl O Thulin, *Corpus agrimensorum Romanorum, I Opuscula agrimensorum veterum* (Teubner 1913). One should note the formidable study by Lucio Toneatto, *Codices artis mensoriae* vol 1 (Centro italiano di studi sull'alto Medioevo 1994) 11f. (hereafter Toneatto, *Codices*), since this subject is again regaining currency; and his 'L'editio princeps del 'Liber regionum I' (1983) 1.1 (s 3) DdA 87–95.

characterized by exhaustive inventory of existing knowledge and data, in hindsight rekindled historiographical interest in the territorial structure of Roman power in Italy. This shift had been anticipated by a brilliant article by Zdzislaw Zmigryder-Konopka,[39] although still focused on the Roman municipal system, and would find its full expression in the fundamental work by Adrian Nicholas Sherwin White on Roman citizenship, which appeared in 1939.[40]

This latter work also touched on the history of colonization in more than one respect. In his analysis of the way Roman legal categories expanded in Italy (with the nucleus constituted by *civitas optimo iure*), Sherwin White in fact highlighted the fragmentation and heterogeneity of Roman territorial power, which was also reflected in the rich Roman terminology for the various forms of rural settlements: *fora*, *conciliabula*, *pagi*, *vici*, *territoria*. These multifaceted forms of rural settlement, in part deriving originally from older systems of territorial organization, attest to the limits of the municipal and colonial organization and at the same time to the dangers of any kind of generalization, for a better understanding of Roman institutional history. Sherwin White's multilayered understanding of the Roman territorial system showed also the relatively disadvantageous situation of the Roman citizens who enrolled in new colonies, compared to other settlement forms and even to the municipal experiment itself. Moreover, the relatively low numbers of colonists reported to have settled in citizen colonies motivated him to accept the older view that 'the earlier Republican colonies were *praefecturae* and received their jurisdiction from itinerant prefects'.[41] In spite of these insights, Roman colonization remained on the margins of Sherwin White's book, which centred instead on the expansion of Roman citizenship, *civitas sine suffragio*, and the municipalization of Italy.

This minor interest in the history of colonies changed significantly,[42] in the immediate aftermath of the Second World War, when a new and a more specific

[39] Zdzislaw Zmigryder-Konopka, 'Les rélations politiques entre Rome et la Campanie' (1929) 32 Eos 596ff.

[40] Adrian N Sherwin White, *The Roman Citizenship* (2nd edn, Oxford University Press 1973) (hereafter Sherwin White, *Citizenship*).

[41] Sherwin White, *Citizenship* (n 40) 84. This view he derives from Rudolph, *Staat und Stadt* (n 24).

[42] A study like that by Joshua Whatmough, *The Foundations of Roman Italy* (Methuen & Company 1937), is not relevant, despite the fact that it essentially concerned the structures and configuration of Italic peoples before Rome. Another book that also appeared on the eve of the Second World War, Josef Göhler's highly ideological *Rom und Italien* (Verlag Priebatschs Buchhandlung 1939), also remains in the background, as well as Eugenio Manni, *Per la storia dei municipii fino alla guerra sociale* (Signorelli 1947) which also is marginal. The physiognomy of the study by Adam Afzelius, *Die römische Eroberung Italiens (320–264 v. Chr.)* (Universitetsforlaget I Aarhus 1942), in contrast is quite different. Following in the footsteps of Beloch, Afzelius takes up the quantification of Roman expansion, touching several times on colonial foundations in various Italic regions.

attention to the close ties between the forms of Roman private and public law and territorial and organizational structures emerged.[43] But even as late as 1965, in the fine study by Charles Saumagne,[44] Roman colonization remained relatively sidelined.[45] This study concentrated primarily on Latinity in the imperial age, identified as a particular attribute of *municipia*: the standard status of provincial communities that found themselves in an intermediate position between full citizenship and peregrine status. This evocative reconstruction, albeit not without its difficulties, assumed that the institutional framework of the imperial age was radically different with respect to colonies from the Republican age having, for that reason, a limited relevance for my survey.

With this work, however, and with the early researches of Umberto Laffi, the questions revolving around the nature and history of municipal organization began to take on special significance.[46] Laffi's book, in fact, concerned an argument that was chronologically limited but of the greatest significance for understanding the relevance of cities and their organization in the Roman territorial administration. According to Laffi, the Roman system of territorial control known as *adtributio*, which he places chronologically between the beginning of the last century of the Republic and the age of Augustus, did not, as was assumed before, absorb minor 'cantonal' entities—*vici*, *pagi*, *conciliabula*—into city units but rather served essentially to integrate these autochthonous elements into the Roman colonial and municipal order while preserving their diverse legal statuses.[47]

Another crucial step in the advancement of the discourse was made by Francesco Grelle. For our purposes, his study on city autonomy in the age

[43] As in the difficult and elusive problem of *praefecturae*. cf Wilhelm Ensslin, 'praefectus iure dicundo', *Realencyclopädie XXII* (1954) 1309–23; Erich Sachers, 'praefectura', ibid 2347–52; Wilhelm Ensslin, 'Praefectus iure dicendo', ibid 2378–91. Particularly noteworthy for its modern approach, anticipating more recent findings and successfully combining profound knowledge of history, law, and archaeology in the same scholar, is the work of Giuseppe Ignazio Luzzatto now conveniently collected in Giuseppe Ignazio Luzzatto, *Scritti minori epigrafici e papirologici* (Forni 1984). See especially the articles titled 'La riscossione tributaria in Roma e l'ipotesi della proprietà-sovranità' (1953); 'In tema di limitatio' (1963); 'In tema di processo provinciale e autonomia cittadina' (1964); 'rec. a Sordi' (1960); 'rec. a Simshäuser' (1974).

[44] Who continued earlier research on the important city of *Volubilis*.

[45] Charles Saumagne, *Le droit romain et les cités romaines sous l'empire. Essai critique* (Publications de l'Institut de droit romain de l'Université de Paris 1965).

[46] The later study by Dieter Nörr, *Imperium und polis in der hohen Principatszeit* (Beck 1969), was also important.

[47] Umberto Laffi, *'Adtributio' e 'contributio'. Problemi del sistema politico-amministrativo dello Stato romano* (Nistri-Lischi 1966). The importance of his findings for better understanding the effects of establishing new colonial centres, as well as for more precisely assessing the more general dynamics of urbanization and the administrative regrouping of populations under Roman power, has proven to be especially obvious as other aspects of the original simplification of the Romans' methods of organizing their territory have been called into question over the last fifteen years.

of Trajan published in 1972, is particularly significant.[48] In focusing on the polycentric institutional nature of the Roman imperial system, which he explored as it trended downward, Grelle also seized the opportunity to devote a detailed discussion to the famous passage of Gellius in which he reports Hadrian's opinions on the nature of colonies and *municipia*. This text is indeed as important as it is difficult, and it has—as is well known—tormented many historians, from Mommsen down to the most recent scholars today. Taking seriously the ideas exposed in Hadrian's *horatio de Italicensibus*, referred to by Gellius, Grelle could develop a sound analysis of the different features of colonies and *municipia* which gave real substance to the debate on municipal autonomy, which had been surveyed only in general terms by most modern historians.

These views and topics, although very promising, failed to bear immediate fruit, or rather failed to elicit an adequate response. In particular this is true for Anglophone scholarship, which has always been less sensitive to more strictly institutional and legal aspects of Roman history. These scholars, instead, were more interested in the political dimension of colonization,[49] as we can see, first of all, in Toynbee's *Hannibal's Legacy*.[50] In this wide-ranging and dramatic sketch of post-Hannibalic Italy, the author recognizes the decisive value of Roman colonization in creating the 'Roman commonwealth' that was put to the test by Hannibal's arrival. As Toynbee saw as one of the principal reasons of the Roman victory the endurance of that commonwealth system, Roman colonies become a crucial component of the Roman imperial success story.

The relevance of political-military effects of Roman colonization, in contrast to the social role that many previous historians had attributed to it, would be taken up vigorously by Edward Togo Salmon a few years later. In two brief papers that appeared in the mid-1950s, he insisted that the founding of new Latin colonies prior to 338 BCE took place strictly outside Roman power.[51] Although

[48] Francesco Grelle, *L'autonomia cittadina fra Traiano e Adriano. Teoria e prassi dell'organizzazione municipale romana* (Edizioni Scientifiche Italiane 1972); see also Francesco Grelle, *'Stipendium vel tributum'. L'imposizione fondiaria nelle dottrine giuridiche del II e III secolo* (Pubblicazioni della Facoltà Giuridica dell'Università di Napoli 1963).

[49] Peter A Brunt, *Italian Manpower 225 BC. –AD. 14*, (Oxford University Press 1971) (hereafter Brunt, *Italian Manpower*) is less interesting for our purposes.

[50] See especially the first volume of Arnold Toynbee, *Hannibal's Legacy* vol 1 (Oxford University Press 1965) (hereafter Toynbee, *Legacy*). Given the scope of the work, it is unsurprising that the author pays particular attention to the type of human resources the Romans had to draw upon to pursue the creation of new Latin colonies—although, in this colossal effort, the author does not deny interest in other more specific aspects relevant to the topic (cf 387–91 on the colony of Ostia, and 391–97 for a discussion of the nature of the colonies cited in the first decade of Livy).

[51] Edward Togo Salmon, 'Rome and the Latins, I–II' (1953) 7 Phoenix 93–104, 123–35; Edward T Salmon, 'Roman Expansion and Roman Colonization in Italy' (1955) 9 Phoenix 63–75 (hereafter Salmon, 'Roman Expansion').

it is difficult, today, to accept his idea that the formal sovereignty of the Latin League defined the legal condition of the new colonies,[52] it is interesting that Salmon's interpretation of the institutional structure of pre-338 colonization allowed him to give a plausible explanation for the difficulties Rome subsequently encountered in pursuing its policy of founding new colonies. That is one of the aspects Salmon illuminates best in *Roman Colonization*, one of the first twentieth-century monographs dedicated to the subject.[53]

In considering Salmon's work, we are obliged to deal with the article by Pelgrom and Stek, which pays appropriately close attention to the thought of Salmon, who, in contrast to his Italian colleagues—above all Pais, but also Fraccaro and his pupils—emphasized the importance of political-military aspects rather than the potential social functions of Roman settlement policy.[54] Their assumption is strongly supported by their analysis of Salmon's book, where the 'potential importance of the Roman colonization program in creating and supporting the crucially important peasant-soldier communities and connected civic virtues' was marginalized. Despite the fact that, during the same years, the important findings of new research on traces of ancient colonial centuriation seemed to point to the opposite conclusion, Salmon reaffirmed the virtually exclusive military function of colonies as 'road-blocks, barring the advance of any enemy in the territory of Rome or her allies'.[55]

These ideas undoubtedly have their roots in the way in which ancient historians did describe the new colonial foundations of the fourth and third centuries BCE. It was a period full of wars and political conflicts in central Italy. On the other hand, this evaluation had as a consequence to dismiss the impact of Roman colonization in reinforcing the Roman economy and society.[56] But, in my opinion, it was exactly the economic and social resilience of the Romans and their allies that did play a key part in the Rome's success against Carthage.

Salmon's position certainly had an ideological background: Pelgrom and Stek have recently highlighted this and the considerable weakness of this

[52] For that reason the different interpretation given by Kornemann (n 3) seems to me more likely.

[53] Edward T Salmon, *Roman Colonization under the Republic* (Thames & Hudson 1969) (hereafter Salmon, *Colonization*).

[54] Pelgrom and Stek, 'Roman Colonization' (n 1) , 26–31, emphasize the potential ideological background that they suspect influenced Salmon's approach. Particularly striking is their interpretation (ibid 32) as to why Salmon downplays the social role of Roman colonization for purposes of redistribution and agricultural exploitation of the land, on the one hand, and the creation of small-scale and middle-size peasant property holdings, on the other, as part of a wave of urbanization across the Peninsula. According to Pelgrom and Stek, this 'may perhaps be explained in part by his personal background. Salmon had strong anti-Soviet and more generally anti-Russian political views, which may go some way towards explaining why portraying colonies as more or less egalitarian societies did not appeal to him'.

[55] Salmon, 'Roman Expansion' (n 51) 64.

[56] Pelgrom and Stek, 'Roman Colonization' (n 1) 31f.

approach. Here, however, we are more interested in focusing on a particular consequence of this approach, namely, Salmon's special attention to the remarkably small numbers of colonists sent to Roman citizen colonies, at least until the Hannibalic wars. These low numbers reported by the ancient sources led Salmon to ask whether these settlements scattered along the coast could actually have provided military defence during the greatest crisis of Roman power in Italy, the Hannibalic Wars, as intended by the Romans.[57] The nature of these colonies in turn appears to be directly related to the difficulties that beset the condition of the new colonists, which were not offset by the slightest advantages[58] and were such as to discourage them from participating in similar initiatives of the Roman government.

The upshot of all this was Salmon's remarkable claim—generally neglected in subsequent historiographical reflections—that the limited size of these collections of 300 citizens could not permit an 'authentic and effective commonwealth' to exist, casting doubt on their ability to offer military resistance to potential aggressors. And this brings us back yet again to the thorny question of the nature of the 'city-state'.[59] Indeed, as Salmon wrote, the decisive reason for the scarcity of colonists in Roman colonies, besides various secondary factors, will have been a 'constitutional difficulty'.[60] Salmon in fact believed that, for this more remote age, the very foundation of a colony must have seemed of dubious legality.[61]

I confess that when I first read this assertion, I was slightly puzzled; even today, I still think it has little basis in Roman legal and political theory. But the core theme that emerges from this circuitous reconstruction is highly

[57] Salmon, *Colonization* (n 53) 82–91.

[58] Considering the minimal extent of the land assignments, the new settlements were isolated and their inhabitants cut off from the life of Rome. See already Toynbee, *Legacy* (n 50) 184ff.

[59] This aspect is now at the heart of the paper by Jeremia Pelgrom, 'Roman Colonization and the City-State Model, in Stek and Pelgrom, 'Roman Colonization' (n 1) 73–85, which elaborates on the ideas present in Salmon in an original way. I still believe, however, that it is misguided to ask 'whether a *colonia* as a socio-political entity . . . possessed exclusive jurisdiction over a spatial extent' (ibid 79), because the relationship between Rome and its Latin colonies was in essence based on the fact that Rome never surrendered its sovereignty in actuality, even if the extensive power delegated to the colonies by virtue of their internal self-organization and everyday administration masked its force. The fact that this was so is demonstrated by the sudden assumption of powers in exceptional cases: one thinks for example of the intervention on the occasion of the *SC de Bacchanalibus* or of the sanctions imposed on rebellious colonies. And besides that, the *iurisdictio* of the colony over its own territory, mentioned by the *gromatici*, was not in fact insignificant. We find perhaps a different nuance in Salmon, 'Roman Expansion' (n 51) 67ff, where the unique quality of Latin colonies is tied to their nature as 'independent, self-governing communities'. I agree entirely with this definition, on the condition that we recall that this 'independence' is always granted: it does not reflect autonomous sovereignty.

[60] Salmon, *Colonization* (n 53) 72ff.

[61] He cites the difficulty of enrolling citizens for such foundations and the impossibility, under the Republic, of excusing a higher number of citizens from service in the legions, as happened for Roman colonists.

significant. It highlights a fundamental question that the Roman political leadership had to confront and answer in the watershed years that coincided with the beginning of the municipalization and colonization of Italy in 338 BCE. The creation of a different type of colonial community, consisting of groups of Roman citizens that lived organically separated from the territory of Rome, cut off from the *Urbs* in a diaspora, must have been controversial as it is at odds with 'the traditional concept of the city-state' and the rationale of the government on which it was based.[62] The multiplication of Roman colonies on the one hand and of Latin colonies on the other,[63] placed the ancient political configuration, identified as the *polis*, under extreme pressure, affecting its unitary character.

It thus is precisely in a work focused primarily on political-military aspects that we find such an original impetus for reflecting on the fundamental institutional nature of the colonial model and its relationship with the exclusive character of every ancient city. It is rather surprising that this argument has received little attention in the studies that focused on the nature and transformation of Roman institutions. This is the case of the most extensive and exhaustive reconstruction of the 'Roman constitution' undertaken in the twentieth century, namely the work of Francesco De Martino. One searches in vain, particularly in the second volume of his work, which is dedicated to the Republican age, for any mention of possible tension within the institutional structure gradually erected by the Romans that might have stemmed from the crumbling of its civic political unity, whether caused by the colonial system or by the municipal order.[64]

An Alternative Trajectory: Plinio Fraccaro and His Students

Here, however, we must take a step back, because in Italy itself a different trend emerged in the first decades of the twentieth century that would bear ample

[62] Besides the practical difficulties that Salmon cites, the crucial point is the moment in time that this innovation occurred. On this see Colognesi, *Storia di Roma* (n 15) 110–13, which discusses the importance of the 338 BCE date as marking the initial moment when the Roman order moved beyond the basic structure of the 'city-state'. Although Salmon's considerations might now induce me to push this conventional date further back.

[63] In addition to the presence of *fora* and *conciliabula* connected to viritane distributions, the importance of which should not be underestimated.

[64] This is despite the fact, one should note, that the various aspects of Roman colonization receive ample and incisive treatment in the two volumes of Francesco De Martino, *Storia della costituzione romana* (Jovene 1973).

fruit after the Second World War and down to our own days. I mean the work of Plinio Fraccaro, one of the most important historians of the twentieth century. Fraccaro stands out both for the independence of his scholarly career and the originality of his approach, as well as for the high example of civic and academic morality that he set. It is not surprising that his influence has proven to be so far-reaching and broad, even enriching such an important work as Lily Ross Taylor's *Voting Districts*, where political-institutional history and the reconstruction of material information are blended in both an exemplary and so innovative way.[65] It is in fact beyond question that Fraccaro—followed by his students: Tibiletti, Bernardi, and Gabba—dominates the scholarly literature under review here. These scholars, as will be shown, were truly avant-garde at the time, but the impact of their research on the history of Roman settlements and colonization initially did not extend far beyond their own academic circle in the Pavia area.[66]

As early as the 1930s, a dense article by Fraccaro on Greek and Roman colonization appeared in the Treccani *Enciclopedia Italiana*.[67] Fraccaro's article stood out for the breadth of the picture it drew, combining a felicitous perception of the peculiarities of the Roman dealings with a sound interest for the history of the territorial structures and settlement forms of the Italic world. This new sensibility, capable of taking great steps forward, was confirmed by Fraccaro's subsequent career. I refer above all to the task that was then entrusted to him by the organizers of the famous *Mostra Augustea della Romanità* for the bimillennarium of Augustus—and completed as a resounding success: namely, the task of creating a series of maps of Roman centuriation.[68] His attention to the materiality of the landscapes in which ancient history took shape and which were shaped by it in turn never slackened, but took on ever more nuanced forms. In this, after all, Fraccaro followed—albeit in an autonomous and original way—the trail that had been blazed by Beloch, paying constant attention to the *Realien* of the Italic world that inevitably enriched every facet of the colonial system.[69]

[65] Lily Ross Taylor, *Voting Districts of the Roman Republic* (The American Academy in Rome 1960).

[66] Perhaps with the exception of the waves made by the innovative studies of a somewhat anomalous Romanist, Giuseppe Ignazio Luzzatto.

[67] Plinio Fraccaro, 'colonizzazione (greca e romana)', *Enciclopledia Treccani XXI* (1931) 831–36. Gaetano De Sanctis, one should note, oversaw the section of the encyclopaedia dedicated to ancient history.

[68] Unwittingly reminding us of all we know about his early aspirations to a military career. cf Giulio Quirino Giglioli (ed), *Mostra augustea della romanità: catalogo* (Colombo 1938) xxvi and 702–05.

[69] However, the vast range of the great German historian's interests and undertakings led him down paths relatively far removed from those relevant here, which would instead be taken up by Fraccaro: cf Arnaldo Momigliano, *Terzo contributo alla storia degli studi classici e del mondo antico* (Edizioni di Storia e Letteratura 1966) 239–65 (hereafter Momigliano, *Terzo contributo*).

It is obvious that this interest removed him from the prevailing approaches of ancient historians during these decades, aligning him instead with the great traditions of the nineteenth century, and in particular with the work of Mommsen. Fraccaro felt immense admiration for Mommsen, as attested by that magnificent teller of human and intellectual stories, Arnaldo Momigliano, my ever-mourned mentor and *amicus maior*.[70] It is essentially the old positivist model and the 'scholarly' soundness of his research methods that emerges from his scrupulous and meticulous attention to the facts and the significance of each document, which constitute the basis for this systematic exploration of the territorial structures of northern Italy, primarily focused on the area of Lombardy-Veneto. His studies in this field multiplied, highlighting his ever greater interest in topographical aspects, such as his studies of Roman road systems, a legacy he left to his pupils like Pierluigi Tozzi. This exploration, however, was not exhausted by his geographical-topographical approach, although that interest may have dominated. I refer specifically to his youthful but highly influential work on drainage works of Roman Campania.[71] Among other things, this work attests a direct and considerable knowledge of archaeological contexts.[72]

It thus seems obvious that cartographic problems and interest in the geographical framework in which Roman history was located[73] led Fraccaro to occupy himself with agrarian land-divisions, completing notable studies while also making use of aerial photography, then in its highly experimental infancy. Perhaps less obvious—but certainly more 'Mommsenian'—is the fact that in this field he did not content himself with reconstructive and topographic aspects, but strove to uncover their more complex historical and institutional significance. Thus, with his studies of *centuriatio* and the history of particular colonies,[74] he revived the unfinished work of the great

[70] See Arnaldo Momigliano, *Commemorazione del socio Plinio Fraccaro* (Lincei 1960), now in Momigliano, *Terzo contributo* (n 69) 230.

[71] Plinio Fraccaro, 'Di alcuni antichissimi lavori idraulici di Roma e della Campagna' (1919) 56 Bollettino della Reale società geografica italiana186–215. Intimately connected to this topic is his contemporaneous paper 'La malaria e la storia degli antichi popoli classici' (1919) 22 Atene e Roma 186–215.

[72] But see also his review of Thomas Ashby, 'The Roman Campagna' (1928) 16 Atheneaum 274–79, and especially the subject of his reply to Ashby's own objections, published in ibid 367–75. His remark on the absence of maps and illustrations in the text under review is significant (whereas Ashby was probably right concerning the function of *cunicoli*).

[73] We also should not neglect the author's diligence in editing various historical atlases for the Istituto De Agostini in 1926, 1927, 1930, and 1938, as well as a map of ancient Italy in 1935, and a map of Italy in the age of the Congress of Vienna in 1941.

[74] cf Plinio Fraccaro, 'Centuriazione romana dell'agro Ticinese (con una carta topografica)' in *Atti e memorie del IV Congresso storico lombardo* (Giuffrè 1940) 3–13; Plinion Fraccaro, 'La colonia romana di Eporedia (Ivrea) e la sua centuriazione' (1941) Annali dei lavori pubblici 1–24.

scholars of the nineteenth century; yet on account of his multidimensional attention to the agrarian republican society, Fraccaro also inaugurated a new beginning for our studies.

It is perhaps the famous talk he gave in Rome at the *Convegno internazionale di diritto romano* of 1933 on the 'Political Organization of Roman Italy' that gives us an idea of how Fraccaro helped recover the more comprehensive historiographical perspective that was essential for tackling all the problems connected to the expansion of Rome's political territory. To be clear: it is not a vast and exhaustive monograph with an appropriate apparatus of notes, but a handful of extremely nimble pages.[75] In musical terms, it is the overture to a vast work that would coincide not only with so much of his subsequent scholarly work, but also with the major developments it would make with his school.

It was an overture constructed so well that it anticipated with incisive clarity all the themes that would subsequently develop into a vast and complex symphonic orchestration, helping us to grasp the importance and complexity of all those problems. And in this clear enunciation of problematic threads, which would be elaborated over subsequent decades, we can easily grasp how much inspiration Fraccaro drew from the subjects and methods of the masters of the nineteenth century. But here too we should be clear: it was never simply blind adherence; we can also observe how Fraccaro corrects the same Mommsenian constructions in key regards. The link is particularly strong at one point that colours Fraccaro's entire scholarly perspective: the constant and intimate relationship between the political and social aspects of the history of Roman expansion and conquest and the corresponding juridical and institutional forms. This relationship is easy to declare but quite difficult to trace in concrete terms, as Fraccaro always did. The institutional forms that seem to be so clear and precise to us, in the ancients' representations of them and in their actual application, prove to be hazier and more ambiguous.

In reading these pages today, at a distance of more than eighty years, they appear as a very relevant and comprehensive research project for the new generations. The key issues are all there: from relations between Rome and the *prisci Latini*, to what the author describes as 'the beginning of a more ambitious and more energetic Roman policy', to the origin of that remarkable multiplicity of 'political institutions' from various types of *municipia* to the colonies—within

[75] Plinio Fraccaro, 'L'organizzazione politica dell'Italia romana', *Atti del congresso internazionale di diritto romano* (Fusi 1933) 195–208 (hereafter Fraccaro, 'L'organizzazione politica') now in Fraccaro, *Opuscula* vol 1 (Presso la rivista 'Athenaeum' 1956) 103–14.

which the *ius Latii* would evolve. Within this framework, the tensions generated by the expansion of Roman power, destined to bring political unity, first to Italy and then to the Mediterranean world, served as the backdrop against which two opposite processes took shape: the withering of the structures of the 'city-state' and the embryonic development of what Fraccaro calls the 'territorial state'. The entire historiographical perspective thus outlined revolved around this axis.

I wonder to what extent the audience, then, made up of specialists of legal history, could have appreciated the real importance of Fraccaro's talk. But the witnesses have since disappeared: I would like to know what a person like my teacher Volterra thought about it. He took repeated interest in analogous aspects, albeit related to the succeeding period of Roman history, and went on to shape the contours of my own scholarly interests during the years of my apprenticeship under him. What is certain is that, even today, no jurist seems to me to have taken up the formidable challenge Fraccaro made then on the following premises: that with respect to public law and international relations, 'the tweaking and adaptation of institutions diverted from their original purpose to different purposes' necessitated by this process brought about 'phenomena analogous to those presented by the parallel development and adaptation of private law to the new conditions created precisely by the rise of the territorial state'.[76] The perception at the time, especially, but not only, that of the jurists, as throughout almost the entire twentieth century, was somehow clouded over by the complete identification of the Roman polity with the great political structure of modern Europe: the nation-state, which still dominates our thinking today.

The profound historical sensibility of the (then) young scholar easily persuaded him to exercise caution in hazarding comprehensive scholarly interpretations of the processes triggered by Roman policy. He recalled how often the outcomes of political action differed from those anticipated. He moreover abandoned the interpretive paradigm that was then commonly in use, inspired by federalist models, and instead—and here we see the ingeniousness of his intuition, especially as a 'non-jurist'[77]—relied on the logic of the city-state itself, which inspired Roman conduct in suppressing and absorbing neighbouring

[76] Fraccaro, 'L'organizzazione politica' (n 75). His generalized use of the term 'state' does not indicate a limitation in his own language, but rather in the language and associated conceptualization of the nineteenth and twentieth centuries.

[77] I have long been impressed by the special juridical sensibility that Fraccaro and his school have always shown (so different, for example, from the impatience, on this point, of one of their great friends, Momigliano) and which allied him with some rather peculiar figures among Romanists, such as Pietro De Francisci and especially Giuseppe Ignazio Luzzatto.

communities. This modified vision led him to redefine the nature of Rome's possible relations with the other cities of Latium, downplaying the importance of the ethnic and cultural community that had inspired reconstructions of archaic history since Mommsen. Consequently, Fraccaro offered a very different view of the same caesura in Roman policy in the second half of the fourth century BCE. From this change of perspective, not only did Fraccaro cease to understand the assimilative nucleus of rights inherent in the *ius Latii* as the product of an original unity but he interpreted it on the contrary as the result of the need for communication and integration between Rome and its artificially created Latin colonies. Moreover, he shows how this development occurred in a period in which also the *civitas sine suffragio* appeared in all its complexity. This transitory system was undoubtedly a highly useful solution for the increased Roman presence but also the source of tensions and contradictions of which Fraccaro gave a penetrating interpretation.

Naturally, Fraccaro also had to confront the primary question of the general function of Roman colonization as a means of providing security and control: but it is interesting to see how the question was framed, as he tried to take into account conflicting rationales depending on the case and context. Yet again, Fraccaro paid close attention to the morphology and territorial distribution of Roman and Latin colonies. And he was able to give an account of the reality of such exigencies by starting with the geographic properties. But another idea he clearly enunciates appears to be even more important, namely, the 'inability of the citizen state to extend its administration beyond certain limits'—and here he is referring above all to the small number of governing magistrates and the absence of any bureaucratic apparatus at their disposal, excepting a handful of humble executory officials—as the key to understanding the Romans' organizational choices, with the extensive semi-sovereign autonomy of the world of cities that ensued: that too is a topic that warrants further reflection.[78]

Over time, these views, so innovative at the time and in the context in which they were articulated, took on the consistency of finished works and entered into the collective consciousness. This was also possible—and this is not the least of his legacies—because Fraccaro gave rise to a formidable troop of students who adopted his orientation and interests in scholarly work of the highest calibre, revived by the succession of so many worthy students of worthy students, with whom we felicitously arrive at our own time.

[78] cf Fraccaro, 'L'organizzazione politica' (n 75) 111ff.

There is no need for the deleterious modern stupidity of 'impact factor' to acknowledge the success, both in influence and in citations, attained by Giancarlo Tibiletti's studies of *ager publicus*. One of Fraccaro's first pupils, Tibiletti published on the subject between the late 1940s and the first half of the 1950s. Here, I would like to emphasize the lasting success of his ideas, which spans the entire twentieth century down to our own time.[79] Their success is due above all to the fact that the author successfully set forth the variegated and—from a juristic point of view—variously defined concept of *ager publicus* in consistent and plausible terms. This reconstruction was appropriately relocated in the context of the socio-economic changes and political struggles that marked Republican history, from the original patrician-plebeian conflict down to the Licinian-Sextian laws.[80]

Other contributions by Tibiletti seem no less important. These studies illustrate in various ways—but always with notable originality—manifold aspects of the history of Roman colonization, especially during the age of the Gracchi. Drawing on one of Fraccaro's major themes, Tibiletti turned to a watershed moment in the history of Roman colonial structures and forms of gromatic territorial organization. Thus, with similar clarity, the rich legacy of Fraccaro reappears in another line of research pursued by Tibiletti, the various results of which were collected in his book on *Storie locali dell'Italia romana*. In this work, he attempts to reconstruct the specific ways in which Roman law spread across Italy and the role played in the process by Latin colonization. Tibiletti proposed several hypotheses that are notable even now for their originality and raised questions that, in my view, still have not sufficiently been explored.[81]

I believe we also should consider the theme elaborated by another of Fraccaro's great students, Aurelio Bernardi, in his research on the law of Latin colonies and on the *ius Latii*. Immediately after the Second World War, Bernardi had published a study of the legal status of the twelve colonies under the *ius Ariminense*, which historians and jurists since the time of

[79] I have expressed some doubts on these views in chapters 5–7 of my *Cittadini e territorio. Consolidamento e trasformazone della 'civitas Romana'* (La Sapienza 2000) (hereafter Capogrossi, *Cittadini e territorio*). This point is also taken up in Luigi Capogrossi Colognesi, 'La radici storiche della *lex Licinia de modo agrorum*' in *Fides, humanitas, ius, Studi in onore di Luigi Labruna* vol 2 (Editoriale Scientifica 2007) 677–94. See, however, Capogrossi, *Cittadini e territorio* (n 79) xi n4.

[80] Giancarlo Tibiletti, 'Il possesso *dell'ager publicus* e le norme *de modo agrorum* sino ai Gracchi' (1948) 26 Athenaeum 173–236; Giancarlo Tibiletti, 'Ricerche di storia agraria romana' (1950) 28 Athenaeum 183–266.

[81] Giancarlo Tibiletti, *Diritti locali nei municipi d'Italia e altri problemi* (Pàtron Editore 1973), now in Tibiletti, *Storie locali dell'Italia romana* (presso la rivista 'Athenaeum' 1978) 345–71 (hereafter Tibiletti, *Storie locali*), on which cf Capogrossi, *Cittadini e territorio* (n 79) 168ff.

Mommsen had wrestled with. He would take up the subject again in 1973 in his study of the *Nomen Latinum*. Here, in a highly complex and indisputably original analysis, he explored the strictly legal aspects of membership in a colony under Latin law—reiterating the distinction between colonies after 268 BCE and older colonies.[82] His theory overturned the traditional view (held particularly by Romanists, but which had already been criticized by Fraccaro) that Latin colonists' rights of *commercium* and *conubium* derived from the original position of the *prisci Latini* as regulated by the *Foedus Cassianum*. He offers us food for thought that might prove to be vitally important with respect to what seems to me, especially after the research of Saskia Roselaar and other recent authors, to be an issue that can no longer be postponed.[83]

Several times, I myself in my own research on these topics have been struck by the innovative insights of these two authors' essays. I have made reference to Tibiletti in particular in seeking to reconstruct the possible legal conditions that the new processes of the expansion of Roman power must have created after 338 BCE.[84] Yet, in this case as well, only a complete reconsideration of the entire topic could convey the full significance of the many papers Tibiletti dedicated to various aspects of the forms of Roman rule in Italy.

As for the third of Fraccaro's great heirs, and perhaps the first for what concerns the quality and the quantity of his scholarly output, I recall the memory of Emilio Gabba who passed away not long ago. I am immediately

[82] Aurelio Bernardi, *Nomen Latinum* (Collegio Ghislieri 1973).

[83] Saskia Roselaar, *Public Land in the Roman Republic: A Social and Economic History of Ager Publicus in Italy, 396–89 BC* (Oxford University Press 2010).

[84] It would be of enormous interest for better situating this scholar's academic career in its context, if we knew more about what Emilio Gabba told me in his own time (already in the first half of the 1980s, when this conversation took place, as he was well aware of the vital importance of this documentary material for our studies, whether for agrarian history or the history of Roman colonization) about Tibiletti's project of translating the texts of the *gromatici*. He had developed a special (and, for his time, quite original) interest in the *gromatici*, as attested by a letter he sent to Dilke. Published now under the title 'Considerazioni sui gromatici' in Tibiletti, *Storie locali* (n 81) 325–27, this letter contains some very important information. It tells us not only that Tibiletti had effectively undertaken a detailed analysis of the manuscript tradition on which the old edition by Lachmann had been based, coming to the conclusion that 'his [Lachmann's] method should be reversed', but also that he clearly believed that a plurality of traditions were inherent in the very substance of the discipline. It is here that, among other things, he rightly adopted a critical position toward Mommsen's dismissive opinion of the value of the *libri coloniarum*. In contrast, Tibiletti emphasized their practical value as representing a general type of text intended for a purpose no different from that of the texts used in 'our schools for accountants and surveyors'. This is an exceptional realization that permits us to appreciate the significance of legal references in these texts, a view he shared with Luzzatto, whom I have mentioned above. As regards the translation of the texts, Gabba fully shared my belief that it was important and downright essential for any serious new study of the subject to clarify all the extraordinary ambiguities and uncertainties of the evidence and manuscript tradition.

reminded of how much I had to say in a recent commemoration held in his honour at the Accademia dei Lincei. There I stressed the way in which nearly half a century after Fraccaro's paper on the 'Political Organization of Roman Italy,' cited above, his former student undertook a new analysis of the profound transformations that Rome's political expansion caused its institutional framework to undergo. Gabba emphasized the fact that the protagonists of these ancient events lacked the conceptual sophistication that would have enabled them to articulate new and more appropriate reformulations in formal legal terms. In understanding these delays as one of the factors behind the late Republican crisis, he explicitly drew on the references Fraccaro had made to the possible concerns of the Roman ruling class with respect to Rome's territorial expansion and the potential spatial redistribution of its citizenry.[85]

He thus harkened back to the ancients' theorizations about the spatial and quantitative limitations of the ideal city. Gabba observed that even widespread ideas in antiquity about the quantitative and qualitative features of the ideal city did not trigger any particular alarm about 'the unsuitability of the traditional constitutional political structures to the new imperial reality' in the age of Cicero and Sallust.[86] He rightly emphasized that this concern derived, not from the ancients, but rather from 'Enlightenment political reconsiderations', especially Montesquieu. On the contrary, it was obvious to Cicero or Sallust that the Roman state they were discussing was still 'a city state, even if its territory had grown enormously'.[87] It is the tension within this conceptual realm that enabled Gabba to explain how the generalized 'political-administrative restructuration of Roman territory' caused by the extension 'of Roman citizenship to all Italy' and based on *municipia* had not diminished the significance of 'traditional political principles and city-state institutions'.[88] By adding this subjective element—the protagonists' failure to grasp the ultimate consequences of their own political-institutional musings—to the objective factors that had been identified by his teacher, Gabba completed our interpretation and understanding of the historical

[85] Luigi Capogrossi Colognesi, 'Gabba e l'Italia romana' in *Emilio Gabba. Un maestro della storia antica* (Bardi Edizioni 2016) 73–83.

[86] Emilio Gabba, 'Le città italiche del I sec. A.C. e la politica' (1986) 98 Rivista Storica Italiana 653–63, now in Emilio Gabba, *Italia romana* (New Press Edizioni 1994) 124 (hereafter Gabba, *Italia romana)*.

[87] ibid 123.

[88] Emilio Gabba, 'I municipi e l'Italia augustea' in Mario Pani (ed), *Continuità e trasformazioni fra repubblica e principato* (Edipuglia 1991) 69–81, now in Gabba, *Italia romana* (n 86).

drama that convulsed the ancient Republican institutions, bringing to a close the interrupted scholarly trend that had lasted half a century.

In this way, Fraccaro's legacy was reaffirmed and taken further in a plurality of directions that overlapped in the exploration of the territorial forms of Roman power. Hence, adopting a new sensibility—also in response to the changed orientation of European historiography in the late twentieth century—Gabba wondered about the economic, and the specific social impact of the various institutional and territorial systems devised by the Romans. In particular, he picked up the thread left by his teacher in which institutional history and that of physical structures were closely intertwined, as emerges especially clearly in his long study of 1979.[89] It represents another aspect of his uninterrupted and systematic investigation of the territorial and settlement-related impact of Roman expansion in Italy.[90]

His contribution appeared in a book edited by Gabba himself together with his pupil Marinella Pasquinucci, in which the latter published an ample essay on the history of transhumance in Roman Italy. Their studies focused on a type of occupation and land-use radically opposed to the logic of colonization and its intrinsic forms of territorial exploitation: yet precisely for this reason, transhumance is highly significant for establishing the limits of the history of colonization.[91] Since then, research on transhumance has blossomed, thanks to the efforts of a generation of scholars contemporary with or even younger than myself, but their work thus exceeds the chronological scope of these pages.[92] For the same reason, the vast and uninterrupted research of another student of Gabba's over the past decades down to the present also falls outside the scope of this chapter, Umberto Laffi, whom I have already cited for his book on *adtributio* and who remains engaged in full and productive scholarly activity.[93]

[89] Emilio Gabba, 'Sulle strutture agrarie dell'Italia romana fra III e I sec. a.C.' in Emilio Gabba and Marinella Pasquinucci, *Strutture agrarie e allevamento transumante nell'Italia romana (III–I sec. a.C.)* (Giardini 1979) 5–73.

[90] And overall this is well attested by the volume *Italia romana* (n 86), which collects his papers that appeared primarily in the 1970s and 1980s.

[91] Marinella Pasquinucci, 'La transumanza nell'Italia romana' in Emilio Gabba and Marinella Pasquinucci, *Strutture agrarie e allevamento transumante nell'Italia romana (III–I sec. a.C.)* (Giardini 1979) 79–182.

[92] But I must emphasize the extraordinary interest of localized studies of the history of territorial structures and settlement forms published in recent years yet harkening back to these approaches. By way of example, I will cite only the rich material produced by the *Picenum Survey Project*.

[93] For his research down to the 1970s, however, which is covered by the present essay, see the various studies now collected in Umberto Laffi, *Studi di storia romana e di diritto* (Storia e Letteratura 2001) (hereafter Laffi, *Studi di storia*); in particular, his analysis of the inscription of Saepinum (CIL, IX, 2438) (1965); 'Sull'organizzazione amministrativa dell'area cisalpina in età giulio-claudia'(1976); 'La lex aedis Furfensis (1978); and the two papers 'Considerazioni sulle articolazioni del contesto urbano e del contesto rurale nell'Italia romana' (1977) and 'Problemi dell'organizzazione paganico-vicana nelle aree abruzzesi e molisane'(1974).

Recent Developments

The 1970s opened with an interesting contribution by a young Spanish scholar who had been strongly influenced by Giuseppe Ignazio Luzzatto: Armando Torrent, who proposed an interesting interpretation of the legal functions of municipal magistrates.[94] As with other important aspects of the civic order of the Roman Empire,[95] he discussed them while paying particular attention to the multiplicity of statutes and the varying institutional autonomy of civic realities. In this study, he observed that 'the concept of *civitas*, understood as citizenship, has not always had a consistent meaning in the history of Roman law', a question that we shall encounter again below.[96]

This work was followed almost immediately by an important book by Wilhelm Simshäuser that focused essentially on the imperial age, although it also evoked the rationale behind the system of municipal jurisdiction in the Republican period.[97] This paper not only demolished the theories of Rudolph, who had associated the system of municipal jurisdiction with the Caesarian reforms, but also distanced itself from Mommsen, whose approach had led him to focus on the aftermath of the Social War. Wilhelm Simshäuser rightly observes that the long trend of institutional reorganization after 89–88 BCE and the creation of forms of municipal autonomy then underway were the ultimate result of the logic that had always influenced the Roman political fabric, which was quite different from that of the modern unitary state, and which consequently was capable to give way to a form of unsurpassed institutional pluralism. Simshäuser's analysis not only considered the way in which historians interpreted the nature and functions of prefectures *iure dicundo* but also reflected on their assessment of forms of colonial autonomy.

In a wide-ranging study by Helmut Galsterer, *Herrschaft und Verwaltung im republikanischen Italien*, which appeared in 1976, we find many pages dedicated to Roman colonization that are rich with new ideas. In particular, Galsterer criticized Salmon's ideas about the exclusively military character of

94 Armando Torrent, *La 'iurisdictio' de los magistrados municipales* (Universidad, Secretariado de Publicaciones e Intercambio Cientifico 1970) (hereafter Torrent, *La iurisdictio*). It is interesting how Torrent already articulates the idea that important clues preserved in Festus have been obliterated by modern Romanists on account of their 'excessively dogmatic concepts of the idea of citizenship' (ibid 30). And it is no accident, in fact, that the important contribution by Tibiletti that I have cited above consists of an extensive review of this work, seeking to sound out the significance of the jurisdiction of the same local magistrates with respect to the nature of the law in force in various communities.

95 On the margins of his research but not irrelevant, we find an extensive discussion, involving numerous first-rate historians and jurists, of the possible existence of forms of dual citizenship within the municipal system in the imperial age. See the references in Capogrossi, *Cittadini e territorio* (n 79) 178ff.

96 Torrent, *La iurisdictio* (n 94) 30.

97 Wilhelm Simshäuser, *Iuridici und Municipalgerichtsbarkeit in Italien* (Beck 1973).

Roman citizen colonies. Galsterer undermined Salmon's interpretation by emphasizing the fact that the consolidated acquisition of Italy under Roman power brought an end to the founding, not of new colonies *civium Romanorum*, but of Latin colonies. If anything, this proved the strategic value of the Latin colonies in controlling the various territories and communications between them. With the demise of their strategic function as military strongholds after the second century BCE, there was no further need to deploy colonies of this type.[98] Galsterer's new views and the problems he creatively addressed were by no means limited to this: a case in point is his analysis of the potential for political hegemony and patronage that the existence or foundation of a new colony might generate; or those in which he investigates how the founding of a new colony potentially affected the pre-existing legal positions of Roman citizens, along with specific modifications to their personal status. In contrast, he reasonably attributes the extremely limited size of assignations for Roman citizens in the most ancient phase to the availability and exploitation of vast areas of public lands, to be exploited by the colonists without being distributed in private property.[99]

Two years later, in 1978, the publication of Michel Humbert's monograph on the Roman municipal system and to *civitates sine suffragio*, in my view, marked the completion of a true shift in the historiography of the processes of territorial and legal integration of Roman Italy in the Republican age. We still consider *'Municipium' et 'civitas sine suffragio'* as a cornerstone of our studies.[100] Even if this work represented a major step forward primarily for our understanding of the processes of Italian municipalization, the colonies which had a great importance in his reconstruction are discussed rather marginally. Nevertheless, Humbert shows that it was precisely through the *ius migrandi* of the colonists that the proximity of *Latinitas* to Roman citizenship was demonstrated. In that way the French scholar did propose a more direct relationship between Latin colonization and Roman citizenship, different from that which was generally accepted by modern historians and jurists.

Historians' interest in these problems was further revived by the appearance of Giorgio Luraschi's study of the concession of colonial Latinity to the

[98] Hartmut Galsterer, *Herrschaft und Verwaltung im republikanischen Italien* (Beck 1976) 43ff, 63 (hereafter Galsterer, *Herrschaft*). See also Wilhelm Simshäuser, 'Stadtromisches Verfahrensrecht im Spiegel der lex Irnitana' (1992) 109 Zeitschrift der Savigny-Stiftung für Rechtsgeschichte, romanistische Abteilung 163–208.

[99] Galsterer, *Herrschaft* (n 98) 47ff.

[100] Michel Humbert, *'Municipium' et 'civitas sine suffragio'. L'organization de la conquête jusqu'à la guerre sociale* (École française de Rome 1978).

communities of Transpadana.[101] Its importance was not immediately recognized, particularly since the scope of the book seemed limited to that of a 'local history', as the late author himself let slip in the opening discussion.[102] However, what stands out in this book above all else, in my view, is the convergence of a precious strand of the historiography of places and territories—of 'local history', in a word, of the physical history of territory, elements of the precious legacy of Fraccaro—and the most traditional forms of institutional and political history. The topic Luraschi wrestled with is well known: the Romanization of northern Italy upon the permanent acquisition of Gallia Cisalpina and Roman expansion into Gallia Transalpina after the *lex Pompeia de Transpadanis* of 89 BCE.

The grant of *Latinitas* to the communities of Gallia easing their assimilation, as is well known, helped to define one of the key arenas where the struggle between Caesar and the senatorial party would play out. Referring to that process, the author did go beyond a simple discussion on the various legal statuses, fruitful exploring their impact on the transformation (or continuity) of physical forms in territories and settlements. In Luraschi, we discover how difficult this line of investigation is. Contrary to the widespread classical model that underlay the colonial foundations of the middle Republic, the scenario which was originated by *lex Pompeia*, at least according to the interpretation of my deceased colleague and friend, was absolutely unusual. The concession of *Latinitas* to autochthonous populations, in fact, was followed neither by typical processes of urbanization, represented by the demarcation of a new colonial community, nor by extensive intervention in the territory attributed to it by way of the usual workings of *limitatio*.[103]

[101] Giorgio Luraschi, *Foedus, ius Latii, civitas. Aspetti costituzionali della romanizzazione in val Padana* (Pubblicazioni della Università di Pavia 1979) (hereafter Luraschi, *Foedus*). This was followed by Werner Eck's work on the civil organization of Italy under the Principate, whose chronological perspective did largely exceed the temporary limits of this review. Werner Eck, *Die staatliche Organization Italiens in der hohen Kaiserzeit* (Beck 1979).

[102] Luraschi, *Foedus* (n 101) xviff. But we never can rely on the general pronouncements of an author, even one as careful and distinguished as Luraschi. Instead one should peruse the ample notes that enrich the text, weighing it down *more italico*, and see the calibre of the bibliography it features, paying the greatest attention to specific local histories, the archaeology of places, and documentation for subsequent developments in individual settlements. That is what truly stands out in the book and from which much of its novelty derives. It moreover should not be forgotten that, in certain regards, the development—intended in the 'high' sense—of his numerous earlier studies is on display, which were destined to be brought together in Giorgio Luraschi, *Storia di Como antica. Saggi di archeologia, diritto e storia* (New Press edizioni 1997) (hereafter Luraschi, *Storia*).

[103] Giorgio Luraschi, *Foedus* (n 101) 210ff, 373ff. See also Giorgio Luraschi, 'Nuove riflessioni sugli aspetti giuridici della romanizzazione in Transpadana' in *Atti del 2° Convegno Archeologico regionale: la Lombardia tra protostoria e romanità* (Società Archeologica Comense 1986), also in Luraschi, *Storia* (n 102) 289ff, 298ff.

It is noteworthy that, until now, the term *limitatio* has not appeared in my survey. This fact is not an obvious one, given how *limitatio* is intimately associated with the founding of Roman and Latin colonies in even the most banal and superficial histories of Rome. If I have referred to it (indirectly, in mentioning the writings of the *gromatici*), it is only in connection with Pais and Fraccaro and his school. That is because, apart from them, scarce mention is made about this peculiar Roman institution in the other works we have encountered. The focus of these studies, I repeat, was on purely institutional or political aspects. On the contrary, Luraschi's book help us to acquire a better understanding of the nature of Roman colonization and its multiple effects during the Republican period. Not only does he attract our attention to the peculiar forms of *Latinitas coloniaria*, without *centuriatio*,[104] but he illustrates also other systems of *adsignatio* of land (following different unspecified property laws) to certain groups of *coloni*.[105] Moreover, he shows cases of new *centuriatio* that coincided with the redefinition of the settlement status of a colony,[106] and cases of *centuriatio* that were applied to *municipia* that, in theory, should have been remained outside them.[107]

With these studies and those that immediately followed over the course of the 1990s,[108] however, the story of our generation begins and I entrust it to whoever is mature and ready to take our place. Authors I have mentioned, such as Laffi,[109] Grelle, Galsterer, and Eck, have continued to make fundamental and innovated contributions to this field, followed by an even greater number of younger scholars who have enriched this extraordinary field of knowledge. But that, indeed, is another story. Hence, rather than offer impossible conclusions on a scholarly development that fortunately is destined to continue, I will limit

[104] The characteristic practice of demarcating the territory that is generally considered the normal consequence of the foundation of a new *colonia*.

[105] This interpretation was founded by Luraschi on the well-known evidence of Appian concerning the colonial measures of Scipio. Luraschi, *Foedus* (n 101) 365ff.

[106] Being anyhow its legal status already determined by previous concessions.

[107] I will not attempt to pursue Luraschi's reconstruction further, but rather will refer to what has already been written, with *pietas* and intelligence, by Stefano Barbati: cf in particular: Stefano Barbati, 'Gli studi sulla cittadinanza romana prima e dopo le ricerche di Giorgio Luraschi' (2012) 12 Rivista di Diritto Romano 1–21, and especially Stefano Barbati, 'Asc., in Pis. 3 Clark: sulle cosiddette "colonie fittizie" transpadane' (2013) 3 Quaderni Lupiensi 59–106.

[108] Particularly important during these years is the book by Gino Bandelli, *Ricerche sulla colonizzazione romana della Gallia Cisalpina* (Quasar 1988), followed by Tim J Cornell, 'The Conquest of Italy' in *Cambridge Ancient History* 7.2 (2nd edn, Cambridge University Press 1990) and by Werner Eck and Hartmut Galsterer, *Die Stadt in Oberitalien und in den nordwestlichen Provinzen des Römischen Reiches* (Zabern 1991).

[109] cf above all, but not exclusively, the vast array of works collected in Laffi, *Studi di storia* (n 93) concerning which, for a close assessment of the aspects relevant here, cf also Luigi Capogrossi Colognesi, 'Gli studi di storia romana e di diritto di Umberto Laffi' (2003) 69 Studia et documenta historiae et iuris 401–10.

myself to raising some questions and giving research suggestions for those who come after us.

Challenges for the Future

In this kind of inventory of what has been done and what remains to do, I believe we can distinguish the following important challenges for future research:

1. Although in many archaeological studies we can register a growing, praiseworthy attention to the complex system of relations between the material history of territory, its different legal conditions (*ager publicus*, *privatus*, object to *dominium ex iure Quiritium*), and the various forms of territorial organization under the supervision of Roman *agrimensores*, a general survey of the different territorial systems and of their various institutional aspects favoured or created by Rome is still missing.

Recently, as I already mentioned above, the lack of interest in the study of the *Gromatici veteres* and their complex implications for so many aspects of ancient history, which emerged in the late nineteenth century and lasted virtually until the second half of the ensuing century, has begun to be filled. Particularly important in this respect is the unrelenting interpretive work of Ferdinando Castagnoli,[110] who combined detailed knowledge of the *argimensores* with the discovery of traces of ancient centuriation in these years, above all by means of the—at the time new—tool of aerial photography carried out by people like John Bradford, Raymond Chevallier, or Giulio Schmiedt.[111] In this way, the previously striking lack of interest in a crucial page in the material and institutional history of Roman colonization began to be overcome. From the end of the 1970s, this shift undoubtedly accelerated with the publication of two important books by Oswald Dilke and Focke Tannen Hinrichs on the work of the Roman *agrimensores* and their practical and institutional significance.[112] In the

[110] The studies I refer to here, dating from 1943 to his well-known 'Sulle più antiche divisioni agrarie romane' (1984), have been collected in Ferdinando Castagnoli, *Topografia antica. Un metodo di studio* vols 1–2 (Istituto Poligrafico dello Stato 1993) (hereafter Castagnoli, *Topografia*). The material tackled by Ferdinando Castagnoli, *Le 'formae' delle colonie romane e le miniature dei codici dei gromatici* (Anno Edizione 1943), now in Castagnoli, *Topografia* (n 110) 703–32, remains to be explored. In this substantial essay, Castagnoli discussed for perhaps the first time in such systematic fashion (the earlier remarks by Ettore Pais were not sufficiently developed) the problem of the documentary value of the illustrations that accompany the text of the *gromatici* in various manuscript traditions. And it is with great awareness that the distinguished topographer revealed in them not only a purely illustrative value, but also their supplementary function in the text as a general hermeneutic criterion.

[111] cf Pelgrom and Stek, 'Roman Colonization' (n 1) 31 and n125, who discuss these studies to demonstrate the limitations of certain assessments of Salmon that I have discussed above.

[112] Oswald A W Dilke, *The Roman Land Surveyors. An introduction to the Agrimensores* (David and Charles 1971); Focke T Hinrichs, *Die Geschichte der gromatischen Institutionen. Untersuchungen zu*

meantime a new and strong interest in the history of territory was stimulated by the research centre of the University of Besançon, spurred on by Monique Clavel-Lévêque. The movement was shaped by two directives: on the one hand, a systematic approach to the study of archaeological evidence of ancient *limitationes*,[113] and, on the other, a comprehensive translation project of the ancient texts. This second was in my view the most productive way to plan for and obtain conditions for the surest utilization of this kind of evidence, on the basis of a reliable interpretation of these difficult texts. This not only produced a series of good results in specialized areas, but also constituted a basis for new developments that followed over the past twenty years by Gérard Chouquer and François Favory,[114] marking, together with the valuable undertaking of Brian Campbell,[115] a true and proper watershed in this area of study, as well as of renewed interest in the manuscript tradition, on which the work of our friend Lucio Toneatto represents an undeniable high point.[116]

Much recent work has been done since, mitigating the preceding stagnation, but much still remains to be done, above all with respect to the systematic comparison of material information recovered by archaeologists and the ever more refined interpretation of the various writing of Roman land surveyors.[117] Of course, we already have new studies that pay new attention to this area, but we also must engage in a more subtle rereading of the various types of evidence we possess, taking sufficiently into account—certainly more than we have done so far—various overlapping land division systems and the different rationales

Landverteilung, Landvermessung, Bodenverwaltung und Bodenrecht im römischen Reich (Franz Steiner 1974), and François Favory, 'Détection des cadastres antiques par filtrage optique' (1980) 92 Mélanges de l'École française de Rome, Antiquité 347–86.

[113] Obviously, we cannot pinpoint the precise constellation at the University of Besançon insofar as this reawakening interest also manifested itself in broader and more articulate terms, and where contributions (albeit always very specialized) by several different major authors came together. The concentration of studies, research, and, above all, scholarly initiatives that took shape from the early 1980s there is highly significant. These revolved around names such as Monique Clavel-Lévêque, François Favory, Gerard Chouquer, and Jean Pierre Vallat. It began with the doctoral theses of Vallat and Chouquer and the pioneering (as far as I recall) roundtable of Basançon in 1980, published as Monique Clavel-Lévêque (ed), *Cadastres et espaces rurales. Approches et réalités antiques* (Éditions du Centre national de la Recherche scientifique 1983). Certainly the tireless work of Ella Hermon is linked to the Besançon group, although its significance is diminished by methodological uncertainty and the lack of clarity concerning technical-institutional topics (a limited verdict that does not extend, of course, to the many scholarly collaborators involved). The work of Rita Compatangelo Soussignan on the remains of centuriation is also very significant.

[114] cf on all this Gérard Chouquer and François Favory, *L'arpentage romain* (Errance 2001).

[115] Brian Campbell, *The Writings of the Roman Land Surveyors* (Roman Society Publications 2000).

[116] Toneatto, *Codices* (n 38).

[117] A particularly important effort in this sense is represented by the collective volume edited by Gérard Chouquer and others (eds), *Structures agraires en Italie centro-méridionale. Cadastres et paysages ruraux* (École Française de Rome 1987), the findings of which remain quite interesting.

they followed over the long history in which we are interested. A stratigraphic reading is indispensable, not only of the archaeological evidence, but also of the most difficult texts of the *agrimensores*. In sum, the necessary approach, as I imagine it, is a kind of 'institutional stratigraphy': that is, a reading of the ancient testimony dominated by constant awareness of how much these texts, written in the first centuries AD, did preserve testimonies of earlier periods, but without any chronological order. Consequently, it is very difficult for us to understand their real meaning about the morphology of various Roman settlements, and even the very notion of a *colonia*, *municipium*, *forum*, and *conciliabulum*, changed over time, varying in function and significance.

2. Another pressing issue is the question of how different forms colonial settlements changed over time, and how they relate to each other. For example, to what extent is a *colonia* under *ius Latinum*, founded by Rome on behalf of the League, the same as a colony founded after 338 BCE, with respect to the legal situations it created and its institutional physiognomy? And, as for those 'ancient' colonies, to what extent do they differ from the more recent Latin colonies, such as the twelve founded under the *iure Ariminensi*? To answer such questions, an understanding of the temporal context is crucial, as the territorial and demographic impact of such new colonial settlements can differ significantly in time. Similarly, for colonies *civium Romanorum*, it is also difficult to imagine that their physiognomy and function in the first centuries of the Republic and the continuation of the experiment after the Hannibalic Wars were identical.

But, above all, it is difficult to decipher the complex mosaic of different legal, political, and territorial situations connected to Roman citizenship and the extension of forms of *dominium ex iure Quiritium* in Italy. For example, it remains unclear how viritane distributions and the related nuclei of landowner-cultivators, such as *fora*, *conciliabula*, etc can be interpreted. Were they an alternative to or in competition with Roman colonies? What was the reason that induced the Romans to adopt one form or another of these different types of land distributions? Even more puzzling is the issue of the potential impact on the territory and the institutional result of the creation of *praefecturae*.[118]

[118] Precisely the multiplicity of initial situations in which the various types of colonies found themselves, as I have repeatedly mentioned, ruled out any correlation between the form of *limitatio* and the progressive expansion of *dominium ex iure Quiritium* (property under Roman civil law) to all Italic lands. The reasons of the substantial incongruity between the criteria for the application and extension of forms of Roman *ius civile*, on the one hand, and the intentional expansion of the Roman surveyors' techniques to such an extensive part of Italic and provincial territory, on the other, are not always clear. It seems certain to me, however, that *dominium* under Roman civil law played a relatively secondary role in the legal-institutional reconfiguration of most Italic territories prior to its unexpected expansion

3. With regard to the colonial projects of the late Republic crucial questions that need further research include: how much did the Gracchan policy change the very idea of colonization? It is clear that these changes were significant in social and economic terms, and especially their increasing usage as a political tool is evident. However, the new way colonial foundations were used makes us wonder why such a political usage (which has a reasonable precedent in Flaminius' management of the Gallic conquests and of Picenum) did not occur in another episode equally associated to plebeian magistrates: the conquest of the Sabines by Manius Curius Dentatus.

With respect to the political impact of colonization, the last century of the Republic appears even more dramatic. Even for the better documented end of the first century, we don't have any substantial study of the impact on the social structure of Rome and other Italian cities of land allotments for veterans and the ensuing colonization. And even where relevant references appear, as in some fleeting remarks in the new edition of the *Cambridge Ancient History*,[119] one searches in vain for a possible connection between such measures and the contextual transformation of territorial structures and economic forms of property in the various regions of Italy. The only exceptions, I should say, are the studies of Peter Brunt and, more recently, the work of Lawrence Keppie, but that is all.[120] This is clearly insufficient to give an exhaustive answer to many of our questions.[121]

4. Many questions also remain, regarding the impact, with respect to social equilibrium, of the unforeseen invasion of a multitude of small or middling landowners, introduced forcibly by the process of colonization to an

after 89–88 BCE. This hypothesis constitutes an essential interpretive key for better understanding the peculiar physiognomy of Roman political expansion. Then again, it is true that, over time, some territories that belonged to individual *municipia* were subjected to the work of *gromatici*, resulting in their reorganization in the form of *limitatio*. This phenomenon is anything but exceptional in many areas of the Peninsula and above all in Gallia Cisalpina, where we find the most extensive evidence of the massive systematization carried out by Julius Caesar. But these processes raise further problems: why did these territorial reorganizations occur? And when they were carried out, what sections of municipal territory did they affect? We thus fund ourselves confronted by a considerable host of problems, for which there are relatively few answers and none of them certain. These uncertainties, even at the level of general statements (how many times do we find the generic idea of the 'private property' of colonial lands in scholarly works without any indication that it was not the 'private' known to Roman law?), have long failed to attract much attention on the part of historians. This substantial weakness of twentieth-century historiography pertains not only to Roman colonization; equally serious problems are raised by the parallel development of *municipia*, whether *sine suffragio* or *optimo iure*.

[119] Robin Seager, 'Sulla' in *Cambridge Ancient History* vol 9 (2nd edn, Cambridge University Press 1994) 203ff.

[120] cf Brunt, *Italian Manpower* (n 49) 394–44, Lawrence Keppie, *Colonization and Veteran Settlement in Italy 47–14 BC* (British School at Rome 1983).

[121] cf Brunt, *Italian Manpower* (n 49).

agrarian landscape. What did this unforeseen reappearance of small peasant holdings mean (if that is indeed what it happened)? And, for the last century of Republic, what do the followers of Catiline tell us about the outcome of this phenomenon? Is it perhaps that, over the medium-term, it helped accelerate the expansion of large landholdings even further? But, more than anything else, what could have been the impact on Italian agrarian property and its economy, of Silla's proscriptions, and still more of the continuous land settlement of veterans during the years of the civil wars? To all these problems, for which frequently we don't dispose of sufficient historical evidences, we have to add also how difficult it is for us to follow the fate of every community and its particular its institutional development that is anything but linear and also marked by the great institutional revolutions that shaped the history of the Italian peninsula.[122]

5. A general history, in particular for the period between the innovations of Caesar to the systematization of Augustus down to the great work under Vespasian, remains to be written. It can, I believe, be attempted with success only by broadening our attention, which threatens to become devoted exclusively to inscriptions, and by recovering in full the other important body of evidence represented by the *gromatici*. But, we must note, it can be done only on the condition that we subject this evidence to a stratigraphic reading, because virtually every passage in this corpus is bursting with overlapping, interwoven, and even contradictory references to situations from different eras.[123]

This profound heterogeneity of material presented in seemingly coherent form frustrated the formidable efforts of Rudorff in his day. But more than a century and a half have passed since then. Might the time have come to

[122] When the general process of assimilation initiated by the Romans resulted in the transformation of an ancient peregrine community into a *municipium sine suffragio* and then a *civitas optimo iure*, the altered legal system governing land held as private property by these new citizens, now using Roman law exclusively, did not entail the complete reorganization of this land by forms of *limitatio*. Over the entire Republican era, in an ever more massive and macroscopic fashion the autonomy, semi-sovereignty, and sovereign independence of innumerable Italic *municipia* with autonomous private legal systems, extending to private land ownership, were transformed in consequence to the measures following the Social War, while the greater and more extensive part of private lands, now subject to *dominium ex iure Quiritium*, remained outside the scope of Roman gromatic systems. On the contrary, these were applied not only to Roman public lands—which per se fell outside the scope of civil-law forms of property—but also to the lands of Latin colonies that were, instead, not only outside Roman law, but formally governed by legal systems that I would designate by no other term than 'pseudo-sovereign'.

[123] The person who undoubtedly grasped this particular reconstructive approach is Tibiletti, in his remarkable letter to Dilke (in Tibiletti, *Storie locali* (n 81)), in which he pointed out the profound differentness of the way in which the legal material was treated by the *gromatici* in contrast to the canonical method of Romanists. From this necessarily sprung a different way of interrogating the ancient text: a work that remains to be done.

prepare a new venture? Perhaps it is necessary for this enterprise, not the work of a single scholar, but of a community of scholars that could integrate different competences and specializations. Today, we not only possess the knowledge and the competences that were once inconceivable, but the proliferation of scholarly initiatives—conferences, journals like *Agri centuriati*, individual research—reveals how the path taken by the most recent generation of scholars has proceeded ever more effectively and rapidly. And nonetheless, because we can obtain a new, richer crop of results, I believe we must also see to it that a more intimate fusion occurs between our study of Roman gromatic history and that of the institutional organization and legal forms of its territory, bridging the gap that we still occasionally observe.

7
Epilogue

Reflections on the Past and Future of the Roman Colonial Discourse

Christopher Smith

The study of colonization in the Roman world has, as this volume amply demonstrates, a long and venerable history. The intensive study of Livy and other ancient sources revealed to scholars from Niccolò Machiavelli on the peculiar Roman practice of sending individuals and sometimes families outside Rome to establish a settlement which would operate to some extent independently of Rome, and to some extent in subordination to Rome. Livy and others regarded this practice as something which could be traced back to the beginning of the Roman Republic.[1] They were patchily informed about and interested in who these individuals were, what rights they had and what function the colonies had. Later, towards the end of the Republic, colonies were being used to settle veterans from the legions and their constitutional position was defined by substantial pieces of legislation.[2] Thereafter the foundation and maintenance of overseas colonies represented a new organizational structure in conquered provinces, often explicitly tied to the imperial cult. Their names, officials, and public art all brought the Roman empire into the civic heart of provincial life.[3]

The significant differences between the various forms of colonies are not well represented by our sources. Our sources fail to be able fully to imagine the evolution of warfare, and assume that the armies and wars of the early Republic were similar in scale to those of later periods; therefore they systematically overstate the size and impact of early military activity. Similarly, they fail completely to follow through the logic of their own narrative about the

[1] For a thorough account of the literary sources for early colonization see Monica Chiabà, *Roma e le priscae Latinae coloniae. Ricerche sulla colonizzazione del Lazio dalla costituzione della repubblica alla guerra Latina* (Edizioni Università di Trieste 2011).

[2] Lawrence Keppie, *Colonization and Veteran settlement in Italy 47–14 BC* (British School at Rome 1983).

[3] Rebecca J Sweetman, *Roman Colonies in the First Century of their Foundation* (Oxbow Books 2011).

Christopher Smith, *Epilogue* In: *The Renaissance of Roman Colonization.* Edited by: Jeremia Pelgrom and Arthur Weststeijn, Oxford University Press (2020). © the Several Contributors. DOI: 10.1093/oso/9780198850960.003.0007

small scale of early colonies, often acknowledging small numbers of colonists but assuming high levels of autonomy and impact, which are more relevant to later large-scale and state-driven veteran settlement.[4]

The work of teasing this out has taken some time. Although by the nineteenth century, Barthold Niebuhr and Theodor Mommsen were making substantial progress, they still thought in increasingly rigid categories, elaborating Carlo Sigonio's ground-breaking reconstruction of Roman colonization. So much ink has been spilt over whether colonies had Latin or Roman rights, which is certainly not trivial, but to some extent reflects modern preoccupations. We have made the Romans perhaps a little more precise than they ever were.[5]

The process of easing the rigidity of these distinctions, and insisting on local variation and adaptability has reached its furthest point perhaps in the recent work of Jeremia Pelgrom and Tesse Stek. Their painstaking work of identifying presuppositions in scholarship, especially the standard work of Edward Togo Salmon, which significantly shaped Anglophone scholarship in the last part of the twentieth century, of identifying variability in foundations, and in assessing the limited immediate impact of early colonies, has opened up the debate. We are now faced with some very significant questions about the motivation and mechanisms of Roman colonization in the early and middle Republic, that is, before the Second Punic War.[6]

There are several different and competing problems in play, and one of the most significant questions is the extent to which they coalesce or are distinct. For instance, it is tempting to assume that the motivation of colonization is to be found in another aspect of the ancient historical record, the discussion of a number of significant social and economic problems which beset Roman citizens and the Roman polity. Poverty and indebtedness on the one hand was a social challenge, but given the way the Roman army worked, it also reduced numbers of soldiers. Land redistribution offered solutions for those who for one reason or another had lost land, or who had never had it, but also increased possibilities for mobilization.[7] In the later Republic, this was regarded as a way of removing potentially disruptive

[4] On early Roman warfare, see especially Jeremy Armstrong, *War and Society in Early Rome: From Warlords to Generals* (Cambridge University Press 2016).

[5] See Paul J du Plessis, Clifford Ando, and Kaius Tuori (eds) *The Oxford Handbook of Roman Law and Society* (Oxford University Press 2016) for an up-to-date survey.

[6] Tesse D Stek and Jeremia Pelgrom (eds), *Roman Republican Colonization. New Perspectives from Archaeology and Ancient History* (Palombi 2014) (hereafter Stek and Pelgrom, *Roman Republican Colonization*); previous standard account in Edward Togo Salmon, *Roman Colonization under the Republic* (Thames & Hudson 1969) (hereafter Salmon, *Roman Colonization*).

[7] The agrarian problems of the early Republic are immensely complex. See for an introduction Saskia T Roselaar, *Public Land in the Roman Republic* (Oxford University Press 2010).

individuals from the city, although that was a tendentious comment and there were other discursive descriptions of this practice.[8] Sigonio argued that this was also a factor in early colonization, but this works awkwardly for an earlier situation in which the colonies were being used as part of an aggressive territorial strategy, and where the numbers involved were low, and the individuals not necessarily Romans.

So early Roman colonization at any rate has to be conceptualized rather differently, and not just from the orthodoxy of Salmon but essentially from the whole tradition studied in this volume, and taking its lead from Sigonio. The shift reflects in part our changing understanding of the kind of city Rome was. The more institutionalized Rome was seen to be (a tradition driven in a sense by starting from law), the more we might expect the colonies to follow suit. However there have been attempts to suggest that we should imagine both Rome, and the colonies before the fourth century BCE, as still partly dominated by individuals and their followers. So a powerful model has been developed of individual military leaders generating colonial foundations in the period before the fourth century BCE, a model which sees the colony as a perpetuation of the warrior band. This would offer the possibility of seeing colonies as effectively fissive moments. If this is combined with the idea that a colony could be the result of popular agitation, then we have a complex picture of settlements which were far less related to state decisions.[9]

It remains a reasonable question to ask why their foundation was recorded at all. Livy often gives the information about the foundation of a colony as if it were a formal notice. Now one might argue that this reflects Livy's assumption that any settlement outside Rome was the same as the formal settlements of a later period, and so he (or his sources) invented an official notice for something that was in fact very different. That is indeed possible, and raises the chances that in fact we have far fewer notices of such activity than may have been the case.[10]

[8] Cicero, *Epistulae ad Atticum* 1.19.4; *De Lege agraria* 2.70. See now Evan Jewell, '(Re)moving the Masses: Colonization as Domestic Displacement in the Roman Republic' (2019) 8 Humanities 66.

[9] Guy Bradley, 'Colonization and Identity in Republican Italy' in Guy Bradley and John-Paul Wilson (eds), *Greek and Roman Colonization: Origins, Ideologies and Interactions* (Classical Press of Wales 2006) 161–87.

[10] Salmon, *Roman Colonization* (n 6) 166n7 dismisses Greek sources which claimed that the Romans settled colonies in Corsica and Sardinia in the fourth century, saying that 'they must be in error'. Of the two passages, Diodorus Siculus 15.27.4 is readily amended to refer to Satricum (cf Livy 6.7.1, and cf Diodorus Siculus 14.102). However, Theophrastus, *Historia Plantarum* 5.8.1 records an abortive expedition to Corsica, primarily to found a city, but then to gather timber, and which is so peculiar that it might reflect some sort of more independent mission.

There is however a slightly different version of this which is to suppose that the act of fission was recorded and respected by the Roman authorities. That is to say, that it somehow entered the pontifical records. Why might this be? The best way to understand the nascent Roman politics of the fifth and fourth centuries BCE may well be to accept that the sources reflect a genuine argument between fissive and communal activity, between groups seeking to retain independence, or to retrench their position or break into power, and the increasingly significant polity. We can then envisage a variety of ways in which what may have been predominantly driven by familial ambition or popular agitation was in fact also brought within the purview of the wider community. So retrospective sanction, a formal recognition of continuing rights and shared religious practices, a claim on loyalty might all be relevant. It is notable that if this activity is, as Guy Bradley suggests, compared to a *ver sacrum* or sacred spring the custom of sending out the first born males from communities to found their own settlements, which operated in the Sabine and Samnite worlds, then what we know of that also had a strong communal element.[11]

As we move into the fourth century BCE and beyond, it is harder to sustain the idea that colonial settlements have only a familial element, although it remains arguably a significant element.[12] Critically, as the institutions of the Roman Republic firm up, issues of citizenship, voting, senatorial approval, and so forth become more significant. Salmon, who took a strong statist viewpoint, had reduced the motivation for colonies to being simply a military manoeuvre.[13] That proposal was made much more plausible by the old idea that road-building was followed by colonies, but that looks much less likely now and so colonies preceded roads in many instances.[14] Moreover, the idea that they were starkly independent of their surroundings, or coercive of local populations is, even if Livy's numbers of some thousands of colonists are right, rather difficult to sustain.[15] Equally, colonies were expected to remain tied to Rome; patterns of loyalty and disloyalty in the Second Punic War were of great

[11] Bradley, 'Colonization and Identity in Republican Italy' (n 9) 169; analysis of sources at Luciana Aigner Foresti, 'La tradizione antica sul ver sacrum' in Marta Sordi (ed) *Coercizione e mobilità umana nel mondo antico* (Vita e Pensiero 1995) 141–47; wider considerations in Elena Isayev, *Migration, Mobility and Place in Ancient Italy* (Cambridge University Press 2017).

[12] The thesis was made by Filippo Cassola, *I gruppi politici romani nel III secolo a. C.* (Università degli studi di Trieste 1962); reprised by Nicola Terrenato, *The Early Roman Expansion into Italy. Elite Negotiation and Family Agendas* (Cambridge University Press 2019).

[13] Salmon, *Roman Colonization* (n 6).

[14] Guy Bradley, 'The Nature of Roman Strategy in Mid-Republican Colonization and Road Building' in Stek and Pelgrom, *Roman Republican Colonization* (n 6) 60–72.

[15] Saskia T Roselaar, 'Colonies and Processes of Integration in the Roman Republic' (2011) 123–2 Mélanges de l'École française de Rome, Antiquité 527–55.

concern to the Romans.[16] It may well be that we should envisage that the foundation of colonies which offered advantages to those who participated, with some additional expectations, were increasingly instrumentalized as a set of sometimes unnerving obligations at distance and in potentially dangerous circumstances, but accompanied by minimal privilege. Small wonder that colonies became less appealing over time, and petered out for a while after the early second century BCE.

However, it remains challenging to see military reasons as the only cause for colonial foundations, and one might start to wonder about the economic impacts of colonies.[17] Were they more significant as organizers of territory, or attractors of labour and creators of opportunity? This is an interesting path to follow, and needs to be incorporated into conversations about the development of Roman coinage. While there is some coherence to the location of colonies in terms of military strategy, insofar as we allow that for the Roman Republic, there is also an economic benefit to expanding markets and increased production. Whilst this might seem anachronistically modernist in tone, it is easy to reframe it in the kinds of moral discourses of the time. The role of the farmer, the value of cultivation, and discourses of civilization (even if actually inappropriate) may have been important in rhetoric we sadly no longer have, except in the context of the rather different land distributions of the late Republic. We still lack a comprehensive attempt to read through the distorting lens of Cicero's aggressive rejection of the land redistribution plans of the 60s BCE in the speeches *de lege agraria* in order to determine how the argument in favour might have been expressed and how this fitted into broader conversations about land use. On this specific point however, the speeches are shot through with a discourse of the value of cultivation and the creation of agricultural surplus. It is easy to imagine something similar for the colonies of northern Italy, especially given the ethnographic characterization of the Gauls as poor farmers.[18]

Much of this is reasoning relatively foreign to Sigonio. Although a profound thinker and a good historian, as this volume shows, much of the more recent debate was foreign to his and subsequent systematization. The recognition that

[16] Important discussions in Michael P Fronda, *Between Rome and Carthage: Southern Italy during the Second Punic War* (Cambridge University Press 2010).

[17] See now Tesse D Stek, 'Early Roman Colonization beyond the Romanizing Agro-Town: Village Patterns of Settlement and Highland Exploitation in Central Italy' in Bleda Düring and Tesse D Stek (eds), *The Archaeology of Imperial Landscapes* (Cambridge University Press 2018) 145–72; Saskia T Roselaar, *Italy's Economic Revolution Integration and Economy in Republican Italy* (Oxford University Press 2019).

[18] General account in Carolynn E Roncaglia, *Northern Italy in the Roman World From the Bronze Age to Late Antiquity* (Johns Hopkins University Press 2017). Polybius 2.17.7 and Caesar, *De Bello Gallico* 3.17 both hint at the Gallic disinterest in agricultural efficiency.

the Roman world was different, perhaps very different, from that of Livy, was relatively late in coming and even when it did, the kind of world which we are sketching was rather different from that which Louis de Beaufort or others contemplated. So one question might be to ask what sort of intellectual enterprise we are engaged in here?

One answer might be that we are watching the way that modern scholarship fashioned a discourse around the ancient evidence for Roman colonization. In other words we are seeing the contours of modern thought as it evolves in dialogue with historical study. Sigonio was drawing on and feeding into traditions of scholarship which were fascinated by the Roman example. But they were not obviously likely to deploy the specific example of colonization. When Machiavelli proposed colonization as potentially advantageous, he did not persuade anyone to follow his advice. Sigonio's careful attempts to understand colonization were no doubt influential in legal arguments for instance over the contemporary extension of control over the New World and later America, as the volume shows, but they do not seem to have made a determining impact on overseas policy.

However, I venture to suggest that what this volume is demonstrating is the way that Roman history was used to illuminate two central problems. The first is the problem of sovereignty over distance and the second is the nature of imperialism. Both would require substantial treatments. Here I want simply to outline how the rather theoretical problem of what the Romans were doing when they founded colonies in fact has huge theoretical impact. Once one has recognized that until very recently Roman colonization was regarded as a relatively uniform and state-run operation, a central concern becomes the status of that colony vis-à-vis Rome. Were the colonists citizens? Citizens of where? What were the limits and theoretical understanding of their autonomy?

In the absence of the possibility of significant consent, and in the presence of the Roman paradox of the double loyalty to Rome and to the local community, the colony is an interesting thought experiment. This thought experiment would become extremely significant in the context of various imperial enterprises, including the British expansion in North America, as shown above. But the problem has an even wider relevance.

Lauren Benton's pathbreaking volume on geography and law in European imperialism tells a story which is absolutely comparable to ours, precisely because her subjects are tackling the same problem.[19] What does it mean to

[19] Lauren Benton, *A Search for Sovereignty. Law and Geography in European Empires, 1400–1900* (Cambridge University Press 2009).

exercise power at and over distance? The production of imperial space offered the same challenge in antiquity as it did in the early modern and modern periods. Benton argues that 'descriptions of geographic elements such as rivers, oceans, islands and highlands were creatively combined with discourses about law and with reports about patterns of legal practice'.[20] So exploration, especially via rivers, mapping, and eventually the definition of territorially bounded imperial spaces are a chronological sequence which is extremely close to the Roman capillary processes of expansion. In this way, colonies in a sense are part of the process of testing out the eventual snaking road network; and one can also think perhaps of the importance of the Tiber and the Po among other rivers in guiding expansion.

Benton turns to the challenge of the sea. In due course, Roman notions of the *mare nostrum* would feed into the larger Grotian challenge of the specific legal nature of the sea, but at an earlier point the sea could be regarded as 'a space of intersecting corridors'. This seems to me to be a very interesting concept in relation to the work of the Roman maritime colonies. The early ones were small and relatively unpopular, and perhaps more connected to the defence of the hinterland, but at the same stage they were defined to a degree by pirate routes and the challenge of maritime violence. The move to found such colonies was a critical step in shaping a Roman view of the connectivity of land and sea. The fact that they had a specific legal requirement (not to be away for more than thirty days) perhaps reinforces the sense of the exceptionalism of the coastal façade, but it also indicates a remarkable challenge for citizenship—these citizens were more constrained than non-citizens.

When it comes to landlocked colonies, Benton extracts a discourse of the town as domesticating the surrounding countryside which is identical to the sorts of notions of the interaction between Roman and native which Pelgrom in particular has effectively critiqued in his work.[21] Some of the discourse around hill dwellers no doubt borrowed its rhetoric from classical texts. Benton rightly draws a direct line from narratives of the conquest of the New World to Roman overseas conquest, but the experience of empire, the need to permit a certain degree of local invention and the debate over the peculiar legal statuses of colonial towns is a perfect match to what we have just described. What the Romans actually did in engaging

[20] ibid 9.

[21] Jeremia Pelgrom, 'Roman Colonization and the City-State Model' in Stek and Pelgrom, *Roman Republican Colonization* (n 6) 73–87.

with other Italians, and how they ended up defining that process in a legalistic language that was more straightforward than the messy reality is exactly Benton's story too. The intellectual background to the modern struggles with empire is precisely the subject of this book.

Benton concludes with a very complex picture of partial and divided sovereignty, far from the classic notion of indivisible sovereignty coterminous with national boundaries. What this covers was a great deal of violence and repression; it was a steady working out of the process of imperialism. It is noticeable that Sigonio's concentration on different sorts of *jura* gave way to rather more direct applications to practice in for instance the North American context. Livy and his sources' occlusion of both local participation and the potential independence of the colonies offers an interesting parallel with the problems of colonies being both inventive and constrained. Niebuhr and Mommsen bring us to rather similar versions of Roman systematization as we find in the nineteenth-century discussions of imperialism, where the subtle differences are rather driven out. But Roman lawyers were not nineteenth-century lawyers, even if they did systematize more complex situations. One of the many fascinating aspects of the twentieth-century scholarship was the road which Giancarlo Tibiletti opened, but which we are only beginning to take, which is a recognition of the fact that structures of power are co-produced and locally variable.[22] The scaffolding of sovereignty, like the artifice of empire, is an exercise in overt and concealed violence, in visible and internalized exercises of power.

In short, the historiography of Roman colonization runs parallel to the historiography of imperialism more generally. Our modern messy and complex pictures of agency are comparable to the acute and sensitive accounts we now write about the emergence of modern imperial space. Nineteenth-century systematizing approaches are mirrored in the organizational approach to empire; earlier still, the Roman understanding of the peculiarities of the Roman colony map on to the experience of exercising power over distance. This volume has shown how the intellectual history of one byway of the renewing explication of the Roman world contributes profoundly to the understanding of later imperialism, and of the history of our own times.

[22] Giancarlo Tibiletti, *Storie locali dell'Italia romana* (presso la rivista 'Athenaeum' 1978).

Bibliography

Abbott, Frank F and Johnson, Allan C *Municipal Administration in the Roman Empire* (Princeton University Press 1926)

Abercromby, James, *Magna Charta for America: James Abercromby's 'An examination of the acts of Parliament relative to the trade and the government of our American colonies' (1752) and 'De jure et gubernatione coloniarum, or An inquiry into the nature, and the rights of colonies, ancient, and modern' (1774)* (JP Greene, CF Mullett, and EC Papenfuse eds, American Philosophical Society 1986)

Afzelius, Adam, *Die römische Eroberung Italiens (320–264 v. Chr.)* (Universitetsforlaget I Aarhus 1942)

Agustín, Antonio, *De legibus et senatus consultis liber* (Basa 1583)

Agustín, Antonio, *Dialogos de medallas, inscriciones y otras antiguedadas* (Felipe Mey 1587)

Aigner-Foresti, Luciana, 'La tradizione antica sul ver sacrum' in Marta Sordi (ed) *Coercizione e mobilità umana nel mondo antico* (Vita e Pensiero 1995) 141–47

Alciato, Andrea, *De verborum significatione* (Gryphius 1530)

Alciato, Andrea, *Rerum patriae libri IIII* (Bidelli 1625)

Anghie, Anthony, *Sovereignty, Imperialism and the Making of International Law* (Cambridge University Press 2004)

Apianus, Petrus and Amantius, Bartolomaeus, *Inscriptiones sacrosanctae vetustatis non illae quidem Romanae, sed totius fere orbis* (Apianus 1534)

Arbel, Benjamin, 'Colonie d'Oltremare' in Alberto Tenenti and Ugo Tucci (eds), *Storia di Venezia dalle origini alla caduta della Serenissima, vol. 5: Il Rinascimento. Società ed economia* (Istituto della Enciclopedia Italiana 1996) 947–85

Arbel, Benjamin, 'Venice's Maritime Empire in the Early Modern Period' in Eric Dursteller (ed), *A Companion to Venetian History, 1400–1797* (Brill 2013) 125–253

Arena, Valentina, *Libertas and the Practice of Politics in the Late Roman Republic* (Cambridge University Press 2012)

Armitage, David, 'Empire and Liberty: A Republican Dilemma' in Martin van Gelderen and Quentin Skinner (eds), *Republicanism: a Shared European Heritage*, vol 2, (Cambridge University Press 2002) 29–46

Armitage, David, *The Ideological Origins of the British Empire* (Cambridge University Press 2004)

Armstrong, Jeremy, *War and Society in Early Rome: From Warlords to Generals* (Cambridge University Press 2016)

Arneil, Barbara, *Domestic Colonies: The Turn Inward to Colony* (Oxford University Press 2017)

Bacon, Francis, 'Of Plantations' (1625) in Michael Kiernan (ed), *The Essayes or Counsels, Civill and Morall* (Oxford University Press 1985)

Balbo, Mattia, 'La *lex Licinia de modo agrorum*: riconsiderazione di un modello storiografico' (2010) 138 Rivista di Filologia e di Istruzione Classica 265–311

Balbo, Mattia, '*Lex tam acerba*: la sanzione per i trasgressori del modus agrorum nella Roma repubblicana' (2014) 142 Rivista di Filologia e di Istruzione Classica 75–90

Bandelli, Gino, *Ricerche sulla colonizzazione romana della Gallia Cisalpina* (Quasar 1988)

Bannister, Turpin C, 'Oglethorpe's Sources for the Savannah Plan' (1961) 20 The Journal of the Society of Architectural Historians 47–62

Barbati, Stefano, 'Gli studi sulla cittadinanza romana prima e dopo le ricerche di Giorgio Luraschi' (2012) 12 Rivista di Diritto Romano 1–21

Barbati, Stefano, 'Asc., in Pis. 3 Clark: sulle cosiddette "colonie fittizie" transpadane' (2013) 3 Quaderni Lupiensi 59–106

Barron, William, *History of the Colonization of the Free States of Antiquity Applied to the Present Contest between Great Britain and Her American Colonies* (Cadell 1777)

Bartolucci, Guido, *La Repubblica ebraica di Carlo Sigonio: modelli politici dell'età moderna* (Olschki 2007)

Bartolucci, Guido, 'Carlo Sigonio and the "Respublica Hebraeorum": A Re-evaluation' (2008) 3 Hebraic Political Studies 19–59

Bartolucci, Guido, 'The Hebrew Republic in the Political Debate of Sixteenth-Century Europe: The Struggle for Jurisdiction' in Wyger Velema and Arthur Weststeijn (eds), *Ancient Models in the Early Modern Republican Imagination* (Brill 2017) 214–33

Baudouin, François, *De institutione historiae universae et eius cum iurisprudentiae coniunctione* προλεγομένων *libri II* (André Wechel 1561)

Beaufort, Louis de, *La république romaine, ou plan général de l'ancien gouvernement de Rome* (Nicolas van Daalen 1766)

Bell, Duncan (ed), *Empire, Race and Global Justice* (Cambridge University Press 2019)

Belloni, Annalisa, *L'Alciato e il diritto pubblico romano: I Vat. Lat. 6216, 6271, 7071* (Biblioteca Apostolica Vaticana 2016)

Beloch, Karl Julius, *Der italische Bund unter Roms Hegemonie* (Teubner 1880)

Beloch, Karl Julius, *Römische Geschichte bis zum Beginn der Punischen Kriege* (Walter de Gruyter 1926)

Benton, Lauren, *A Search for Sovereignty. Law and Geography in European Empires, 1400–1900* (Cambridge University Press 2009)

Béranger, Jean, 'Les jugements de Cicéron sur les Gracques' (1972) 1 Aufstieg und Niedergang der römischen Welt 732–63

Bernardi, Aurelio, *Nomen Latinum* (Collegio Ghislieri 1973)

Bernays, Jakob, 'Die Behandlung des römischen Staatsrechts bis auf Theodor Mommsen' in Jacob Bernays and Hermann Usener (eds), *Gesammelte Abhandlungen* (Hertz 1885) vol 2, 255–75

Bersani, Silvia Giorcelli, *Torino capitale degli studi seri. Carteggio Theodor Mommsen—Carlo Promis* (Celid 2014)

Bianchi, Lorenzo, 'Machiavelli e Cardano. Note su naturalismo e fortuna' in Lorenzo Bianchi and Alberto Postigliola (eds), *Dopo Machiavelli/Après Machiavel* (Liguori 2008) 53–73

Biondo, Flavio, *De roma triumphante* (Froben 1559)

Bispham, Edward, 'Coloniam deducere: How Roman was Roman Colonization During the Middle Republic?' in Guy J Bradley and John-Paul Wilson (eds), *Greek and Roman Colonization* (Classical Press of Wales 2006) 73–160

Bispham, Edward, *From Asculum to Actium. The Municipalization of Italy from the Social War to Augustus* (Oxford University Press 2007)

Bland, Richard, *An Inquiry into the Rights of the British Colonies* (Alexander Purdie 1766)

Blume, Friedrich, Lachmann, Karl, and Rudorff, Adolf, *Die Schriften der römischen Feldmesser* (Georg Reimer 1848)

Boralevi, Lea Campos, 'Classical Foundational Myths of European Republicanism: The Jewish Commonwealth' in Martin van Gelderen and Quentin Skinner (eds), *Republicanism: A Shared European Heritage*, vol 1, (Cambridge University Press 2002) 247–61

Botero, Giovanni, *Della ragion di stato libri dieci. Con tre libri delle cause della grandezza e magnificenza delle città* (Gioliti 1589)
Bracke, Wouter, 'La première "édition" humaniste du *De verborum significatione* de Festus (Vat. Lat. 5958)' (1995) 25 Revue d'histoire des textes 189–215
Bradley, Guy, 'Colonization and Identity in Republican Italy' in Guy J Bradley and John-Paul Wilson (eds), *Greek and Roman Colonization* (Classical Press of Wales 2006) 161–87
Bradley, Guy, 'The Nature of Roman Strategy in Mid-Republican Colonization and Road Building' in Tesse Stek and Jeremia Pelgrom (eds), *Roman Republican Colonization* (Palombi 2014) 60–72
Bradley, Guy and Wilson, John-Paul (eds), *Greek and Roman Colonization. Origins, Ideologies and Interactions* (The Classical Press of Wales 2006)
Bridges, John, *A defence of the gouernment established in the Church of Englande for ecclesiasticall matters* (John Windet 1587)
Brown, Frank, *Cosa. The Making of a Roman Town* (University of Michigan Press 1980)
Brunt, Peter A, *Italian Manpower 225 BC–AD 14* (Oxford University Press 1971)
Brunt, Peter A, '*Nobilitas* and *novitas*' (1982) 72 Journal of Roman Studies 1–17
Brunt, Peter A, *The Fall of the Roman Republic and Related Essays* (Clarendon Press 1988)
Budé, Guillaume, *Annotationes priores et posteriores . . . in Pandectas* (De Vascosan 1556)
Calvelli, Lorenzo, 'Novità sulla fortuna del Codex unicus di Velleio Paterculo' (2016) 58 Rivista di cultura classica e medioevale 357–72
Campbell, Brian, *The Writings of the Roman Land Surveyors: Introduction, Text, Translation and Commentary* (Institute of Classical Studies 2000)
Capogrossi Colognesi, Luigi, *Cittadini e territorio. Consolidamento e trasformazione della 'civitas Romana'* (La Sapienza 2000)
Capogrossi Colognesi, Luigi, 'Gli studi di storia romana e di diritto di Umberto Laffi' (2003) 69 Studia et Documenta Historiae et Iuris 401–10
Capogrossi Colognesi, Luigi, *De Ruggiero e l'Italia romana* (Arbor Sapientiae 2004)
Capogrossi Colognesi, Luigi, 'Le radici storiche della lex Licinia de modo agrorum' in Cosimo Cascione and Carla Masi Doria (eds), *Fides humanitas ius: Studii in onore di Luigi Labruna* (Editoriale scientifica 2007) vol 2, 677–94
Capogrossi Colognesi, Luigi, *Scritti scelti* (Jovene 2010)
Capogrossi Colognesi, Luigi, *Padroni e contadini nell'Italia repubblicana* ('L'Erma' di Bretschneider 2012)
Capogrossi Colognesi, Luigi, *Storia di Roma tra diritto e potere* (2nd edn, Il Mulino 2014)
Capogrossi Colognesi, Luigi, 'Gabba e l'Italia romana' in *Emilio Gabba. Un maestro della storia antica* (Bardi Edizioni 2016) 73–83
Cardano, Girolamo, *De sapientia* (Iohannes Petreius 1544)
Carocci, Giampiero, 'Problemi agrari del Lazio nel '500' (1959) 1 Studi storici 3–23
Casali, Battista, *In legem agrariam pro communi utilitate, et ecclesiastica libertate tuenda, ad Clementem VII Pont. Max. oratio* (De Henricis and Perusinus 1524)
Cassola, Filippo, *I gruppi politici romani nel III secolo a. C.* (Università degli studi di Trieste 1962)
Castagnoli, Ferdinando, *Le 'formae' delle colonie romane e le miniature dei codici dei gromatici* (Anno Edizione 1943)
Castagnoli, Ferdinando, *Topografia antica. Un metodo di studio* (Istituto Poligrafico dello Stato 1993)
Ceserani, Giovanna, *Italy's Lost Greece. Magna Graecia and the Making of Modern Archaeology* (Oxford University Press 2012)
Chiabà, Monica, *Roma e le priscae Latinae coloniae. Ricerche sulla colonizzazione del Lazio dalla costituzione della repubblica alla guerra Latina* (Edizioni Università di Trieste 2011)

Chouquer, Gérard and Favory, François, *L'arpentage romain* (Errance 2001)

Chouquer, Gérard and others (eds), *Structures agraires en Italie centro-méridionale. Cadastres et paysages ruraux* (École française de Rome 1987)

Clavel-Lévêque, Monique (ed), *Cadastres et espaces rurales. Approches et réalités antiques* (Éditions du Centre national de la Recherche scientifique 1983)

Codicis Theodosiani Libri XVI (Johannes Sichardus ed, Henricus Petrus 1528)

Cohen, Benjamin, 'La notion d'*ordo* dans la Rome antique' (1975) 4-2 Bulletin de l'Association Guillaume Budé 259–82

Coles, Amanda J, 'Founding Colonies and Fostering Careers in the Middle Republic' (2017) 112 Classical Journal 283–87

Consideratien als dat de negotie op Brasil behoort open gestelt te worden (1638)

Copie consideratien van d'edele Pieter van Hoorn wegens de Nederlantse colonie in dese Indische gewesten, National Archive, The Hague, 1.04.02, 1297 Batavia, fols. 685–702

Cornell, Tim J, 'The Conquest of Italy' in Frank W Walbank (ed), *The Cambridge Ancient History* vol 7.2 (2nd edn, Cambridge University Press 1990) 351–419

Coşkun, Altay, *Bürgerrechtsentzug oder Fremdenausweisung? Studien zu den Rechten von Latinern und weiteren Fremden sowie zum Bürgerrechtswechsel in der römischen Republik (5. bis frühes 1 Jh. v. Chr.)* (Steiner 2009)

Coşkun, Altay, 'The Latins and Their Legal Status in the Context of the Cultural and Political Integration of Pre- and Early Roman Italy' (2016) 98 Klio 526–69

Crawford, Michael H (ed), *Antonio Agustín between Renaissance and Counter-Reform* (The Warburg Institute 1993)

Crawford, Michael H, 'La storia della colonizzazione romana secondo i Romani' in Alfredina Storchi Marino (ed), *L'incidenza dell'antico. Studi in memoria di Ettore Lepore* 1 (Luciano 1995) 187–92

Crawford, Michael H (ed), *Roman Statutes* (Institute of Classical Studies 1996)

Crawford, Michael H, 'How to Create a *municipium*: Rome and Italy after the Social War' in Michel Austin, Jill Harries, Christopher Smith (eds), *Modus Operandi: Essays in Honour of Geoffrey Rickman* (Institute of Classical Studies 1998)

Cuddihy, William J, 'Paxton's Case and the Writs of Assistance Controversy in Massachusetts, 1755–1762' in William J Cuddihy (ed), *The Fourth Amendment: Origins and Original Meaning, 602–1791* (Oxford University Press 2009)

Cunaeus, Petrus, *The Hebrew Republic* (Peter Wyetzner tr, Shalem Press 2006)

D'Alessandro, Alessandro, *Genialium dierum libri vi* (De Vascosan 1549)

Dart, Christopher J, *The Social War, 91 to 88 BCE. A History of the Italian Insurgency Against the Roman Republic* (Ashgate 2014)

De agrorum conditionibus, & constitutionibus limitum (Turnèbe 1554)

De Divitiis, Bianca, Lenzo, Fulvio and Miletti, Lorenzo (eds), *Ambrogio Leone's* De Nola, *Venice 1514* (Brill 2018)

De Martino, Francesco, *Storia della costituzione romana* (Jovene 1973)

De Nolhac, Pierre, *La bibliothèque de Fulvio Orsini* (Bouillon & Vieweg 1887)

De Nolhac, Pierre, 'Piero Vettori et Carlo Sigonio. Correspondance avec Fulvio Orsini' (1889) 10 Studi e documenti di storia e diritto 138–49

De Ruggiero, Ettore, *La 'gens' in Roma avanti la formazione del commune* (Tipografia del Genio Artistico 1872)

De Ruggiero, Ettore, *Le colonie dei Romani* (Tipografia dell'Umbria 1896)

De Ruggiero, Ettore, 'colonia', *Dizionario Epigrafico II* (Pasqualucci 1900)

De Ruggiero, Ettore, 'Lo Stato e la città capitale nel mondo romano' (1918) 2 Nuova Rivista Storica 3

De Ruggiero, Ettore, *La Patria nel diritto pubblico romano* (Maglione 1921)
De Sanctis, Gaetano, *Storia dei Romani* (2nd edn, La Nuova Italia 1960)
Días Fernández, Alejandro, Provincia et Imperium. *El mando provincial en la República romana (227–44 a. C.)* (Universidad de Sevilla 2015)
Dietler, Michael. *Archaeologies of Colonialism: Consumption, Entanglement, and Violence in Ancient Mediterranean France* (University of California Press 2010)
Dilke, Oswald AW, *The Roman Land Surveyors. An introduction to the Agrimensores* (David and Charles 1971)
Dionisotti, Anna Carlotta, 'On Fragments in Classical Scholarship' in Glenn W Most (ed), *Collecting Fragments—Fragmente sammeln* (Vandenhoeck & Ruprecht 1997) 1–33
Drogula, Fred K, '*Imperium*, *potestas* and the *pomerium* in the Roman Republic' (2007) 56 Historia 419–52
Drogula, Fred K, *Commanders and Command in the Roman Republic and Early Empire* (University of North Carolina Press Chapel 2015)
Du Rivail, Aymar, *Civilis historiae iuris, sive in XII tab. leges commentarii* (Schoeffer 1527)
Eck, Werner, *Die staatliche Organization Italiens in der hohen Kaiserzeit* (Beck 1979)
Eck, Werner and Galsterer, Hartmut, *Die Stadt in Oberitalien und in den nordwestlichen Provinzen des Römischen Reiches* (Zabern 1991)
Elliott, John H, *Empires of the Atlantic World. Britain and Spain in America, 1492–1830* (Yale University Press 2006)
Ensslin, Wilhelm, 'praefectus iure dicundo', *Realencyclopädie XXII* (Druckenmüller 1954) 1309–23
Erasmus, Hendrik J, *The Origins of Rome in Historiography from Petrarch to Perizonius* (Van Gorcum 1962)
Kornemann, Ernst, 'municipium', *Realencyclopädie XVI* (Druckenmüller 1933) 570–638
Favory, François, 'Détection des cadastres antiques par filtrage optique' (1980) 92 Mélanges de l'École française de Rome - Antiquité 347–86
Fentress, Elizabeth, 'Frank Brown, Cosa and the Idea of a Roman City' in Elizabeth Fentress (ed), *Romanization and the City: Creation, Transformation and Failures* (2000) 38 Journal of Roman Archaeology Supplementary Series 11–24
Ferguson, Adam, *The History of the Progress and Termination of the Roman Republic* (Strahan 1783)
Ferrary, Jean-Louis, *Onofrio Panvinio et les antiquités romaines* (École française de Rome 1996)
Ferrary, Jean-Louis, 'Onofrio Panvinio' in Colette Nativel (ed), *Centuriae Latinae: Cent une figures humanistes... offertes à Jacques Chomarat* (Droz 1997) 595–99
Ferrary, Jean-Louis, 'Rome et Venise dans la pensée politique et chez les antiquaires du XVIe siècle: à propos des *Antiquitates Romanae* de Paul Manuce' (1997) 141–2 Comptes Rendus de l'Academie des Inscriptions et Belles-Lettres 491–514
Ferrary, Jean-Louis, *Recherches sur les lois comitiales et sur le droit public romain* (Pavia University Press 2012)
Finley, Moses I, *Ancient History. Evidence and Models* (Chatto & Windus 1985)
Fiocchi, Andrea, *De potestibus romanorum libri II* (Plantin 1561)
Fitzmaurice, Andrew, 'The Commercial Ideology of Colonization in Jacobean England: Robert Johnson, Giovanni Botero, and the Pursuit of Greatness' (2007) 64 The William and Mary Quarterly 791–820
Fitzmaurice, Andrew, *Sovereignty, Property and Empire, 1500–2000* (Cambridge University Press 2014)
Flower, Harriet I, *Ancestor Masks and Aristocratic Power in Roman Culture* (Clarendon Press 1999)

Flower, Harriet I, *Roman Republics* (Princeton University Press 2010)
Forni, Giovanna M, 'Tribù romane e problemi connessi dal Biondo Flavio al Mommsen' in *Studi di storia antica in memoria di Luca de Regibus* (Universitá di Genova 1969) 17–90
Fraccaro, Plinio, 'Di alcuni antichissimi lavori idraulici di Roma e della Campagna' (1919) 56 *Bollettino della Reale società geografica italiana* 186–215
Fraccaro, Plinio, 'La malaria e la storia degli antichi popoli classici' (1919) 22 Atene e Roma 186–215
Fraccaro, Plinio, 'colonizzazione (greca e romana)', *Enciclopledia Treccani XXI* (Treccani 1931) 831–36
Fraccaro, Plinio, 'L'organizzazione politica dell'Italia romana', *Atti del congresso internazionale di diritto romano* (Fusi 1933) 195–208
Fraccaro, Plinio, 'Centuriazione romana dell'agro Ticinese (con una carta topografica)' in *Atti e memorie del IV Congresso storico lombardo* (Giuffrè 1940) 3–13
Fraccaro, Plinio, 'La colonia romana di Eporedia (Ivrea) e la sua centuriazione' (1941) 79 *Annali dei lavori pubblici* 1–24
Fraccaro, Plinio, *Opuscula I. Scritti di carattere generale, studi catoniani, i processi degli Scipioni* (La Rivista 'Athenaeum' 1956)
Frede, Dorothea, 'Citizenship in Aristotle's *Politics*' in Richard Kraut and Steven Skultety (eds), *Aristotle's Politics: Critical Essays* (Rowman & Littlefield 2005) 167–84
Freeman, Samuel, 'Constitutional Democracy and the Legitimacy of Judicial Review' (1990–91) 9 Law and Philosophy 327–70
Fronda, Michael P, *Between Rome and Carthage: Southern Italy during the Second Punic War* (Cambridge University Press 2010)
Fryde, Edmund B, *Humanism and Renaissance Historiography* (Hambledon Press 1983)
Gabba, Emilio, 'Sulle strutture agrarie dell'Italia romana fra III e I sec. a.C.' in Emilio Gabba and Marinella Pasquinucci (eds), *Strutture agrarie e allevamento transumante nell'Italia romana (III–I sec. a.C.)* (Giardini 1979) 5–73
Gabba, Emilio, *Italia romana* (New Press Edizioni 1994)
Galsterer, Helmut, *Herrschaft und Verwaltung im republikanischen Italien. Die Beziehungen Roms zu den Italischen Gemeinden vom Latinerfrieden 338 v. Chr. bis zum Bundesgenossenkrieg 91 v. Chr.* (CH Beck 1976)
Gargola, Daniel J, *Lands, Laws and Gods: Magistrates and Ceremony in the Regulation of Public Lands in Republican Rome* (University of North Carolina Press 1995)
Gargola, Daniel J, 'Appian and the Aftermath of the Gracchan Reform' (1997) 118 American Journal of Philology 555–81
Gargola, Daniel J, 'The Gracchan Reform and Appian's Representation of an Agrarian Crisis' in Luuk de Ligt and Simon Northwood (eds), *People, Land and Politics. Demographic Developments and the Transformation of Roman Italy, 300 BC–AD 14* (Brill 2008)
Gargola, Daniel J, *The Shape of the Roman Order: The Republic and its Spaces* (University of North Carolina Press 2017)
Garnsey, Peter, *Thinking about Property. From Antiquity to the Age of Revolution* (Cambridge University Press 2007)
Gelderen, Martin van and Skinner, Quentin (eds), *Republicanism: a Shared European Heritage* 2 vols (Cambridge University Press 2002)
Gelzer, Matthias, 'Latium', *Realencyclopädie XII* (Druckenmüller 1924) 940–63
Gelzer, Matthias, *The Roman Nobility* (R Seager tr, Blackwell 1969)
Giardina, Andrea and Vauchez, André, *Il mito di Roma. Da Carlo Magno a Mussolini* (Laterza 2000)
Giglioli, Giulio Quirino (ed), *Mostra augustea della romanità: catalogo* (Colombo 1938)

Ginzburg, Carlo, 'Machiavelli: L'eccezione e la regola' (2003) 38 Quaderni storici 195–213
Godwyn, Thomas, *Romanae historiae anthologia* (John Lichfield 1631)
Goffart, Walter, *Historical Atlases: The First Three Hundred Years* (Chicago University Press 2003)
Göhler, Josef, *Rom und Italien* (Verlag Priebatschs Buchhandlung 1939)
Grafton, Anthony, *Joseph Scaliger. A Study in the History of Scholarship, vol. 1: Textual Criticism and Exegesis* (Oxford University Press 1983)
Grafton, Anthony, *Defenders of the Text* (Harvard University Press 1991)
Grafton, Anthony, *The Footnote: A Curious History* (Harvard University Press 1997)
Grafton, Anthony, 'Conflict and Harmony in the *Collegium Gellianum*' in Leofranc Holford-Strevens and Amiel Vardi (eds), *The Worlds of Aulus Gellius* (Oxford University Press 2004) 318–42
Grafton, Anthony, *What Was History? The Art of History in Early Modern Europe* (Cambridge University Press 2007)
Greene, Molly, *A Shared World. Christians and Muslims in the Early Modern Mediterranean* (Princeton University Press 2002)
Gregorovius, Ferdinand, 'Alcuni cenni storici sulla cittadinanza romana' (1876–77) 274 Atti della R. Accademia dei Lincei 342
Grelle, Francesco, *'Stipendium vel tributum'. L'imposizione fondiaria nelle dottrine giuridiche del II e III secolo* (Pubblicazioni della Facoltà Giuridica dell'Università di Napoli 1963)
Grelle, Francesco, *L'autonomia cittadina fra Traiano e Adriano. Teoria e prassi dell'organizzazione municipale romana* (Edizioni Scientifiche Italiane 1972)
Grift, Liesbeth van de and Forclaz, Amalia Ribi (eds), *Governing the Rural in Interwar Europe* (Routledge 2017)
Grol, Gerrit Johan van, *De grondpolitiek in het West-Indisch domein der Generaliteit* (Algemeene Landsdrukkerij 1934)
Hammersley, Rachel, *James Harrington. An Intellectual Biography* (Oxford University Press 2019)
Harrington, James, *The Commonwealth of Oceana and a System of Politics* (John GA Pocock ed, Cambridge University Press 1992)
Harris, William V, *War and Imperialism in Republican Rome 327–70 BC* (Clarendon Press 1979)
Haverfield, Francis J, *Ancient Town Planning* (Clarendon Press 1913)
Herklotz, Ingo, *Cassiano dal Pozzo und die Archäologie des 17. Jahrhunderts* (Himer 1999)
Herklotz, Ingo, 'Arnaldo Momigliano's "Ancient History and the Antiquarian": A Critical Review' in Peter N Miller (ed), *Momigliano and Antiquarianism: Foundations of the Modern Cultural Sciences* (Toronto University Press 2007) 127–53
Heuss, Alfred, *Barthold Georg Niebuhrs wissenschaftliche Anfänge. Untersuchungen und Mitteilungen über die Kopenhagener Manuscripte und zur europäischen Tradition der lex agraria (loi agraire)* (Vandenhoeck & Ruprecht 1981)
Heyne, Christian G, *Opuscula academica collecta et animadversionibus locupletata* (Dieterich 1796)
Hinrichs, Focke T, *Die Geschichte der gromatischen Institutionen. Untersuchungen zu Landverteilung, Landvermessung, Bodenverwaltung und Bodenrecht im römischen Reich* (Franz Steiner 1974)
Hooke, Nathaniel, *Roman History. From the Building of Rome to the Ruin of the Commonwealth* (reprint Thomas Davison 1830)
Hörnqvist, Mikael, *Machiavelli and Empire* (Cambridge University Press 2004)
Hotman, François, *De legibus populi romani liber* (Episcopius 1557)

Hulsebosch, Daniel, *Constituting Empire: New York and the Transformation of Constitutionalism in the Atlantic World, 1664–1830* (University of North Carolina Press 2005)

Humbert, Michel, *Municipium et civitas sine suffragio. L'organization de la conquête jusqu'à la guerre sociale* (École française de Rome 1978)

Hunt, Isaac, *The Political Family: or a discourse, pointing out the reciprocal advantages, which flow from an uninterrupted Union between Great-Britain and her American Colonies* (James Humphreys 1775)

Huschke, Philipp E *Über die Stelle des Varros von den Licinien (de re rust. I, 2. §. 9), nebst einer Zugabe über Fest. v. Possessiones und Possessio: Zwei Abhandlungen aus dem Gebiete der Alterthumswissenschaft und Rechtsgeschichte* (JCB Mohr 1835)

Isayev, Elena, *Migration, Mobility and Place in Ancient Italy* (Cambridge University Press 2017)

Ittersum, Martine van, *Profit and Principle. Hugo Grotius, Natural Rights Theories and the Rise of Dutch Power in the East Indies, 1595–1615* (Brill 2006)

Jacks, Philip, 'The *Simulachrum* of Fabio Calvo: A View of Roman Architecture all'antica in 1527' (1990) 72 Art Bulletin 453–81

Jacobs, Jaap, 'Dutch Proprietary Manors In America: The Patroonships In New Netherland' in Louis Roper and Bertrand Van Ruymbeke (eds), *Constructing Early Modern Empires. Proprietary Ventures in the Atlantic World, 1500–1750* (Brill 2007) 301–26

Jewell, Evan, '(Re)moving the Masses: Colonization as Domestic Displacement in the Roman Republic' (2019) 8 Humanities 66

Jhering, Rudolf von, *Geist des römischen Rechts auf den verschiedenen Stufen seiner Entwicklung* (Breitkopf und Härtel 1854)

Johnson, Curtis, 'Who is Aristotle's Citizen?' (1984) 29 Phronesis 73–90

Jones, William (ed), *The Speeches of Isæus in Causes Concerning the Law of Succession to Property at Athens* (J Nichols 1779)

Jonge, Jan KJ de (ed), *Opkomst van het Nederlandsch gezag over Java*, vol 3 (Martinus Nijhoff 1872)

Kelley, Donald R, *Foundations of Modern Historical Scholarship: Language, Law and History in the French Renaissance* (Columbia University Press 1970)

Kendall, Seth, *The Struggle for Roman Citizenship. Romans, Allies and the Wars of 91–77 BCE* (Gorgias Press 2013)

Keppie, Lawrence, *Colonization and Veteran Settlement in Italy 47–14 BC* (British School at Rome 1983)

King, Russell, *Land Reform: The Italian Experience* (Butterworth-Heinemann 1973)

Kingsbury, Benedict and Straumann, Benjamin (eds), *The Roman Foundations of the Law of Nations. Alberico Gentili and the Justice of Empire* (Oxford University Press 2010)

Knorr, Klaus E, *British Colonial Theories, 1570–1850* (University of Toronto Press 1944)

Kornemann, Ernst, 'coloniae', *Realencyclopädie IV* (Druckenmüller 1901) 511–88

Koskenniemi, Martti, Rech, Walter, and Fonseca, Manuel Jiménez (eds), *International Law and Empire. Historical Explorations* (Oxford University Press 2017)

Kremer, David, *Ius Latinum. Le concept de droit latin sous la république et l'empire* (De Boccard 2006)

Kremer, David, 'À propos d'une tentative récente de déconstruction des privilèges latins et en particulier du *ius migrandi*' (2014) 102 Athenaeum 226–37

Kumar, Krishan, 'Greece and Rome in the British Empire: Contrasting Role Models' (2010) 51 Journal of British Studies 76–101

Kunkel, Wolfgang, *Staatsordnung und Staatspraxis der römischen Republik, II: Der Magistratur* (Beck 1995)

Laffi, Umberto, *'Adtributio' e 'contributio'. Problemi del sistema politico-amministrativo dello Stato romano* (Nistri-Lischi 1966)
Laffi, Umberto, 'La provincia della Gallia Cisalpina' (1992) 80 Athenaeum 5–23
Laffi, Umberto, *Studi di storia romana e di diritto* (Storia e Letteratura 2001)
Laffi, Umberto, 'Leggi agrarie e coloniarie' in Jean-Louis Ferrary (ed), *Leges publicae. La legge nell'esperienza giuridica romana* (Pavia University Press 2012) 429–61
Lanfranchi, Thibaud, *Les tribuns de la plèbe et la formation de la République romaine, 494–287 avant J.-C. Rome* (École Française de Rome 2015)
Laureys, Marc, 'At the Threshold of Humanist Jurisprudence: Andrea Fiocchi's *De potestatibus Romanis*' (1995) 65 Bulletin de l'Institut historique belge de Rome 25–42
Lazius, Wolfgang, *Commentariorum Reipublicae Romanae illius, in exteris provinciis, bello acquisitis, constitutae, libri duodecim* (Oporinus 1551)
Lazius, Wolfgang, *Commentariorum rerum Graecarum libri II* (Raphael Hoffalter 1558)
Lewis, George Cornewall, *An Inquiry into the Credibility of the Early Roman History* (JW Parker 1855)
Ligota, Christopher R, 'Annius of Viterbo and Historical Method' (1987) 50 Journal of the Warburg and Courtauld Institutes 44–56
Liljegren, Sten B (ed), *James Harrington's Oceana* (Winter 1924)
Lintott, Andrew W, 'What was the "Imperium Romanum"?' (1981) 28 Greece & Rome 53–67
Lintott, Andrew W, 'The So-Called Tabula Bembina and the Humanists: A Chapter Rewritten in the Renaissance Discovery of Classical Epigraphy' (1983) 61 Athenaeum 201–14
Lintott, Andrew W, *Imperium Romanum: Politics and Administration* (Routledge 1993)
Lintott, Andrew W, *The Constitution of the Roman Republic* (Oxford Unversity Press 1999)
Lipsius, Justus, *Admiranda, sive de magnitudine Romana* (Jan Moretus 1598)
Livy, *Titi Livii Historiarum libri, ex recensione I.F. Grouovii* (Elzevier 1644–45)
Livy, *Titi Livii Historiarum quod extat, cum perpetuis Car. Sigonii et J. F. Gronovii Notis. Jac. Gronovius probavit, suasque et aliorum Notas adjecit* (Elzevier 1679)
Long, George, 'Colonia' in William Smith (ed) *A Dictionary of Greek and Roman Antiquities* (Taylor and Walton 1842) 256–61
Luraschi, Giorgio, *Foedus, ius Latii, civitas. Aspetti costituzionali della romanizzazione in val Padana* (Pubblicazioni della Università di Pavia 1979)
Luraschi, Giorgio, *Storia di Como antica. Saggi di archeologia, diritto e storia* (New Press edizioni 1997)
Luzzatto, Giuseppe Ignazio, *Scritti minori epigrafici e papirologici* (Forni 1984)
Machiavelli, Bernardo, *Libro di ricordi* (Cesare Olschki ed, Le Monnier 1954)
Machiavelli, Niccolò, *Il Principe* (Luigi Firpo ed, Einaudi 1961)
Machiavelli, Niccolò, *Discorsi sopra la prima Deca di Tito Livio* (Mario Martelli ed, Sansoni 1971)
Machiavelli, Niccolò, 'Del modo di trattare i popoli della Valdichiana ribellati' in Niccolò Machiavelli, *Opere* vol 1 (Corrado Vivanti ed, Einaudi 1997)
Macrae, Duncan, '*Diligentissimus investigator antiquitatis*? "Antiquarianism" and Historical Evidence between Republican Rome and the Early Modern Republic of Letters' in Kaj Sandberg and Christopher J Smith (eds), Omnium annalium monumenta. *Historical Writing and Historical Explanation in Republican Rome* (Brill 2017) 137–56
Madvig, Johann N, 'De iure et condicione coloniarum populi Romani quaestio historica' in Johann Madvig *Opuscula Academica* (Gyldendal 1834) 228–55
Mancini, Giovanna, 'I codici Vaticani Latini 1549 e 3369 e le pagellae perdute del Codex Farnesianus' in Fay Glinister and others (eds), *Verrius, Festus, and Paul: Lexicography, Scholarship, and Society* (BICS supplement 93) (Institute of Classical Studies 2007) 137–58
Manni, Eugenio, *Per la storia dei municipii fino alla guerra sociale* (Signorelli 1947)

Manuzio, Paolo, *Antiquitatum romanarum liber de legibus* (Bernard Turrisan 1557)

Manuzio, Paolo, *Antiquitatum romanarum Paulli Mannuccii liber de ciuitate Romana* (Bartholomaeus Grassus 1585)

Marcocci, Giuseppe, 'Machiavelli, la religione dei romani e l'impero portoghese' (2008) 41–42 Storica 35–68

Marquardt, Joachim, *Römische Staatsverwaltung* (Hirzel 1881)

Marsilius of Padua, *Writings on the Empire* (Cary Nederman ed, Cambridge University Press 1993)

Masters, Roger D, *The Political Philosophy of Rousseau* (Princeton University Press 1968)

Mastrorosa, Ida Gilda, 'Biondo Flavio e i *Militiae romanae instituta*: Una lezione "moderna" su fondamenti e caratteri dell'impero di Rome' (2011) 2 Technai 85–103

Mazzarino, Santo, 'Storia e diritto nello studio delle società classiche' in *La storia del diritto nel quadro delle scienze storiche* (Olschki 1966)

Mazzocco, Angelo, 'Biondo Flavio and the Antiquarian Tradition' in Richard J Schoeck (ed), *Acta Conventus Neo-Latini Bononiensis: Proceedings of the Fourth International Congress of Neo-Latin Studies* (University Centre at Binghamton 1985) 123–36

Mazzocco, Angelo, 'A Reconsideration of Renaissance Antiquarianism in light of Biondo Flavio's *Ars Antiquaria*' (2014–15) 59/60 Memoirs of the American Academy in Rome 121–59

McCuaig, William, 'Sigonio and Grouchy: Roman Studies in the Sixteenth Century' (1986) 74 Athenaeum 147–83

McCuaig, William, *Carlo Sigonio: The Changing World of the Late Renaissance* (Princeton University Press 1989)

McCuaig, William, 'The Fasti Capitolini and the Study of Roman Chronology in the Sixteenth Century' (1991) 79 Athenaeum 141–59

McDaniel, Iain, *Adam Ferguson in the Scottish Enlightenment* (Harvard University Press 2013)

McKee, Sally, *Uncommon Dominion. Venetian Crete and the Myth of Ethnic Purity* (University of Pennsylvania Press 2010)

Mecca, Ippolita, 'Borghi e paesaggi rurali della Basilicata: tipologie edilizie e tecniche costruttive' (November 2012) Esempi di Architettura 1–10

Molmenti, Pompeo, *La storia di Venezia nella vita privata dalle origini alla caduta* (Roux and Vavalle 1885)

Momigliano, Arnaldo, 'Camillus and Concord' (1942) 36 Classical Quarterly 111–20

Momigliano, Arnaldo, 'Ancient History and the Antiquarian' (1950) 13 Journal of the Warburg Institute 293

Momigliano, Arnaldo, *Contributo alla storia degli studi classici* (Edizioni di Storia e Letteratura 1955)

Momigliano, Arnaldo, *Terzo contributo alla storia degli studi classici e del mondo antico* (Edizioni di Storia e Letteratura 1966)

Momigliano, Arnaldo, 'New Paths of Classicism in the Nineteenth Century' in Glen W Bowersock and Tim J Cornell (eds), *Studies on Modern Scholarship* (University of California Press 1994) 223–87

Mommsen, Theodor, '*Die* libri coloniarum' in Friederich Blume, Karl Lachmann, and Adolf Rudorff, *Die Schriften der römischen Feldmesser* vol 2 (Georg Reimer 1852) 143–220

Mommsen, Theodor, *Römische Geschichte* (3rd edn, Weidmann 1861)

Mommsen, Theodor, *Römisches Staatsrecht* (3rd edn, Hirsel 1887)

Mommsen, Theodor, 'Die Interpolationen des gromatischen Corpus' (1895) in Theodor Mommsen (ed), *Gesammelte Schriften* vol 7 (Weidmann 1909) 464–82

Montesquieu, Charles-Louis de Secondat, Baron de La Brède et de, *Considérations sur les causes de la grandeur des Romains et de leur decadence* (Jacques Desbordes 1734)
Montesquieu, Charles-Louis de Secondat, Baron de La Brède et de, *De l'esprit des lois* (2nd edn, London 1768)
More, Thomas, *Utopia* (Clarence Miller tr, 2nd edn, Yale University Press 2014)
Mossé, Claude, 'La conception du citoyen dans la *Politique* d'Aristote' (1967) 6 Eirene 17–21
Mouritsen, Henrik, *Italian Unification. A Study in Ancient and Modern Historiography* (University of London, Institute of Classical Studies 1998)
Mouritsen, Henrik, 'The *civitas sine suffragio*: Ancient Concepts and Modern Ideology' (2007) 56 Historia 141–58
Moyle, Walter, *An Essay upon the Constitution of the Roman Government* in *Works of Walter Moyle, none of which were ever before published* (Thomas Sergeant ed, 1726)
Muecke, Frances, '"Fama superstes?": Soundings in the Reception of Biondo Flavio's *Roma triumphans*' in Angelo Mazzocco and Marc Laureys (eds), *A New Sense of the Past: The Scholarship of Biondo Flavio (1392–1463)* (Leuven University Press 2016) 219–41
Muecke, Frances and Maurizio Campanelli (eds), *The Invention of Rome: Biondo Flavio's Roma triumphans and its Worlds* (Droz 2017)
Nelson, Eric, *The Greek Tradition in Republican Thought* (Cambridge University Press 2004)
Nelson, Eric, *The Hebrew Republic. Jewish Sources and the Transformation of European Political Thought* (Harvard University Press 2011)
Nicolet, Claude 'Le cens sénatorial sous la République et sous Auguste' (1976) 66 Journal of Roman Studies 20–38
Nicolet, Claude, 'Le *stipendium* des alliés Italiens avant la Guerre Sociale' (1978) 46 Papers of the British School at Rome 1–11
Nicolet, Claude (ed), *Des ordres à Rome* (Université de Paris I 1984)
Niebuhr, Barthold G, *Römische Geschichte* (Realschulbuchhandlung 1811–12)
Niebuhr, Barthold G, *The Roman History* (Francis A Walter tr, Rivington 1827)
Niebuhr, Barthold G, *Römische Geschichte* (2nd ed, Reimer 1828–32)
Niebuhr, Barthold G, *Storia romana* (Bizzoni 1832–33)
Niebuhr, Barthold G, *Vorträge über römische Geschichte, an der Universität zu Bonn gehalten* (Meyer Isler ed, Reimer 1846–48)
Niebuhr, Barthold G, *The History of Rome* (Julius C Hare and Connop Thirlwall eds, Taylor, Walton, Maberly 1851)
Niebuhr, Barthold G, *Lectures on Roman History* (Havilland M Chepmell and Franz Demmler tr, Chatto & Windus 1875)
Niese, Benedictus, 'Das sogenannte Licinisch-Sextische Ackergesetz' (1888) Hermes 410
Nippel, Wilfried, 'Das *Staatsrecht* in der Diskussion—von 1871 bis heute' in Wilfried Nippel and Bernd Seidensticker (eds), *Theodor Mommsens langer Schatten: Das römische Staatsrecht als bleibende Herausforderung für die Forschung* (Olms 2005) 9–60
Nippel, Wilfried, 'The Structure and Legacy of Mommsen's Staatsrecht' in Jean-Louis Ferrary and John Scheid (eds), *Il princeps romano: autocrate o magistrato?* (IUSS Press 2015) 35–53
Nörr, Dieter, *Imperium und polis in der hohen Principatszeit* (Beck 1969)
Northwood, Simon J, 'Asconius' Fifty-Three Colonies: A Regal Solution' (2008) 58 Classical Quarterly 353–62
O'Callaghan, Edmund B (ed), *Laws and Ordinances of New Netherland, 1638–1674* (Weed, Parsons and Co 1868)
O'Flanagan, Patrick, 'Mediterranean and Atlantic Settler Colonialism from the Late Fourteenth to the Early Seventeenth Centuries' in Edward Cavanagh and Lorenzo

Veracini (eds), *The Routledge Handbook of the History of Settler Colonialism* (Routledge 2017) 37–48

Oakley, Stephen P, *A Commentary on Livy Books VI–X. Vol. 2: Books VII–VIII* (Clarendon Press 1998)

Ohlmeyer, Jane H, 'A Laboratory of Empire?: Early Modern Ireland and English Imperialism' in Kevin Kenny (ed), *Ireland and the British Empire* (Oxford University Press 2006) 26–59

Osler, Douglas J, 'Humanist Philology and the Text of Justinian's *Digest*', in Paul J du Plessis and John Cairns (eds), *Reassessing Legal Humanism and its Claims:* Petere Fontes? (Edinburgh Unversity Press 2016) 41–58

Osmond, Patricia J, '"Princeps Historiae Romana": Sallust in Renaissance Political Thought' (1995) 40 Memoirs of the American Academy in Rome 101–43

Otis, James Jr, *The Rights of British Colonies Asserted and Proved* (Edes and Gill 1764)

Ott, Martin, *Die Entdeckung des Altertums: Der Umgang mit der römischen Vergangenheit Süddeutschlands im 16. Jahrhundert* (Lassleben 2002)

Oudaan, Joachim, *Roomsche Mogentheyt, of naeuwkeurige beschryving, van de macht en heerschappy der oude Roomsche keyseren* (Daniel Baccamude 1670)

Pais, Ettore, *Ancient Legends of Roman History* (Mario E Cosenza tr, Dodd, Mead, and Company 1905)

Pais, Ettore, *Storia della colonizzazione di Roma antica* (Nardecchia 1923)

Pais, Ettore, 'Serie cronologica delle colonie romane e latine dall'età regia fino all'impero' (1924–25) 5.17 Atti della Reale Accademia nazionale dei Lincei – Memorie della Classe di scienze morali, storiche e filologiche 311–55 and 1.6, 345–412

Paleario, Aonio and others, *ΘΕΣΙΣ positio, sive constitutio causae, et distributio patrium actionis pro lege agraria* (Moschenius 1557)

Panvinio, Onofrio, *Reipublicae Romanae Commentariorum libri tres* (Valgrisi 1558)

Paping, Richard and Tassenaar, Vincent, 'Levenskansen, levensstandaard en integratie in de Koloniën van de Maatschappij van Weldadigheid' (2018) 135 Nieuwe Drentse Volksalmanak 21–48

Pasquinucci, Marinella, 'La transumanza nell'Italia romana' in Emilio Gabba and Marinella Pasquinucci, *Strutture agrarie e allevamento transumante nell'Italia romana (III–I sec. a.C.)* (Giardini 1979) 79–182

Patterson, John, 'Colonization and Historiography: the Roman Republic' in Guy J Bradley and John-Paul Wilson (eds), *Greek and Roman Colonization* (Classical Press of Wales 2006) 189–219

Pedullà, Gabriele, '"Concedere la civiltà a' forestieri". Roma, Venezia e la crisi del modello municipale di res publica nei *Discorsi* di Machiavelli' (2003) 25–26 Storica 105–73

Pedullà, Gabriele, 'Giro d'Europa. Le mille vite di Dionigi di Alicarnasso (XV–XIX secolo)' in Dionigi di Alicarnasso (ed), *Le antichità romane* (Einaudi 2010) lix–cxlvi

Pedullà, Gabriele, *Machiavelli in Tumult: The* Discourses on Livy *and the Origins of Political Conflictualism* (Cambridge University Press 2018)

Pelgrom, Jeremia, 'Roman Colonization and the City-State Model' in Tesse Stek and Jeremia Pelgrom, *Roman Republican Colonization* (Palombi 2014) 73–87

Pelgrom, Jeremia, 'The Roman Rural Exceptionality Thesis Revisited' (2018) 130 Mélanges de l'École française de Rome—Antiquité 69–103

Pelgrom, Jeremia and Stek, Tesse D 'Roman Colonization under the Republic: Historiographical Contextualization of a Paradigm' in Tesse Stek and Jeremia Pelgrom (eds), *Roman Republican Colonization* (Palombi 2014) 10–41

Perini, Davide A, *Onofrio Panvinio e le sue opere* (Popaganda Fide 1899)

Pettingal, John, *An Enquiry into the Use and Practice of Juries among the Greeks and Romans* (Cadell 1769)

Pitts, Jennifer, *Boundaries of the International. Law and Empire* (Harvard University Press 2018)

Plessis, Paul J du, Ando, Clifford, and Tuori, Kaius (eds) *The Oxford Handbook of Roman Law and Society* (Oxford University Press 2016)

Pobjoy, Mark P, 'The First *Italia*' in Kathryn Lomas and Edward Herring (eds), *The Emergence of State Identities in Italy in the First Millenium BC* (Accordia Research Institute 2000) 187–211

Pobjoy, Mark P and Rich, John W, 'From Riccoboni to Roth: Early Editions of the Fragments of the Roman Historians' in Tim J Cornell and others, *The Fragments of the Roman Historians* (Oxford University Press 2013) vol 1, 652–60

Pocock, John GA, *The Machiavellian Moment. Florentine Political Thought and the Atlantic Republican Tradition* (Princeton University Press 1975)

Pocock, John GA, 'Political Thought in the English-speaking Atlantic, 1760–1790. Part I: The Imperial Crisis' in John GA Pocockand others (eds) *The Varieties of British Political Thought* (Cambridge University Press 1993) 246–82

Pocock, John GA, *Barbarism and Religion, vol. 3: The First Decline and Fall* (Cambridge University Press 2003)

Poldo d'Albenas, Jean, *Discours historiale de l'antique et illustre cite de Nismes* (Roville 1559)

Premerstein, Anton von, 'ius Italicum' *Realencyclopädie X* (Druckenmüller 1918) 1238–53

Puchta, Georg F, *Cursus der Institutionen* (Breitkopf und Härtel 1841)

Puchta Georg F, 'Remarks on Professor Long's Paper on the Licinian Law *de modo agri*' (1846) 3 Classical Museum 67–77

Quinn, David B, 'Renaissance Influences in English Colonization' (1976) 26 Transactions of the Royal Historical Society 73–93

Raggi, Andrea, 'Senatus consultum de Asclepiade Clazomenio sociisque' (2001) 135 Zeitschrift für Papyrologie und Epigraphik 73–116

Rainolds, John, *The summe of the conference betwene Iohn Rainoldes and Iohn Hart* (John Wolfe 1584)

Raskolnikoff, Mouza, *Des Anciens et des Modernes* (Publications de la Sorbonne 1990)

Raskolnikoff, Mouza, *Histoire romaine et critique historique dans l'Europe des lumières. La naissance de l'hypercritique dans l'historiographie de la Rome antique* (École Française de Rome 1992)

Rathbone, Dominic W, 'The Control and Exploitation of *ager publicus* in Italy under the Roman Republic' in Jean-Jacques Aubert (ed), *Tâches publiques et entreprise privée dans le monde romain, Actes du Diplôme d'Études Avancées* (Université de Neuchâtel 2003) 135–78

Reid, John Phillip, *Constitutional History of the American Revolution: The Authority to Tax* (University of Wisconsin Press 1987)

Reynolds, Leighton D (ed), *Texts and Transmission: A Survey of the Latin Classics* (Oxford University Press 1983)

Rhenanus, Beatus, *Briefwechsel* (Adalbert Horawitz and Karl Hartfelder eds, Teubner 1886)

Rich, John W, 'Treaties, Allies and the Roman Conquest of Italy' in Philip de Souza and John France (eds), *War and Peace in Ancient and Medieval Italy* (Cambridge University Press 2008) 51–75

Rich, John W, 'Lex Licinia, Lex Sempronia: B.G. Niebuhr and the Limitation of Landholding in the Roman Republic' in Luuk de Ligt and Simon Northwood (eds), *People, Land and Politics. Demographic Developments and the Transformation of Roman Italy, 300 BC–AD 14* (Brill 2008) 519–72

Richardson, John S, *Hispaniae: Spain and the Development of Roman Imperialism 218–82 BC* (Cambridge University Press 1986)

Richardson, John S, *The Language of Empire: Rome and the Idea of Empire from the Third Century BC to the Second Century AD* (Cambridge University Press 2008)

Ridley, Ronald T, *Gibbon's Complement: Louis de Beaufort* (Istituto Veneto di Scienze, Lettere ed Arti 1986)

Ridley, Ronald T, '*Leges agrariae*: Myths Ancient and Modern' (2000) 95 Classical Philology 459–67

Riesbeck, David J, *Aristotle on Political Community* (Cambridge University Press 2016)

Robbins, Caroline, 'The "Excellent Use" of Colonies. A Note on Walter Moyle's Justification of Roman Colonies, ca. 1699' (1966) 23 The William and Mary Quarterly 620–26

Robortello, Francesco, *De uita et uictu populi Romani sub impp. Caess. Augg. tomus primus . . . Disputationes nouem, de prouinciis Romanorum et earum distributione atque administratione, etc.* (Benati 1559)

Roda, Sergio, *Il modello della repubblica imperiale romana fra mondo antico e mondo modern* 'Fecisti patriam diversis gentibus unam' (Monduzzi 2011)

Roncaglia, Carolynn E, *Northern Italy in the Roman World From the Bronze Age to Late Antiquity* (Johns Hopkins University Press 2017)

Roselaar, Saskia T, *Public Land in the Roman Republic. A Social and Economic History of Ager Publicus in Italy, 396–89 BC* (Oxford University Press 2010)

Roselaar, Saskia T, 'Colonies and Processes of Integration in the Roman Republic' (2011) 123-2 Mélanges de l'École française de Rome – Antiquité 527–55

Roselaar, Saskia T, 'The Concept of *commercium* in the Roman Republic' (2012) 66 Phoenix 381–413

Roselaar, Saskia T, 'The Concept of *conubium* in the Roman Republic' in Paul du Plessis (ed), *New Frontiers: Law and Society in the Roman World* (Edinburgh Universty Press 2013) 102–22

Roselaar, Saskia T, *Italy's Economic Revolution: Integration and Economy in Republican Italy* (Oxford University Press 2019)

Rosenberg, Arthur, *Der Staat der alten Italiker* (Weidmann 1913)

Rosinus, Johannes, *Antiquitatum romanarum corpus absolutissimum* (Chouët 1558)

Rousseau, Jean-Jacques, *Oeuvres* (Déterville et Lefèvre 1817)

Rousseau, Jean-Jacques, *Du contrat social* (Edmond Dreyfus ed, Alcan 1896)

Rousseau, Jean-Jacques, *Oeuvres complètes* (Robert Derathé ed, Gallimard 1964)

Rousseau, Jean-Jacques, *The Discourses and Other Early Political Writings* (Victor Gourevitch tr, Cambridge University Press 1997)

Rousseau, Jean-Jacques, *The Social Contract* (Christopher Betts tr, Oxford University Press 1999)

Rowland, Ingrid, *The Culture of the High Renaissance: Ancients and Moderns in Sixteenth-Century Rome* (Cambridge University Press 1998)

Rudolph, Hans, *Staat und Stadt im römischen Italien. Untersuchungen über die Entwicklung des Munizipalwesens in der republikanischen Zeit* (Dieterich 1935)

Rudorff, Adolf AF, *Römische Rechtsgeschichte* (Bernhard Tauchnitz 1857)

Russell, Sir Edward J, 'Agricultural Colonization in the Pontine Marshes and Libya' (1939) 94 The Geographical Journal 273–89

Rytkönen, Seppo, *Barthold Georg Niebuhr als Politiker und Historiker. Zeitgeschehen und Zeitgeist in der geschichtlichen Beurteilungen von B.G. Niebuhr* (Suomalainen Tiedeakatemia 1968)

Sachers, Erich, 'praefectura', *Realencyclopädie XXII* (1954) 2347–52

Sachers, Erich, 'Praefectus iure dicendo', *Realencyclopädie XXII* (Druckenmüller 1954) 2378–91

Salmon, Edward Togo, 'Rome and the Latins, I–II' (1953) 7 Phoenix 93–104, 123–35

Salmon, Edward Togo, 'Roman Expansion and Roman Colonization in Italy' (1955) 9 Phoenix 63–75
Salmon, Edward Togo, *Roman Colonization under the Republic* (Thames & Hudson 1969)
Sánchez, Pierre, '*Latini, id est foederati.* Le statut juridique des colonies latines sous la république' (2016) 104 Athenaeum 50–82
Sandys, John E, *A History of Classical Scholarship* (Cambridge University Press 1908)
Saumagne, Charles, *Le droit romain et les cités romaines sous l'empire. Essai critique* (Publications de l'Institut de droit romain de l'Université de Paris 1965)
Savigny, Friedrich C von, *Das Recht des Besitzes. Ein civilistische Abhandlung* (6th edn, Heyer 1837)
Savigny, Friedrich C von, *Vermischte Schriften* (Veit und Comp 1850)
Saxius, Christophorus, 'Επίκρισις φιλολογική, sive stricturae in nuperum Franci cuiusdam libellum de incerto historiae Romanorum antiquissimae' (1742) 1 Miscellanea Lipsiensia nova ad incrementum scientiarum 40–79; (1743) 2 Miscellanea Lipsiensia 409–95, 620–712; (1744) 3 Miscellanea Lipsiensia 235–329, 743–49
Senatore, Felice, '"Der Staat der alten Italiker" nella storia degli studi sull'Italia antica' in Arthur Rosenberg (ed), *Lo stato degli antichi Italici* (Scienze e Lettere 2011) 235–95
Sens, Angelie, *De kolonieman. Johannes van den Bosch (1780–1844), volksverheffer in naam van de Koning* (Balans 2019)
Serjeantson, Richard, 'Francis Bacon, Colonization, and the Limits of Atlanticism' conference paper (2014), <https://docplayer.net/65319781-Francis-bacon-colonization-and-the-limits-of-atlanticism.html>
Shackleton Bailey, David R, 'Nobiles and Novi reconsidered' (1986) 107 American Journal of Philology 255–60
Shatzman, Israel, *Senatorial Wealth and Roman Politics* (Latomus 1975)
Sherk, Robert K, *Roman Documents from the Greek East.* Senatus Consulta *and* Epistulae *to the Age of Augustus* (Johns Hopkins Press 1969)
Sherwin White, Adrian N, *The Roman Citizenship* (2nd edn, Clarendon Press 1973)
Sigonio, Carlo, *In fastos Romanos ac triumphos Romanos commentarius* (Paolo Manuzio 1556)
Sigonio, Carlo, *Fragmenta Ciceronis, variis in locis dispersa* (Giordano Ziletti 1559)
Sigonio, Carlo, *De antiquo iure ciuium Romanorum libri II* (Giordano Ziletti 1560)
Sigonio, Carlo, *De antiquo iure Italiae libri III* (Giordano Ziletti 1560)
Sigonio, Carlo, *Disputationes Patauinae aduersus Franciscum Robortellum* (Percacino 1562)
Sigonio, Carlo, *De antiquo iure prouinciarum libri II* (Giordano Ziletti 1567)
Sigonio, Carlo, *De antiquo iure populi Romani libri undecim* (Societas Typographiae Bononiensis 1574)
Sigonio, Carlo, *Opera Omnia* (Argelati 1732–37)
Simpson, Richard, 'Sir Thomas Smith (1513–77). An Overview of his Life and Works' in Andrew Burnett and Richard Simpson (eds), *Roman Coins. Money, and Society in Elizabethan England: Sir Thomas Smith's* On the Wages of the Roman Footsoldier (The American Numismatic Society 2017) 1–71
Simshäuser, Wilhelm, *Iuridici und Municipalgerichtsbarkeit in Italien* (Beck 1973)
Simshäuser, Wilhelm, 'Stadtromisches Verfahrensrecht im Spiegel der lex Irnitana' (1992) 109 Zeitschrift der Savigny-Stiftung für Rechtsgeschichte, romanistische Abteilung 163–208
Smith, Christopher, *The Roman Clan: The* Gens *from Ancient Ideology to Modern Anthropology* (Oxford University Press 2006)
Smith, Maurice H, *The Writs of Assistance Case* (California University Press 1978)
Smith, William, *A Dictionary of Greek and Roman Antiquities* (Taylor and Walton 1842)

Somos, Mark, 'Irenic Secularization and the Hebrew Republic in Harrington's *Oceana*' in Gaby Mahlberg and Dirk Wiemann (eds), *European Contexts for English Republicanism* (Ashgate 2013) 81–103

Somos, Mark, '*Mare clausum*, *Leviathan*, and *Oceana*: Bible Criticism, Secularisation and Imperialism in Seventeenth-Century English Political and Legal Thought' in Carly Crouch and Jonathan Stökl (eds), *In the Name of God: The Bible in the Colonial Discourses of Empire* (Brill 2013) 85–133

Somos, Mark, *Varieties of Secularisation in English and Dutch Public and International Law* (PhD dissertation Leiden University 2014)

Somos, Mark, 'Harrington's Project: The Balance of Money, A Republican Constitution for Europe, and England's Patronage of the World' in Béla Kapossy, Isaac Nakhimovsky, and Richard Whatmore (eds), *Commerce and Peace in the Enlightenment* (Cambridge University Press 2017) 20–43

Somos, Mark, *American States of Nature: The Origins of Independence, 1761–1775* (Oxford University Press 2019)

Spenser, Edmund, *A View of the Present State of Ireland* (William L Renwick ed, Clarendon Press 1970)

Stallsmith, Allaire B, 'One Colony, Two Mother Cities: Cretan Agriculture under Venetian and Ottoman Rule' (2007) 40 Hesperia Supplements 151–71

Steinwenter, Arthur, 'ius Latii', *Realencyclopädie X* (Druckenmüller 1918) 1267–70

Stek, Tesse D and Pelgrom, Jeremia (eds), *Roman Republican Colonization: New Perspectives from Archaeology and Ancient History* (Palombi 2014)

Stek, Tesse D, 'The Impact of Roman Expansion and Colonization on Ancient Italy in the Republican Period. From Diffusionism to Networks of Opportunity' in Gary D Farney and Guy J Bradley (eds) *The Peoples of Ancient Italy* (De Gruyter 2017) 269–94

Stek, Tesse D, 'Early Roman Colonization beyond the Romanizing Agro-Town: Village Patterns of Settlement and Highland Exploitation in Central Italy' in Bleda Düring and Tesse D Stek, *The Archaeology of Imperial Landscapes* (Cambridge University Press 2018) 145–72

Stenhouse, William, *Reading Inscriptions and Writing Ancient History: Historical Scholarship in the Late Renaissance* (Institute of Classical Studies 2005)

Stenhouse, William, 'Flavio Biondo and Later Renaissance Antiquarianism' in Frances Muecke and Maurizio Campanelli (eds), *The Invention of Rome: Biondo Flavio's* Roma triumphans *and its Worlds* (Droz 2017) 259–73

Stephens, Walter, 'When Pope Noah Ruled the Etruscans: Annius of Viterbo and his Forged *Antiquities*' (2004) 119 Modern Language Notes 201–23

Stevenson, George H, *Roman Provincial Administration till the Age of the Antonines* (Blackwell 1949)

Straumann, Benjamin, *Roman Law in the State of Nature. The Classical Foundations of Hugo Grotius' Natural Law* (Cambridge University Press 2015)

Sullivan, Vickie B, 'Walter Moyle's Machiavellianism, Declared and Otherwise, in *An Essay upon the Constitution of the Roman Government*' (2011) 37 History of European Ideas 120–27

Sweetman, Rebecca J, *Roman Colonies in the First Century of their Foundation* (Oxbow Books 2011)

Tan, James, 'The *dilectus-tributum* System and the Settlement of Fourth Century Italy' in Jeremy Armstrong and Michael P Fronda (eds), *Romans at War: Soldiers, Citizens and Society in the Roman Republic* (Routledge 2020) 52–75

Tarcov, Nathan, 'Machiavelli and the Foundations of Modernity: A Reading of Chapter 3 of The Prince' in Mark Blitz and William Kristol (eds), *Educating the Prince: Essays in Honor of Harvey Mansfield* (Rowman and Littlefield 2000) 30–44

Tarpin, Michel H, 'Strangers in Paradise. Latins (and Other Non-Romans) in Colonial Context: A Short Story of Territorial Complexity' in Tesse Stek and Jeremia Pelgrom (eds), *Roman Republican Colonization* (Palombi 2014) 161–91

Taylor, Lily Ross, 'Cicero's Aedileship' (1939) 60 American Journal of Philology 194–202

Taylor, Lily Ross, *Voting Districts of the Roman Republic* (The American Academy in Rome 1960)

Tenenti, Alberto, *Cristoforo da Canal: La marine vénitienne avant Lépante* (SEVPEN 1962)

Terrenato, Nicola, *The Early Roman Expansion into Italy. Elite Negotiation and Family Agendas* (Cambridge University Press 2019)

Thomas, Yan, *Mommsen et l'"isolierung' du droit (Rome, l'Allemagne et l'État)* (De Boccard 1984)

Thulin, Carl O, *Corpus agrimensorum Romanorum, I Opuscula agrimensorum veterum* (Teubner 1913)

Tibiletti, Giancarlo, 'Il possesso *dell'ager publicus* e le norme *de modo agrorum* sino ai Gracchi' (1948) 26 Athenaeum 173–236

Tibiletti, Giancarlo, 'Ricerche di storia agraria romana' (1950) 28 Athenaeum 183–266

Tibiletti, Giancarlo, *Diritti locali nei municipi d'Italia e altri problemi* (Pàtron Editore 1973)

Tibiletti, Giancarlo, *Storie locali dell'Italia romana* (presso la rivista 'Athenaeum' 1978)

Toneatto, Lucio, 'Ancora sull'editio princeps del "Liber regionum I"' (1985) 3 Dialoghi di archeologia 125–29

Toneatto, Lucio, 'Dalla biblioteca privata del giurista Jean Matal (Metellus Sequanus, 1510 ca.–1597): una copia annotata della 'princeps' turnebiana dei Gromatici (Codici d'agrimensura perduti o non identificati. Notizie e dati filologici, II)' (2004) 32 Index: Quaderni camerati di studi romanistici 123–58

Toneatto, Lucio, 'L'editio princeps del 'Liber regionum I'' (1983) 1 Dialoghi di archeologia 87–95

Toneatto, Lucio, *Codices artis mensoriae. I manoscritti degi antichi opuscoli latini d'agrimensura* (V–XIX sec.) (Centro italiano di studi sull'alto medioevo 1994–95)

Torrent, Armando, *La 'iurisdictio' de los magistrados municipales* (Universidad, Secretariado de Publicaciones e Intercambio Cientifico 1970)

Toynbee, Arnold, *Hannibal's Legacy* (Oxford University Press 1965)

Turmair, Johannes, *Annalium Boiorum libri septem* (Weissenhorn 1554)

Vagenheim, Ginette, 'La critique épigraphique au XVIe siècle: Ottavio Pantagato, Paolo Manuzio, Onofrio Panvinio, Antonio Agustín et Pirro Ligorio: à propos des tribus romaines' (2012) 86 Aevum 949–68

Vaughan, Charles E, *The Political Writings of Jean-Jacques Rousseau* (Cambridge University Press 1915)

Velema, Wyger RE, *Republicans. Essays on Eighteenth-Century Dutch Political Thought* (Brill 2007)

Veracini, Lorenzo, *Settler Colonialism. A Theoretical Overview* (Palgrave Macmillan 2010)

Verlinden, Charles, *The Beginnings of Modern Colonization* (Cornell University Press 1970)

Vervaet, FJ, *The High Command in the Roman Republic. The Principle of the* summum imperium auspiciumque *from 509 to 19 BCE* (Steiner 2014)

Vico, Giambattista, *The First New Science* (Leon Pompa ed, Cambridge University Press 2002)

Viglietti, Cristiano, *Il limite del bisogno. Antropologia economica di Roma arcaica* (Il Mulino 2011)

Walther, Gerrit, *Niebuhrs Forschung* (Steiner Verlag 1993)

Watkins, Thomas H, '*Coloniae* and *ius Italicum* in the Early Empire' (1983) 78 Classical Journal 319–36

Weststeijn, Arthur, 'Republican Empire: Colonialism, Corruption and Commerce in the Dutch Golden Age' (2012) 26 Renaissance Studies 491–509

Weststeijn, Arthur, 'Dutch Brazil and the Making of Free Trade Ideology' in Michiel van Groesen (ed), *The Legacy of Dutch Brazil* (Cambridge University Press 2014) 187–204

Weststeijn, Arthur, 'The VOC as Company-State: Debating Seventeenth-Century Dutch Colonial Expansion' (2014) 38 Itinerario 13–34

Whately, Thomas, *The Regulations Lately Made Concerning the Colonies* (J Wilkie 1765)

Whatmough, Joshua, *The Foundations of Roman Italy* (Methuen & Company 1937)

Whitman, James Q, *The Legacy of Roman Law in the German Romantic Era* (Princeton University Press 1990)

Wilson, Tom D, *The Oglethorpe Plan: Enlightenment Design in Savannah and Beyond* (University of Virginia Press 2012)

Wirszubski, Chaim, *Libertas as a Political Idea at Rome during the Late Republic and Early Principate* (Cambridge University Press 1950)

Wiseman, Timothy P, *Unwritten Rome* (University of Exeter Press 2008)

Wood, Ian, *The Modern Origins of the Early Middle Ages* (Oxford University Press 2013)

Yarrow, Liv M, '*Decem legati*: A Flexible Institution, Rigidly Perceived' in Christopher J Smith and Liv M Yarrow (eds), *Imperialism, Cultural Politics, and Polybius* (Oxford University Press 2012) 168–83

Yirush, Craig, *Settlers, Liberty, and Empire: The Roots of Early American Political Theory, 1675–1775* (Cambridge University Press 2011)

Zaggia, Massimo, 'La traduzione latina da Appiano di Pier Candido Decembrio: per la storia della tradizione' (1993) 34 Studi Medievali 193–243

Zasius, Ulrich, *Catalogus legum antiquarum* (Guillaume Cavellat 1555)

Ziskind, Jonathan R, 'Petrus Cunaeus on Theocracy, Jubilee and the Latifundia' (1978) 68 The Jewish Quarterly Review 235–54

Zmigryder-Konopka, Zdzislaw, 'Les rélations politiques entre Rome et la Campanie' (1929) 32 Eos 596

Index

For the benefit of digital users, indexed terms that span two pages (e.g., 52–53) may, on occasion, appear on only one of those pages.